Lecture Notes in Computer Science

Lecture Notes in Artificial Intelligence 13997

Founding Editor

Jörg Siekmann

Series Editors

Randy Goebel, *University of Alberta, Edmonton, Canada*
Wolfgang Wahlster, *DFKI, Berlin, Germany*
Zhi-Hua Zhou, *Nanjing University, Nanjing, China*

The series Lecture Notes in Artificial Intelligence (LNAI) was established in 1988 as a topical subseries of LNCS devoted to artificial intelligence.

The series publishes state-of-the-art research results at a high level. As with the LNCS mother series, the mission of the series is to serve the international R & D community by providing an invaluable service, mainly focused on the publication of conference and workshop proceedings and postproceedings.

Tobias Ahlbrecht · Jürgen Dix · Niklas Fiekas ·
Tabajara Krausburg

Editors

The Multi-Agent
Programming Contest 2022

Coordinating Agents in a Dynamic World:
Agents Follow the Rules, or Not

 Springer

Editors
Tobias Ahlbrecht (iD)
Clausthal University of Technology
Clausthal-Zellerfeld, Germany

Jürgen Dix (iD)
TU Clausthal
Clausthal-Zellerfeld, Germany

Niklas Fiekas (iD)
TU Clausthal
Clausthal-Zellerfeld, Germany

Tabajara Krausburg (iD)
TU Clausthal
Clausthal-Zellerfeld, Germany

ISSN 0302-9743   ISSN 1611-3349 (electronic)
Lecture Notes in Artificial Intelligence
ISBN 978-3-031-38711-1   ISBN 978-3-031-38712-8 (eBook)
https://doi.org/10.1007/978-3-031-38712-8

LNCS Sublibrary: SL7 – Artificial Intelligence

This Springer imprint is published by the registered company Springer Nature Switzerland AG
The registered company address is: Gewerbestrasse 11, 6330 Cham, Switzerland

Preface

In this volume, we present the sixteenth edition of the Multi-Agent Programming Contest, an annual international competition amongst researchers and enthusiasts in the field of agent-oriented programming.

The first paper describes the contest in general and this edition in particular, focusing on the organizers' observations. The following papers are written by the participants of the contest, describing their team of agents and its performance in more detail.

The review process was single blind and each paper got three reviews. Seven papers were submitted and passed the review process. We would like to thank the tireless efforts of our reviewers, without whom this would of course not have been possible.

June 2023

Tobias Ahlbrecht
Jürgen Dix
Niklas Fiekas
Tabajara Krausburg

Organization

Program Committee Chairs

Ahlbrecht, Tobias	TU Clausthal, Germany
Dix, Jürgen	TU Clausthal, Germany
Fiekas, Niklas	TU Clausthal, Germany
Krausburg, Tabajara	TU Clausthal, Germany

Program Committee Members

Ahlbrecht, Tobias	TU Clausthal, Germany
Dix, Jürgen	TU Clausthal, Germany
Fiekas, Niklas	TU Clausthal, Germany
Hübner, Jomi F.	Federal University of Santa Catarina, Brazil
Krausburg, Tabajara	TU Clausthal, Germany

Reviewers

Amaral, Cleber J.	Federal Institute of Santa Catarina, Brazil
Cardoso, Rafael C.	University of Aberdeen, UK
Ciortea, Andrei	University of St. Gallen, Switzerland
Esfandiari, Babak	Carleton University, Canada
Pantoja, Carlos Eduardo	Centro Federal de Educação Tecnológica Celso Suckow da Fonseca, Brazil
Sardina, Sebastian	RMIT University, Australia
Sarmas, Evangelos	Greece
Schlesinger, Federico	Google, Switzerland
Zatelli, Maicon Rafael	Federal University of Santa Catarina, Brazil

Contents

The Multi-Agent Programming Contest 2022

Tobias Ahlbrecht[1]([✉])[iD], Jürgen Dix[1][iD], Niklas Fiekas[1][iD],
and Tabajara Krausburg[1,2][iD]

[1] Department of Informatics, Clausthal University of Technology,
Clausthal-Zellerfeld, Germany
{tobias.ahlbrecht,dix,niklas.fiekas}@tu-clausthal.de
[2] School of Technology, Pontifical Catholic University of Rio Grande do Sul,
Porto Alegre, Brazil
tabajara.rodrigues@edu.pucrs.br

Abstract. We present the 16th edition of the Multi-Agent Programming Contest, an annual competition designed to increase interest and further research in the area of Multi-Agent Systems development. This is the third version of the Agents Assemble scenario in which the agents inhabit a grid and must build specific shapes out of blocks scattered in the environment to win a match. Six teams from five different countries were involved in the contest. Each team has shown a solid performance. Given the current state of the Multi-Agent Programming Contest, we envision the matches in the next edition to be run in a more automated fashion. This way, decentralized agents can be enforced, and network latency avoided, while simulations can run for a longer time and with various different parameters.

Keywords: multi-agent systems · agent-based simulation · decentralized computing · cooperation · artificial intelligence · simulation platforms · norms · competition

1 Introduction

The Multi-Agent Programming competition is an (almost) annual competition between people interested in Multi-Agent Systems. The organizers provide the scenario description, i.e. the rules of the game and the necessary software to run the environment. Participants implement a team of agents which then autonomously play said game. The contest has seen a variety of scenarios so far, from gathering food and gold pieces on a grid, over-herding cows into corrals, gathering water by obtaining favorable positions on a graph (on Mars), navigating realistic road networks, to finally moving blocks around and arranging them in specific patterns.

The aims of this are mainly twofold. On the one hand, the idea is to stimulate research in the area of multi-agent system programming by providing a

T. Ahlbrecht et al. (Eds.): MAPC 2022, LNAI 13997, pp. 1–18, 2023.
https://doi.org/10.1007/978-3-031-38712-8_1

challenging test environment and benchmark. On the other hand, the contest can serve as an opportunity for people who are new to the field of agent-oriented programming, mainly students, to get familiar with unconventional programming concepts and frameworks.

This year's contest is certainly the most mature one, both in terms of the used scenario and the performance of the teams attending it. Still, there is room for improvement as in several situations a team could have scored many more points with just a small bit of cooperation between its agents (see the discussion at the end of Sect. 4). Therefore, efficient cooperation between agents is still a major issue, although there is now much more cooperation than in the first years of the contest.

For the first time, we offered warm-up matches against a team of agents not taking part in the contest. Most participants seized the opportunity.

Our scenario seems complicated enough: Even with only two active tasks and enough agents, for almost all developers, it was often unclear what their programmed team would do (and why it was doing what it did and not something else). All groups gratefully used our graphical interface to find out what happened.

In this contest, we also took the opportunity to introduce the concept of norms. Norms dynamically introduce for a number of steps small changes to the rules of the game. The agents then decide whether to follow them, enduring punishments for any violation.

In the end, we can say that we achieved most of our design goals, while some minor or major transformations of the MAPC might be in order for the next iterations.

1.1   Related Work and Competitions

The results and analyses of the previous MAPC have been published in [4]. Another review spanning all editions up to 2019 can be found in [3].

There are as many programming competitions as sand at sea, one could say. Unfortunately, most of those are not targeted at multi-agent systems. Among the few that are, there is the Intention Progression Competition [8]. It is aimed at finding good solutions for how to work on parallel intentions. The solution in our Contest is an agent program, whereas in the Intention Progression Competition the input is an agent program (i.e., its plans) and the solution is how to select the intentions, which is usually part of the agent interpreter.

There are also a variety of planning competitions under the umbrella of the International Conference on Planning and Scheduling (ICAPS) with similar intentions as the MAPC, only focused on planning. For example, the topic of the 2020 planning competition [5] was hierarchical planning. While the MAPC always has a fixed scenario, the input in a planning competition is given in a fragment of the Planning Domain Definition Language [1]. Since our goal is to examine the application of agent-based programming languages, frameworks, and tools, it has proven useful to confront participants with a concrete problem, which is also not supposed to have an optimal solution or any particular best strategy.

Also simulation-based, the Agile Robotics for Industrial Automation Competition (ARIAC) [10] is an annual contest, established in 2017, to foster research in the area of robot agility, i.e. a robot's ability to act and react in dynamic environments. Compared to the MAPC, it addresses a more realistic problem but apparently a more centralized one.

We also mention the well-known *Robocup*, in particular, the rescue simulation.[1] This competition targets evaluating several A.I. techniques such as planning, task allocation, etc. The scenario usually mimics a map of a city in which an earthquake incident occurred, and the agents representing different sorts of responders must act upon the damaged zone. Competitors implement their agents using the frameworks provided by the organizers so that their A.I. techniques can be compared and evaluated [12]. Furthermore, all teams give final talks about their solutions, which counts towards the final score.

Last but not least, a different flavor of competition is the CARLA autonomous driving leaderboard.[2] It focuses on autonomous agents driving cars in multiple simulated traffic scenarios in which the main goal is crash avoidance. Even though the topic of the competition is already interesting, CARLA is also organized in a different way. Each participating team has at most 5 submissions per month of their code to score against a leaderboard. This provides the participating teams the freedom to decide when it is the best moment to implement and enhance their solutions.

1.2   Outline

The remainder of this paper is organized as follows. In Sect. 2 we introduce the current MAPC scenario explaining how we modified it when compared to the previous edition. Then, in Sect. 3, we introduce the 16th MAPC. It addresses the participants, results, and the teams' overall performance. In Sect. 4 we discuss what has succeeded and what can be improved in the current configuration. To conclude this overview paper, we focus on the challenges ahead in the multi-agent programming contest. We discuss the next steps and how we plan to carry them out.

2   The 2022 Scenario

The scenario is the third iteration of the so-called Agents Assemble scenario, where teams of agents have to cooperate in arranging blocks in specific shapes and delivering those shapes to certain locations. *Tasks* describe which shapes are currently required and what the reward for completing the task is.

As usual, the game takes place in discrete steps. In each step, the environment state is sent to the agents first. Then, the server waits for an answer from each agent in the form of an action. Once all actions are received (or a timeout is

---

[1] https://rescuesim.robocup.org/2022-bangkok-robocup/.
[2] https://leaderboard.carla.org/.

encountered), the actions are executed, and the environment state is updated accordingly. The number of steps to run is set before the simulation.

The environment is a grid world containing agents, obstacles, and a few other things:

Dispensers can be used to acquire blocks of a certain type.

Blocks can be retrieved from dispensers. Agents can `attach` blocks to themselves, `connect` blocks to other blocks with the help of other agents, then `disconnect` blocks again, `detach` themselves from blocks or destroy blocks with the `clear` action.

Zones are areas in the grid allowing an agent to perform specific actions. In a *goal zone*, an agent can submit blocks for any task, while in a *role zone*, an agent can change its role, as explained below.

If the agents do nothing at all, the environment does not change except through *clear events*. These can occur at random times in any location. An area will be marked a few steps in advance so that the agents still have a chance to leave it. Then, all blocks and obstacles in the area are cleared, agents get deactivated, and new obstacles appear around the center of the area.

An agent can perceive anything in its vision range. The actions an agent can take are also explained below. To get the complete picture of the scenario, you can also read the documentation[3].

To encourage cooperation, tasks that can be completed by a single agent, i.e. those requiring only a single block have a very small compensation, while the reward drastically increases with the complexity of a task.

We are also trying to find problems that agent platforms can excel at. Therefore, agents only perceive local information. They especially do not know their absolute position in the world (which is possible but challenging to infer). Therefore, it is usually not helpful to come up with a centralized solution.

It is also one of our goals to come up with a problem that is easy to solve (in a simple, yet unoptimized way) but hard to master, i.e. so that there is a lot of room to improve.

For the third edition of the Agents Assemble scenario, we introduced some important changes to how the game is played by the teams.

2.1 Strictly Limited Number of Tasks

In the previous edition, many tasks could exist simultaneously and would persist until either completed by one of the teams or expired. Now, only a set number of tasks are active in any given step. For example, in the final tournament, there were always two tasks for the teams to complete. Each of these tasks remains, even if completed, until it is completed a certain number of times or until a timer runs out. This allows the agents to come up with a good way to complete a certain task and try to repeat the procedure a number of times. Also, it enables

---

[3] https://github.com/agentcontest/massim_2022/blob/main/docs/scenario.md.

the observer to guess what an agent is trying to achieve, as there are only a very limited number of desirable outcomes.

2.2 Addition of Roles

Agent roles were first introduced in the Agents on Mars scenario of the MAPC. Such a role gives an agent different capabilities or characteristics, e.g., the actions it is allowed to use, or certain attributes, like the amount of energy it has. While the number of agents holding a certain role was fixed at the beginning of each game in the Agents on Mars scenario, we wanted to give the agents more strategic options in the current scenario. Therefore, we introduced the concept of *role zones*, where agents are allowed to adopt a new role at any time. Each role defines the following agent parameters:

Name - of course each role needs an identifier.

Vision describes the maximum (Manhattan) distance at which the agent perceives its environment.

Actions restrict which actions can be used by the agent.

Speed means how many cells the agent may traverse per step, depending on how many blocks it carries, e.g., $[2, 1, 0]$ would mean the agent can move two cells if it doesn't carry anything, one cell if it carries one block, and not at all if it carries two or more blocks.

Clear chance is the probability for a `clear` action to not fail.

Clear max distance imposes a limit on how far away the agent can clear. Additionally, if it is 1, an agent can not damage other agents with the action.

To acquire a role, an agent has to use the `adopt` action inside a role zone. The agent will then keep the role indefinitely but can use another `adopt` action at any time (in a role zone) to pick a new role.

Table 1. The roles in the current scenario

Name	Speed	Vision	Actions	Clear
Default	1 cell with no blocks	5	move, rotate, adopt, clear, detach	1/70%
Worker	1 cell with arbitrary blocks	5	default + request, attach, connect, disconnect, submit	1/70%
Constructor	2 cells empty, 1 cell with up to 2 blocks	5	default + request, attach, connect, disconnect, submit	1/70%
Explorer	3 cells with no blocks	7	default + survey, attach	1/70%
Digger	1 cell with no blocks	5	default	5/100%

For the contest, five roles were predefined and known before the tournament, as summarized in Table 1. The DEFAULT role that each agent starts with offers basic capabilities. Of course, the agent can move, rotate, and adopt new roles. Also, it can detach from possibly attached blocks, but not attach new ones. Finally, it can clear obstacles, so that no agent can ever be stuck, i.e., if it is surrounded by obstacles. A DEFAULT agent has a vision range of 5, can move one cell per step no matter how many blocks it has attached, has a clear chance of 0.7, and can only clear obstacles directly in front of it (at distance 1).

The WORKER and CONSTRUCTOR roles are mainly intended for assembling the required shapes of blocks. They can request blocks from a dispenser, attach those blocks, cooperate with other agents to connect their blocks, disconnect them again, and finally submit the assembled shape in a goal zone. The difference is that the CONSTRUCTOR can move with speed 1 regardless of the number of blocks attached, whereas the WORKER can move with speed 2 if it does not carry anything, while it can only carry up to two blocks maximum.

The EXPLORER role was added to allow agents to scout the environment more easily at the cost of other actions. Therefore, the EXPLORER agent has a vision range of 7 and can move three cells per step. In addition to the default actions, the agent can use the attach action to attach itself to some block. However, the EXPLORER can only move without any attachments. Therefore, this action could only serve to attach the EXPLORER to something carried by another agent, so that it moves together with another agent and can use the survey action in parallel. survey can be used to search nearby targets or inspect visible agents. The EXPLORER can request the distance to the next dispenser, role zone, or goal zone, or give the coordinates of another agent to receive its name, role and energy.

Finally, the DIGGER is more adept at clearing the environment. It can only move without attachments and does not have any more than the default actions. When it comes to clearing though, the action always works (except for the random fail probability of all actions) and it can be used up to 5 cells away, i.e. on everything the agent can see. As it is a ranged clear action, it can also damage other agents, if they are hit by it.

Roles also interact with the second big addition to the scenario: norms.

2.3 Applying Dynamic Norms

A norm dynamically introduces small changes in the rules of a game. Aware of those changes, an agent can reason about them, and decide whether to follow or violate them. We say there is an *officer* in the game who announces a new norm to all agents. It also makes sure every agent violating a norm is caught and punished. To this end, the officer has a global view of the agents in the grid. Punishment is a decrease in the violator's energy level.

A norm contains:

Status: either *announced, active,* or *archived.* An announced norm means that the game's officer has announced the norm, but it has not been put in place,

Algorithm 1. Selection of a role to be constrained.

Require: $p \in [0, 1]$, a percentage of agents that may play a selected role
Ensure: $\hat{r}$, a selected role
Ensure: $\hat{c}$, an upper bound on the number of agents allowed to adopt role $\hat{r}$ per team
    Global R, a set of roles
    Global c_A^r, frequency of agents in team A adopting role $r \in R$ at the current step
    Global c_B^r, frequency of agents in team B adopting role $r \in R$ at the current step
1: sample $\hat{r}$ from a categorical distribution on R whose probabilities are the probabilities of a given agent adopting role $r_i \in R$ at the current step
2: $\hat{c} \leftarrow \lceil \max(c_A^{\hat{r}}, c_B^{\hat{r}}) \times p \rceil$
3: **return** $\hat{r}, \hat{c}$

hence the agents have some steps to prepare for the changes. An active norm states all agents violating it are punished and lasts for a given number of steps. On the other hand, an archived norm means it is no longer in place.

Subject: a characteristic of the scenario. For the 16th MAPC, a norm regulates things an agent can carry (mostly blocks), and roles an agent may adopt. The former case represents a norm influencing each agent's decision (e.g., each agent may carry at most two blocks). The latter regulates at a team level, stating how many agents may adopt any given role.

To generate a norm establishing an upper bound, per team, on the number of agents that may play the chosen role, Algorithm 1 selects a role and a limit based on the currently adopted roles in both teams. The more agents adopt a role, the higher the chance of that role being selected. To determine the limit, we use a percentage value defined in the configuration file, indicating how much usage of the chosen role should be reduced. For instance, the role EXPLORER has been selected, and currently, 20 agents are playing this role (5 agents in *Team A* and 15 agents in *Team B*). The percentage has been set to 50% in the configuration file. Then, the norm will allow 8 agents per team to play the role of explorer. If Team B has (in a step where the norm is active) 9 agents playing the role of explorer, then all 9 agents are punished.

Norms that regulate the agents' carrying skills are slightly simpler. In the configuration file, we determine bounds on things that can be attached to an agent. The generator picks a number between those bounds. Every agent having more attachable things than allowed is punished with a loss in energy points.

For the contest, we defined four norms: two for carrying things and two for roles. They are as follows.

1. Carry at most either 0 or 1 things (to be randomly selected) for $5, \ldots, 10$ steps or get punished with 10 energy points.
2. Carry at most $2, \ldots, 5$ things for $5, \ldots, 10$ steps or get punished with either 2 or 3 energy points.
3. A team must have no agent adopting a selected role for $10, \ldots, 30$ steps or lose $1, \ldots, 3$ energy points.

4. A team must have at most 50% of the upper bound for the selected role for $20, \ldots, 40$ steps either 2 or 3 energy points.

Note that agents are penalized at every step in which a violated norm is active. We designed the punishments so that they do not immediately deactivate an agent (i.e., make it lose attachable things and unable to perform actions for some steps). Also, recall that agents recover one energy point at every step.

3 The Tournament

The 16th MAPC was held on 21st and 22nd September 2022. As always, we planned the contest with 3 phases: (1) registration; (2) qualification; and (3) the contest itself. The registration aims at introducing the teams to one another. Each team briefly describes itself to the general public, pointing out the technologies they intend to use. Five teams registered for the 16th MAPC.

In the qualification phase, each team of agents plays one 400-steps simulation alone in the contest scenario. A team must submit at least one two-or-more-block task and send most of their actions in time (i.e., 70% of all actions must arrive at the contest server where the deadline per action is set to 4 s). A team has at its disposal 20 entities to control. Ultimately, all five teams passed the qualification and participated in the Contest. We introduce them in Sect. 3.1.

Finally, each team plays one match against the other participating teams in the contest. One match consists of three simulations with different parameters. The simulations differ as follows.

Simulation 1: every team has 20 agents for 400 steps in a 70×70 grid, which contains scattered obstacles. A task requires $1, \ldots, 3$ blocks (generated randomly), and a clear event produces new obstacles.

Simulation 2: 600 steps in which the number of agents and grid size remain unchanged. However, the grid is now dense in obstacles, and a clear event is more likely to remove obstacles than to add new ones. Tasks require $1, \ldots, 4$ blocks.

Simulation 3: the number of agents is increased to 40 as well as the grid size to 100x100. The teams play for 800 steps. The number of obstacles, blocks per task, and how a clear event changes the environment, follow from Simulation 2.

We depict in Fig. 1 examples of what an environment looks like in each match simulation. During a match, both teams can monitor only action results (i.e., whether an action was completed successfully or why it failed). That means the teams cannot observe the grid itself, and hence, what the opponent agents are doing. Also, they may reconnect their agents in case of bugs and connection failures, although the simulation never waits for more than 4 s for each agent to submit an action for the current step. After the contest is finished, all teams come together to watch how they performed during the matches. We call this event the "watch party".

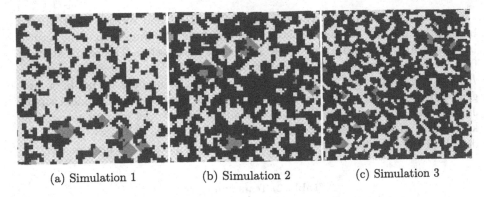

(a) Simulation 1   (b) Simulation 2   (c) Simulation 3

Fig. 1. A match between two teams in the 16th MAPC.

Even though it was not initially planned, in the 16th MAPC we had an additional warm-up phase before the main contest. Every participating team played a full match (i.e., all simulations without a break between them) against a particular adversary. We explain the goal of this phase in Sect. 3.2.

3.1   Participants

Five teams registered for the contest, were able to pass the qualification, and ultimately took part in the contest[4].

FIT BUT. The team that won the previous contest and runner-up from the year before, from Brno University of Technology, Czech Republic, consists of three members. They built on their existing Java-based approach and spent approximately six person weeks in preparation for the contest. In addition to Java, they use JADE [6] for managing agent threads. Their approach is inspired by BDI agents, nonetheless.

GOAL-DTU. Last year's runner-up from Technical University of Denmark consists of three members this time. They invested roughly 60 h in adapting their agent team to the new scenario. As the name suggests, their agents are created using the GOAL agent language [11].

GOALdigger-AIG-Hagen. The second team using GOAL is made up of four people from University of Hagen, Germany. They spent roughly 1200 h hours creating their agent team from scratch.

LI(A)RA. The team from Universidade Federal de Santa Catarina, Brazil, comprises five members: three students and two advisors. They used Jason [7] to program their agents in ca. 80 h, starting two months before the contest.

MMD. The third newcomer, from Eötvös Loránd University, Hungary, is the smallest team in this contest with only two members. The agents are programmed in regular Python. About 896 h were spent in total.

---

[4] An additional sixth team was involved in the warm-up phase.

Two of the teams, *GOAL-DTU* and *FIT BUT* had already participated before, though, in a different constellation of people. We can see that the returning teams had to spend considerably less time, as expected. The teams starting from zero had to invest a fair amount of time to build to viable agent teams. *LI(A)RA* is a bit of an outlier here, not having spent hundreds of hours on programming. Curiously, there was only a single team using Jason this time. Usually, Jason and JaCaMo [2] are the most prevalent frameworks in the contest. The key details of all teams are again summarized in Table 2. It also includes the details of the TU Clausthal student team, which is part of the next section.

Table 2. Team summary

Team	*FIT BUT*	*GOAL-DTU*	*GOALdigger*	*LI(A)RA*	*MMD*	*TUC*
Members	3	3	4	5	2	1
Time	6 p. weeks	60 h	1200 h	80(+40)h	896 h	200–300 h
Platform	Java(+JADE)	GOAL	GOAL	Jason	Python	Kotlin
Lines	12000	2000	10000	1100	5407	5000
Status	Returning	Returning	New	New	New	New

If indicated, the time spent by a team is split into programming and other tasks. As per usual, we see vastly different program sizes. The solution of *GOAL-DTU* is still quite concise, while the other GOAL solution by *GOALdigger* is at the upper end of program sizes. Notably, the Jason solution of *LI(A)RA* is even smaller than the one of *GOAL-DTU*.

3.2   Warm-Up Phase

Usually, it is the case that before a contest takes place, a participating team has not thoroughly tested its agents in environments inhabited by unfamiliar agents (i.e., agents not controlled by the team itself). This leads to many bugs during a team's first matches, eventually converging toward a stable and robust solution.

To try to minimize the chance of bugs that would directly impact the final ranking, we proposed in this contest edition a warm-up match. A master's student at Clausthal University of Technology had implemented a team of agents as part of her master's thesis. The resulting MAS became the participating team's opponent in a warm-up.

All teams played a match[5] and were provided with the corresponding logs and replays so that they could improve their agents afterward. The interested reader can find more information about the warm-up matches in the teams' description papers.

---

[5] *MMD* was the only team to play a warm-up match after the contest started.

3.3   Results

In the main phase of the contest, each team played one match of three simulations against each other team (round robin). As each win awards three points, the maximum score is 36 points this year. A draw awards one point to each of the two teams. Thus, after 10 matches, the ranking of Table 3 was established.

Table 3. Contest ranking

Place	Team	Total score	Simulations won
1	*MMD*	30	10
2	*GOALdigger*	22	7
3	*FIT BUT*	19	6
4	*GOAL-DTU*	9	3
	LI(A)RA	9	3

The team *MMD* won the Multi-Agent Programming Contest by triumphing in 10 out of 12 simulations, netting them 30 points. *GOALdigger* makes this year's runner-up with 22 points, closely followed by *FIT BUT* with 19 points. *GOAL-DTU* and *LI(A)RA* share the fourth place with 9 points each. *GOALdigger* and *FIT BUT* managed to end one simulation in a draw against one another.

4   Lessons Learned

Actions. We added two new actions (adopt and survey) and removed a single action (accept). Out of the 12 available actions, two were barely used by the teams. The action survey was not used at all, while the action disconnect was used only by a single team (i.e., *GOAL-DTU*) a few times. In this scenario, the agents could always find the intended targets (while moving around the grid) and did not need to survey them. While the survey action in the Mars scenario was strictly necessary to reveal the value of a node, here, it was optional. This once again shows that optional features need to be very advantageous to be considered. On the other hand, the effect produced by disconnecting a block is also achieved once a task is submitted, and, most of the time, the teams connect blocks at the goal zone for fast delivery. The disconnect action would be more useful if it would be required to reassemble some complex shape that is not required anymore but instead a similar one. With the smaller shapes that the contest configuration usually requested, though, it is normally not more difficult to just abandon the whole shape and assemble a new one. In order to gain a small advantage here, a potentially complex disconnect behavior would have to be implemented for the agents. Still, the action completes the set of attach/detach, connect/disconnect and could always be used to correct a mistake an agent made.

Roles. This time, we added the concept of roles to the game. Roles were last used in the Agents on Mars scenario. However, at that time, the agents had fixed roles, while this time, agents can adopt a role on demand. Thus, we are interested in how the teams used this new feature.

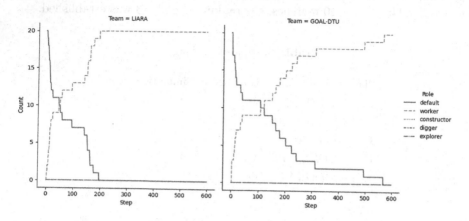

Fig. 2. Role usage in Sim. 2 of *LI(A)RA* vs. *GOAL-DTU*

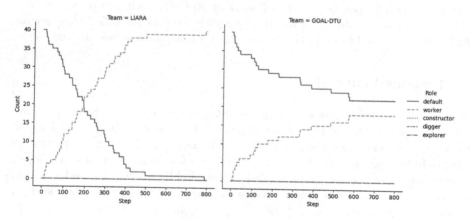

Fig. 3. Role usage in Sim. 3 of *LI(A)RA* vs. *GOAL-DTU*

In Fig. 2, we can see the typical role usage of *LI(A)RA* and *GOAL-DTU*. Both teams essentially use only two roles: the default role and the worker agents. Both teams only convert their default agents into worker agents. Other roles are not being adopted at all. We can also see that *LI(A)RA* converts agents at a higher rate than *GOAL-DTU*.

In their third simulation against each other, see Fig. 3, *GOAL-DTU* even stops with less than 20 (of up to 40) worker agents, while *LI(A)RA* ends up with all 40 agents being workers.

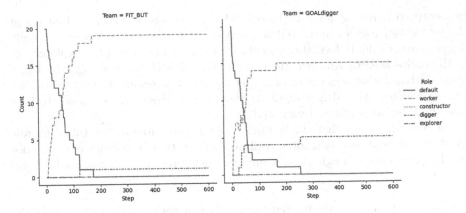

Fig. 4. Role usage in Sim. 2 of *FIT BUT* vs. *GOALdigger*

We see similar behavior from *FIT BUT* in Fig. 4. While default agents are progressively replaced with worker agents, *FIT BUT* also employs a small number (here only one, in later simulations up to 25%) of digger agents. *GOALdigger*, on the other hand, shows a similar strategy, only that more agents take the digger role. For *GOALdigger*, we also see some rare occurrences where the worker graph actually decreases, i.e., worker agents becoming digger agents.

All teams we have seen so far have decided to get many worker agents. This must have led to many norms being created that limit the number of worker agents a team is supposed to have. However, we see almost no corresponding drops in the number of worker agents.

Finally, let us consider the roles in the warm-up match between *MMD* and *Paula* (the TUC student). As pictured in Fig. 5, *MMD* converts many default agents to the WORKER role while simultaneously having a slightly lower number of constructor agents. This makes *MMD* the only team to consider the

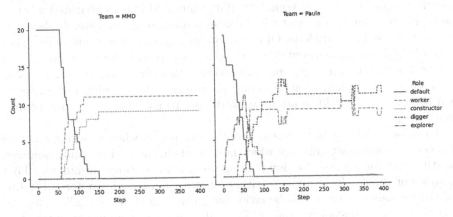

Fig. 5. Role usage in Sim. 1 of *MMD* vs. *Paula*

CONSTRUCTOR role at all. On the other hand, the agents of Paula first adopt the EXPLORER role for up to 100 steps. After that, the explorer agents usually adopt another role. In fact, these agents are the only ones using the explorer role in the entire MAPC. Another difference is that *MMD* is not using any digger agents, while *Paula* uses the most digger agents of all teams. From this, we can already conclude that digger agents cannot be that essential to a good strategy since both teams performed very well.

In general, we see that the WORKER role is preferable to the DEFAULT role (probably since it can assemble). Still, aside from that, the other roles are not strictly necessary, though they seemingly each provide a distinct strategical advantage.

Tasks. This year, we have limited the number of active tasks to 2 so that the agents' intentions become more visible, as they can only be pursuing one task or the other. While this was a step in the right direction, the number of agents and size of the grid still means many different plans are being pursued all at once, which are still not easy enough to follow. To circumvent this, one usually focuses on a specific group of agents in one particular area of the grid.

Of course, one may argue that a MAS technology should provide the means to easily interpret what any single agent or a group of agents is doing. While this is a valid argument, experience has shown we are not at this stage yet. Multiple times the MAS developers seek the MAS's graphical interface assistance to figure out what their agents are doing and what has gone wrong. Therefore, a Multi-Agent Programming Contest goal is also, for the moment, to make this task less complicated.

Norms. Norms were introduced to provide a different approach to modifying the rules of the game dynamically. When designing the norms, we did it in such a way that no agent would end up deactivated in case it decides not to follow any given norm in place. For example, if a norm is designed to reduce at every step a violator's energy in 10 points, it should be active for at most 9 steps (recall an agent's energy is bound by 100 points and it is deactivated when it has 0 energy points). An agent who violates a norm could be severely damaged tough (few energy points left). Of course, in an unpredictable environment such as the MAPC, an agent could get to the deactivated state by a combination of factors. For instance, an agent not complying with a norm and at the same step is targeted by a `clear` action of an opponent agent. Our decision turned out to lead the teams to pay little attention to the norms and just accept any coming punishment.

To enforce the agents to reason about active norms when choosing a course of action, a norm must influence what they can do in the environment. However, we still want the agents' decision-making process to be nondeterministic. That is, an agent should always pursue neither following nor ignoring a norm. Finding the right balance to drive this behavior has proven to be quite challenging and is still an open question to the MAPC. Alternatively, it seems an interesting direction to investigate norms that produce rewards instead of punishments. For example, all well-behaved agents are granted additional speed during some steps after the norm has been deactivated.

Warm-Up Matches. For the first time, we introduced a training team used as a sparring partner for each team right before the contest started. The idea was to provide a last-minute training session (or warm-up phase) to ensure smooth playing. Participants were encouraged to schedule a match against the training team a few days before the contest and most teams actually used this opportunity. The training team was developed within two months from scratch by just one person, Paula Böhm, who did this as her Master's thesis in computer science. She formulated the problem as an optimization problem (because of personal preference) and used available optimization solvers (Google-OR tools). The team was extremely successful and perhaps would end up runner-up in the competition, which was very surprising and shows that even newcomers with fresh ideas can enter the contest successfully and beat teams developed over the years by several people.

After the MAPC, three out of five teams reported that the warm-up match did not bring any new insight into their team of agents, although it helped identify and fix connection issues.

On the other hand, *FIT BUT* reported their match was of paramount importance to improve their team's performance (ending up in third place), while *GOALdigger* identified a missing feature in organizing their agents. This highlights the importance of playing against exogenous agents. However, it also demands effort from the organization side to come up with such a team.

We think the best approach to help the teams become more robust for the contest is to have them play against each other in *anonymous matches*. That is, all teams have only access to their corresponding logs, and no replays are sent afterward to ensure that a team's strategy is not disclosed before the MAPC. We also offered this sort of match to the teams, unfortunately, only one team (*GOAL-DTU*) showed interest in having such a match. This was also the case in the 15th MAPC [4] with little adhesion of participating teams.

The reason why a warm-up match is preferred over an anonymous match remains unclear to us, and further efforts are required to understand it.

Team Performance. Although this is the third edition of the Agents Assemble scenario, we still believe it was not yet mastered by the contestants. That is, there are issues to be overcome in coordination and cooperation that could substantially improve a final score. For instance, in the match between *FIT BUT* versus *GOALdigger*, in the third simulation at step 575[6], *FIT BUT* agents (numbers 2, 5, 17, and 40) managed to collect all blocks required by a four-blocks task and positioned them in a goal zone following the correct shape. However, *FIT BUT* 2 fails to send an action in time at step 576 and tries to send a submit at step 577 even though only 3 blocks are attached to it. What happens next is

---

[6] https://multiagentcontest.org/replays_2022c/?2022-09-22-12-58-01-1663847536037_FIT_BUT_GOALdigger#575.

agent *FIT BUT* 2 continues choosing action `skip` until the deadline for that task is reached (step 612), while *FIT BUT* 17 is trying to connect the fourth block to the required shape. Cooperation between those two agents is never achieved, and *FIT BUT* fails to secure 160 points. In that particular match, *GOALdigger* beat *FIT BUT* by a difference of 30 points.

Design Goals. We have to note that this time, three (i.e. half) of the teams involved (including the warm-up team) opted for using a conventional programming language, while three teams used a strictly agent-oriented platform. While this is only one instance, it might point towards a need of providing agent concepts and programming support in these conventional programming languages in addition to dedicated agent platforms, as most of these teams had to come up with their own implementations instead (the optimization-based warm-up agents being an outlier here). From the code bases, we still see the trend that agent-based platforms require less programming. The platforms already providing many features certainly plays a big role here.

From a cooperation standpoint, we have observed that teams where the agents had more cooperation were able to submit the more complex tasks and therefore the reward structure seems to have paid off.

Also, we did not see a certain strategy that gave the team using it a disproportionate advantage. If one exists, it is at least not obvious, as no team has ever found one in the current series of Agents Assemble scenarios. This is a good thing, as we are more interested in the design and programming than in particular strategies to solve the problem.

5   Outlook

We believe we have reached a moment where the MAPC should provide a way to tell when a team has mastered a given scenario. This feature would then allow us to precisely define when a scenario should be changed. Until now, on average, after three times in a row we design and propose a new scenario. However, that potentially does not mean any team has mastered the current scenario. We usually follow this approach to ensure that the participating teams keep excited about coming over for new contest editions. On the other hand, it provides little feedback on how the agent technologies are being developed and, more importantly, improved to solve complex problems. A quantitative way of determining this would undoubtedly bring forward the multi-agent programming contest.

Another topic that has been taunting the MAPC for some time is the matches duration. Due to various problems (e.g., connection latency, bugs) an agent may fail to deliver an action in time to the server. That results in a step lasting the designed deadline (usually 4 seconds) and ultimately makes a match that is supposed to last 20 to 25 minutes last for 120 minutes. This is not a rare event as it only requires, for instance, a single buggy agent to delay every step transition to their limit. This happens to be a problem because, in our current configuration, we require human operators to run both the MAPC server as well as the participating teams. It is usually the case that those operators find themselves in different time zones and therefore, finding time availability is always tricky.

To cope with no actions from the teams' side, we design the qualification to force the teams to think carefully about this issue when programming their agents. For instance, in the 16th MAPC, we allowed the teams to send a few no action to qualify. The underlying goal was achieved, and all teams came out qualified. However, during the contest, we experienced extremely long-lasting matches. For instance, the match between *GOAL-DTU* versus *FIT BUT* lasted for approximately 117 minutes. In contrast, the match *GOALdigger* versus *MMD* took approximately 31 minutes.

We envision the MAPC to be run automatically and the agents executing in different machines. Given the recent advances in containerized applications, we think the time has come to make it part of the MAPC. This was the initial approach back when it was first organized [9], but the tools at that time were unpractical. Of course, this brings both advantages and disadvantages. To name a few:

- a team will no longer be able to update their code to fix possible bugs;
- we will not encourage the development of tools to analyze and update MAS code on the fly (i.e., while a match is being played);
- we will possibly experience a decrease in interaction among participating teams (they will not be required to be online at the same time);
- we can have many more matches with different configurations;
- all teams will play under the same hardware conditions;
- it will make it possible to compare MAS technologies in terms of CPU usage and memory consumption; and
- decrease in latency and connection problems.

Aware of the implications of such a change, we asked the participating teams in the 16th MAPC their opinions on this matter.[7] To summarize, all teams mentioned the same infrastructure condition as an important advantage and the lack of updates on the code (e.g., to fix bugs) as the main drawback. Therefore, we take an automatic MAPC as a bright direction to follow.

Acknowledgments. The authors would like to thank Springer for their continuous support right from the beginning and for endowing the prize of 500 Euros in Springer books.

References

1. Aeronautiques, C., et al.: PDDL | the planning domain definition language. Technical report (1998)
2. Ahlbrecht, T., Dix, J., Fiekas, N., Krausburg, T.: Accept a challenge: the multi-agent programming contest. In: Baroglio, C., Hubner, J.F., Winikoff, M. (eds.) EMAS 2020. LNCS (LNAI), vol. 12589, pp. 129–143. Springer, Cham (2020). https://doi.org/10.1007/978-3-030-66534-0_9

---

[7] The interested reader can find their answers in the questionnaire at the end of each team description paper.

3. Ahlbrecht, T., Dix, J., Fiekas, N., Krausburg, T.: The multi-agent programming contest: a Résumé. In: Ahlbrecht, T., Dix, J., Fiekas, N., Krausburg, T. (eds.) MAPC 2019. LNCS (LNAI), vol. 12381, pp. 3–27. Springer, Cham (2020). https://doi.org/10.1007/978-3-030-59299-8_1
4. Ahlbrecht, T., Dix, J., Fiekas, N., Krausburg, T.: The 15th multi-agent programming contest. In: Ahlbrecht, T., Dix, J., Fiekas, N., Krausburg, T. (eds.) MAPC 2021. LNCS (LNAI), vol. 12947, pp. 3–20. Springer, Cham (2021). https://doi.org/10.1007/978-3-030-88549-6_1
5. Behnke, G., et al.: Hierarchical planning in the IPC. In: Workshop on HTN Planning (ICAPS) (2019)
6. Bellifemine, F., Poggi, A., Rimassa, G.: JADE–a FIPA-compliant agent framework. In: Proceedings of PAAM, London, vol. 99, p. 33 (1999)
7. Bordini, R.H., Hübner, J.F., Wooldridge, M.: Programming Multi-agent Systems in AgentSpeak Using Jason, vol. 8. Wiley, Hoboken (2007)
8. Castle-Green, S., Dewfall, A., Logan, B.: The intention progression competition. In: Baroglio, C., Hubner, J.F., Winikoff, M. (eds.) EMAS 2020. LNCS (LNAI), vol. 12589, pp. 144–151. Springer, Cham (2020). https://doi.org/10.1007/978-3-030-66534-0_10
9. Dastani, M., Dix, J., Novak, P.: The first contest on multi-agent systems based on computational logic. In: Toni, F., Torroni, P. (eds.) CLIMA 2005. LNCS (LNAI), vol. 3900, pp. 373–384. Springer, Heidelberg (2006). https://doi.org/10.1007/11750734_21
10. Harrison, W., Downs, A., Schlenoff, C.: The agile robotics for industrial automation competition. AI Mag. **39**(4), 73–76 (2018)
11. Hindriks, K.V.: Programming rational agents in GOAL. In: El Fallah Seghrouchni, A., Dix, J., Dastani, M., Bordini, R.H. (eds.) Multi-Agent Programming, pp. 119–157. Springer, Boston, MA (2009). https://doi.org/10.1007/978-0-387-89299-3_4
12. Visser, A., Ito, N., Kleiner, A.: RoboCup rescue simulation innovation strategy. In: Bianchi, R.A.C., Akin, H.L., Ramamoorthy, S., Sugiura, K. (eds.) RoboCup 2014. LNCS (LNAI), vol. 8992, pp. 661–672. Springer, Cham (2015). https://doi.org/10.1007/978-3-319-18615-3_54

Optimization-Based Agents in the 16th Multi-agent Programming Contest

Paula Böhm[✉][iD]

Department of Informatics, Clausthal University of Technology,
Julius-Albert-Strasse 6, 38678 Clausthal, Germany
`paula.boehm@tu-clausthal.de`

Abstract. In this paper we present BLUP, a system designed for the *Agents Assemble III* scenario of the 16th Multi-Agent Programming Contest (MAPC) that took place in 2022. In BLUP, agents collaborate by choosing their actions together. This is implemented by two suitable constraint optimization problems, which are solved using Google OR-Tools. BLUP won 11 out of 15 simulations in 5 games played outside the competition against all participants of the 16th MAPC, which is the second-best result achieved by any team in the contest when including the aforementioned games. We present our approach in detail, analyse the games played, and propose improvements.

Keywords: multi-agent systems · multi-agent programming contest · constraint optimization · Google OR-Tools · artificial intelligence

1 Introduction

Since 2005, 16 iterations of the *Multi-Agent Programming Contest* (MAPC) have taken place to "stimulate research in the area of multi-agent system development and programming"[1] by providing different scenarios in which multiple agents need to fulfil specific tasks. The 16th MAPC, which took place in 2022, used the third revision of the "Agents Assemble" scenario in which "Agents with limited local vision have to organize to assemble and deliver complex structures made of blocks in a grid world"[2]. As part of the MAPC, a server that implements the scenario and communicates the state of the world to the clients, which implement the behaviour of the agents and communicate their actions back to the server, has been provided and used to play all games. Further details about the MAPC, the scenario, and the communication between the server and clients can be found on the official website (see Footnote 1) and in the GitHub repository[3]. Only details that are relevant to illustrate our approach will be explicitly stated in the rest of the paper.

---

[1] https://multiagentcontest.org.
[2] https://multiagentcontest.org/2022/.
[3] https://github.com/agentcontest/massim_2022.

© The Author(s), under exclusive license to Springer Nature Switzerland AG 2023
T. Ahlbrecht et al. (Eds.): MAPC 2022, LNAI 13997, pp. 19–53, 2023.
https://doi.org/10.1007/978-3-031-38712-8_2

We introduce BLUP, a system implemented in the Kotlin programming language that is designed for the *Agents Assemble III* scenario of the 16th MAPC. In BLUP, the agents collaborate to combine their gathered knowledge and decide on their actions together. These actions are computed by solving two *constraint optimization* problems that simulate the actions of the agents and their effects on the world for a few steps ahead. We have chosen this approach because we were aware that current solvers for such problems can be very efficient and because these optimization problems reduce the need for heuristics to coordinate the actions of different agents.

While BLUP did not participate in the contest—to avoid potential bias and partiality as the group in Clausthal is organizing the competition—it played against all five participants of the contest in a warm-up phase before (and during) the games of the contest. Of the fifteen simulations of these five games, BLUP won eleven, which is the second-best result achieved by any team in the contest when taking both the games of the contest and the warm-up games into account.

An overview of the system is presented in Sect. 2, which is accompanied by a detailed discussion of the system design in the four following sections: Sect. 3 describes how groups of agents that have already identified each other share and extend their knowledge; Sect. 4 explains how shortest paths are determined; Sect. 5 discusses how units of agents are formed to work on a goal zone and fulfil tasks together; and Sect. 6 details the constraint optimization problems that are used to explore the world and to fulfil tasks. The games that have been played by BLUP against the participants of the 16th MAPC are analysed in Sect. 7, which motivates the potential improvements that are presented in Sect. 8. The paper concludes with Sect. 9.

2   An Overview of the System

The basis for each agent's actions is the knowledge of the *group* the agent belongs to. A group consists of all agents of the same team that have met and identified each other. These agents collect and extend their shared knowledge about the world (see Sect. 3) and make important decisions together, e.g. which agents should work on which goal zone. However, not every agent of a group necessarily works on a goal zone, and different agents within a group might work on different goal zones.

Each agent itself is in one of multiple different states in each step. At the beginning, each agent has the state SEARCH_ROLE_ZONE while exploring the world until the step in which the first role cell is found by the agent's group. Then, the agents switch to the state GO_TO_ROLE_ZONE, which remains unchanged while the agent goes to a role cell using a shortest path (see Sect. 4). When the agent reaches a role cell, it switches to the state GET_DESIRED_ROLE, which means that the agent performs the *adopt* action—in this situation, the *explorer* role is adopted, since it allows the agent to cover larger distances within one step. After adopting the new role, the agent changes its state to SEARCH_MAP and continues to explore the world. The precise behaviour of the agent when in one of these states is discussed in Subsect. 6.1, especially the optimization problem used when agents are in the state SEARCH_ROLE_ZONE or SEARCH_MAP.

While the agents of a group explore the world, goal zones consisting of adjacent goal cells are stored when found. In each step, an attempt is made for each goal zone to assign agents without a goal zone to it, i.e. to form a *unit* of agents working on the goal zone, if at least one goal zone and role cell has been found (see Sect. 5).

When an agent is assigned to a goal zone, it first changes its role if necessary (states GO_TO_ROLE_ZONE and GET_DESIRED_ROLE) and then moves to the target position corresponding to its job at the goal zone (e.g. a dispenser) in state GO_TO_GOAL_ZONE. To go to a role cell or the target position, a shortest path is computed and followed (see Sect. 4). When the agent reaches its target position, its state changes to WORK_ON_GOAL_ZONE and it starts working on the goal zone, for which another optimization problem is used, as discussed in Subsect. 6.2. When an agent is removed from a goal zone (e.g. because the goal zone has moved), its state is changed to DETACH_THINGS if necessary and then to SEARCH_MAP to explore the world again. An overview of the states can be seen in Fig. 1.

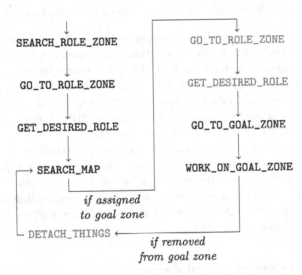

Fig. 1. An overview of the states of an agent, where blue states are only entered if necessary in a given situation. (Colour figure online)

3 Gathering Shared Knowledge

As briefly mentioned in Sect. 2, each agent belongs to a group that contains all the agents that have encountered and identified each other: Each agent forms its own group at the very beginning. The agents in a group know from then on where each agent of the group is and collect information about the world together, which is discussed in Subsect. 3.1. As goal cells and goal zones are handled in a special way, they are explained separately in Subsect. 3.2. The reaction of an agent when it sees another agent and its effect on the group are discussed in Subsect. 3.3, including the procedure to merge two groups.

3.1   The Map of the World

The group's map of the world contains the latest information about every cell (represented as a position in $\mathbb{Z}^2$) that the agents of the group have seen so far. For each seen cell, the last step in which the cell has been seen is stored along with one of the following pieces of information about the content of the cell:

- empty, if there is nothing on the cell;
- obstacle, if there is an obstacle that can be cleared on the cell;
- block together with its type;
- entity together with the team name, if the entity does not belong to the current group;
- agent together with its name, if it is an entity belonging to the current group.

The origin of this map's coordinate system is the position of the first agent of the group at the beginning of the simulation and remains unchanged when the map is updated. Therefore, each agent of the group stores its offset to this origin and updates it in each step based on the parameters and the success of the last action. When the agent's offset is updated, the map of the group is updated with the information that the agent is on its new position (i.e. its offset) and the information about the cells that the agent currently sees.

The positions of role cells, markers (together with their type and the step they were seen in), and dispensers (together with their block type) are stored separately from the map, because there can be e.g. both a dispenser and a block on one cell. Since markers are removed after the corresponding clear event, a stored marker is removed if an agent of the group currently sees the cell of a stored marker but not the marker itself.

3.2   Free Goal Cells and Goal Zones

Each group distinguishes between *goal zones*, which are created from connected goal cells if all their adjacent cells have been seen already, and *free goal cells* that have not been assigned to a goal zone yet. In every step, each group tries to construct new goal zones out of its free goal cells. If a goal zone has moved, it is possible that the agents of the group have only seen a part of the moved goal zone, but classify it as a goal zone because all adjacent cells had been seen in the past (before the goal zone moved). Therefore, more free goal cells are potentially added to a goal zone or goal zones are merged if they become adjacent. The distinction between goal zones and free goal cells is made so that one *unit* of agents per goal zone that works on a single task (see Sect. 5) is formed, which avoids forming multiple units very close to each other and thereby reduces the risk of agents blocking each other. An example showing a goal zone and two free goal cells can be seen in Fig. 2.

Each free goal cell is stored together with the last step in which it has been seen. Goal zones are stored separately, where each goal zone is represented as the set consisting of each goal cell along with the last step in which the goal cell has been seen and may have a unit of agents with different jobs assigned to it. Additionally, for each dispenser type already seen, each goal zone stores the position of the nearest dispenser of that type and its distance. Furthermore, one currently available task is assigned to the goal zone if both possible and reasonable: Tasks that require a block type for which no dispenser has been seen yet are discarded. For each remaining task, the number of steps needed to complete that task is approximated as $\max_{b \in B} 2d_b n_b$, where B is the set of block types that the given task requires, d_b is the distance of the nearest dispenser of block type b (which is doubled because the agent must go from the goal zone to the dispenser and back), and n_b is the number of blocks of type b needed for that task. The maximum is taken because the different block types are delivered in parallel by different agents and, therefore, the block type that is delivered more slowly limits the rate at which tasks are completed. If the approximated number of steps is greater than the number of steps remaining until the deadline of the task, the task is discarded. If all tasks are discarded, no task is assigned to the goal zone. Otherwise, the remaining task with the smallest approximated number of steps per fulfilled task is chosen. The task assigned to the goal zone is only updated when the previously chosen task vanishes, whereas the nearest dispensers and the task of each goal zone are updated in each step as long as no agents are assigned to the goal zone.

If an agent of the group sees a cell that should be a goal cell, but it is not, that goal cell is removed from the information stored by the group. If the goal cell was assigned to a goal zone, the entire goal zone is removed by removing all goal cells and agents assigned to it.

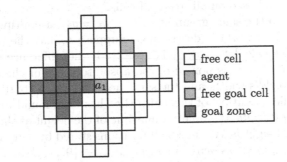

Fig. 2. An example for a goal zone and some free goal cells of a group $g_1 = \{a_1\}$. When all remaining goal cells that are adjacent to the free goal cells as well as their neighbours are discovered, these cells will form another goal zone. (Colour figure online)

3.3 Meeting Other Agents

If agent a_1 of group g_1 with offset $o_1 \in \mathbb{Z}^2$ sees another agent of the same team at position $l_1 \in \mathbb{Z}^2$ in its local coordinate system (where a_1 is at the origin), three different cases can arise:

If an agent is stored in g_1's map at position $o_1 + l_1$, a_1 already knows this agent and nothing is changed. An example of this case can be seen in Fig. 3, where a_1 is able to identify a_2 using the map.

Otherwise, an attempt is made to identify which agent a_1 sees by determining the agents of the team, apart from a_1 itself, which see exactly the same things as a_1 on all cells that both agents see at the moment (for each assuming that it is the agent which a_1 sees). If there are several agents that meet this criterion, nothing is changed. If there is only one, let it be a_2 and part of the group g_2. The further strategy depends on whether a_2 belongs to the same group as a_1, i.e. $g_1 = g_2$, or not.

If $g_1 \neq g_2$, g_2 is merged into g_1: The knowledge collected by g_2 is added to the knowledge of g_1, where each position p_2 in the coordinate system of g_2 is transformed into a position p_1 in the coordinate system of g_1 using $p_1 = p_2 - o_2 + l_1 + o_1$, where o_2 is the offset of the second agent in g_2. If both groups store different information about a cell, the newer information is stored in g_1. An example of a case where two groups are merged can be seen in Fig. 3.

The information about goal zones and free goal cells collected by g_2 is taken into account in multiple ways when merging g_2 into g_1. A goal zone of g_1 is removed together with its agents if g_2 has seen any cell of the goal zone more recently than g_1 and that cell was not a goal cell when seen for the last time by g_2. Moved goal zones are determined and handled in the same manner for the goal zones of g_2 by reversing the roles of g_1 and g_2. Each goal zone of g_2 that is already stored in g_1 is also removed together with its agents to avoid assigning two units per goal zone. If a goal zone of g_2 has not moved and does not exist in g_1 already, the goal zone is added to g_1. Free goal cells of g_2 are added to those of g_1 if they do not belong to a goal zone of g_1 already, after which g_1 tries to find new goal zones based on all free goal cells.

If a_2 belongs to the same group as a_1 (i.e. $g_1 = g_2$), a multiple of the width and/or height of the world is determined: Suppose a_2 has the offset o_2 in g_1, whereas the offset calculated by a_1 is $o_1 + l_1$. If the difference of the x coordinates of o_2 and $o_1 + l_1$ is non-zero, the absolute value of the difference is a multiple of the world's width, and the same holds for the y coordinates and the height. The smallest multiple of the width that has been found up to that point is stored as the *best width*, the smallest multiple of the height as the *best height*. If the best width or height has changed, all positions stored by a group are updated using $x_{new} = (x_{old} \bmod best\,width)$ so that $x_{new} \in \{0, \ldots, best\,width - 1\}$, and analogously for the y coordinate. To ensure that all positions are in the aforementioned value range, the best width and height are always taken into account when adding or subtracting two positions.

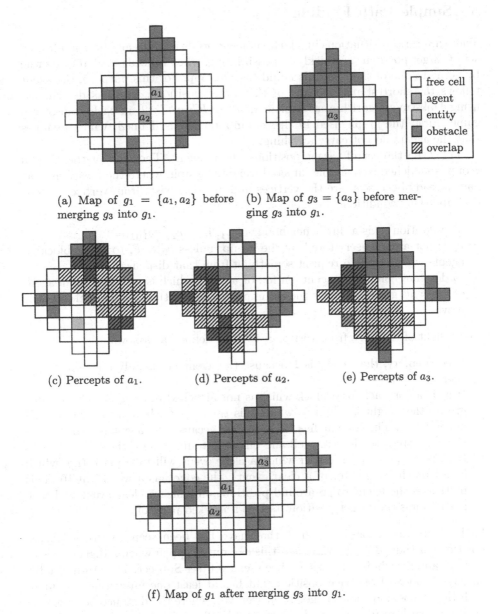

(a) Map of $g_1 = \{a_1, a_2\}$ before merging g_3 into g_1.

(b) Map of $g_3 = \{a_3\}$ before merging g_3 into g_1.

(c) Percepts of a_1.   (d) Percepts of a_2.   (e) Percepts of a_3.

(f) Map of g_1 after merging g_3 into g_1.

Fig. 3. An example for the steps taken when an agent, in this example a_1, sees two other entities. One entity is identified as a_2 by looking at the map of a_1's group. For the other entity, a check is made to see whether $a \in \{a_2, a_3\}$ (i.e. each agent of the team other than a_1) sees exactly the same things as a_1 on all cells that both a and a_1 currently see when assuming that a has the position of the unknown entity, which is visualized by hatching. As only a_3 meets this criterion, g_3 is merged into g_1. The map of g_1 after merging can be seen in Subfig. (f). (Colour figure online)

4   Simple Path Finding

There are various situations in which an agent needs to go to any position from a set of target positions as quickly as possible, e.g. when it needs to change its role by going to one of the role cells found by its group. For this purpose, the agent follows the shortest path to any of the target positions, which is determined using Dijkstra's algorithm as implemented in *JGraphT* [2] in each step of the game. First, the graph used in these computations is defined, which assumes that the agents do not carry anything.

Let T be the set of target positions of the agent. The map of the agent's group is modelled as a simple directed weighted graph, where the positions that have already been seen are the vertices and an edge exists from vertex v_1 to v_2 if all following conditions are met:

- The position v_2 is a direct neighbour of v_1, i.e. $||v_2 - v_1||_1 = 1$.
- v_2 is not a dispenser stored by the group, unless $v_2 \in T$, to avoid blocking agents which want to request something from that dispenser.
- v_2 does not contain an agent, entity, or a block which is attached to an agent of the same group, because the assumption is made that other entities do not move.

The weight of the edge from vertex v_1 to v_2 is defined as follows:

- If v_2 is empty, the weight is 1 because the agent needs only one step to get there.
- If v_2 is an obstacle or a block which is not attached to an agent of the same group, the weight is $\lceil \frac{1}{c} \rceil + 1$, where c is the clear probability of the agent's current role. This weight has been chosen because the agent is expected to need $\lceil \frac{1}{c} \rceil$ steps to clear the cell and one step to move onto the cell.
- If v_2 is a marker position on which a clear event will take place (i.e. which is not on the perimeter of a clear event), the edge has a weight of 10. This motivates the agent to go around positions on which a clear event will take place unless the target position itself is a marked position.

If there are target positions in T that have not been seen yet, these target positions are added to the vertices—this can only happen when a digger goes to its flock and the whole tube has not been seen yet (see Subsect. 5.2). Additionally, an edge is added from each position that has at least one unseen neighbour to each target position that has not been seen yet, where the distance between the positions (with respect to the L_1 norm) multiplied with two (which represents that it is very likely that some unseen cells are not empty) is chosen as the edge weight.

This graph is used to determine the shortest paths from the agent's position to any of the target positions. If there is no reachable target position (which is unlikely), the agent does nothing, i.e. it performs the *skip* action. Otherwise, it follows the shortest path by clearing the next cell on the path if it contains an obstacle or unattached block. If not, it moves at most as far along the path as the agent's current role allows, but stops if it encounters an obstacle or a block on the path.

The same graph is used when determining whether a cell is reachable by checking whether a shortest path exists.

5 Managing Units

5.1 Assigning Agents to Units

For each group and step, an attempt is made to assign agents to each goal zone that has been found by the group and has a task assigned to it (see Subsect. 3.2) if at least one role cell has been found, which enables agents to change their role. The agents that are assigned to the same goal zone form the *unit* working on the goal zone, and each agent that is assigned to a unit gets a *job*. There exist the following jobs:

- A *constructor* waits on the goal zone for the blocks needed for the assigned task, attaches/connects these blocks, and submits the task.
- A *worker* of block type b gathers and delivers blocks of type b.
- A *digger* of block type b clears the world between the closest dispenser of its block type and the goal zone.

The number of agents assigned to each job is required to be between the following predetermined minimum and maximum for each goal zone, where d_b is the distance of the closest dispenser of block type b and the goal zone, n_b the number of blocks of type b needed for the task assigned to the goal zone, $m := \max\{n_b : \text{block type } b \text{ required for the task}\}$, and c the clear distance of the *digger* role:

- *constructor* job: Exactly one is required per unit.
- *worker* job: For each required block type b, there must be at least one worker and there can be at most $\lceil \frac{d_b}{6} \cdot \frac{n_b}{m} \rceil$ workers per unit. Therefore, the maximum number of workers for a block type is higher if the dispenser is further away or if the task needs more blocks of that type than of other types.
- *digger* job: For each required block type b, there must be at least one digger and there can be at most $\lceil \frac{d_b}{c} \rceil$ diggers per unit.

The minimum number of agents is assigned to a goal zone, i.e. a unit is formed, if no agents are assigned to this goal zone yet and there is a sufficient number of agents that are neither assigned to a goal zone nor detaching things—these agents are called *free agents*. If this is the case, the position the constructor will occupy once it reaches the goal zone is determined first, as described in Subsect. 5.4. This position will be called *constructor position*. Then, the free agents closest to the constructor position (with respect to the L_1 norm) are assigned to the goal zone (first to the *constructor* job, then to the remaining jobs and block types in an arbitrary order) until the minimum number of agents is reached. If the goal zone has a unit assigned to it (by now), it is assigned additional free agents which have a distance of less than 20 to the goal zone (with respect to the L_1 norm) until at most the maximum number of agents is reached for all jobs and block types. Here, the algorithm iterates over the block types first and then over the jobs that depend on the block type (worker and digger) in an arbitrary order.

If an agent is assigned to the goal zone, it stores its goal zone, its job, and, if it is a worker or digger, both the block type assigned to it and the position of the nearest dispenser of that type (with respect to its goal zone). Additionally, each digger stores an index that reflects the order in which the diggers of the same block type were assigned to the goal zone and which is used to determine the *flock* of the digger.

5.2   The Flock of a Digger

The flock of a digger with block type b includes all cells which a digger should prefer to clear, which is taken into account in the optimization problem used to submit tasks (see Subsect. 6.2). To determine the flock of a digger, first the cells on the line between the position of its constructor and its dispenser are determined using Bresenham's line algorithm [1]. The set T of all positions that have a distance of at most $\lfloor \frac{c}{2} \rfloor$ to a point on this line form the *tube* between the dispenser and the goal zone, where c is the clear distance of the *digger* role.

Let n be the number of diggers with block type b assigned to the goal zone and $l(u) := (1 - u)p_0 + up_1$, where $p_0 \in \mathbb{Z}^2$ is the constructor position, $p_1 \in \mathbb{Z}^2$ is the dispenser position, and $u \in [0, 1]$. Then the centre of the flock of the digger with index i (starting at 0) is at $d_i := l(\frac{i+0.5}{n})$ (rounded to the nearest integer). The flock itself contains all positions which are in the tube T and have a distance of at most $\lfloor \frac{d+c}{2} \rfloor$ from the centre of the flock, where $d := \lceil n^{-1} ||p_0 - p_1||_1 \rceil$. Therefore, the combined flocks of the diggers assigned to the same goal zone and block type cover the whole line between the dispenser and constructor position (because of $\frac{d}{2}$) as well as the entire tube and the surroundings of both the dispenser and the constructor position (because of $\frac{c}{2}$). An example can be seen in Fig. 4.

5.3   Going to a Goal Zone

If an agent is assigned to a unit, it first changes its role (to the *worker* role if it is a worker or constructor, otherwise to the *digger* role), if necessary. To change its role, it follows the shortest path to any role cell, as described in Sect. 4, by choosing the set of role cells found by the agent's group as the set T of target positions.

After adopting the corresponding role, the agent goes to a target position by following a shortest path again, as described in Sect. 4, where the set T of target positions depends on the job of the agent:

– constructor: T consists only of the constructor position;
– digger: T is the flock of the digger;

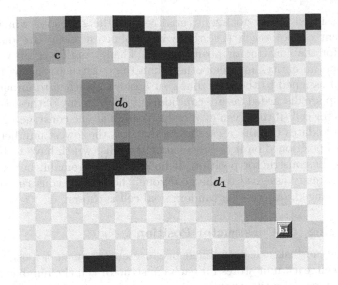

Fig. 4. An example for the flocks of two diggers. **c** represents the constructor position, d_0 the centre of the first digger's flock, which is coloured cyan, and d_1 the centre of the second digger's flock, which is coloured yellow. The overlap of the flocks is coloured green, the remaining appearances are identical to the replays (see Sect. 7). (Colour figure online)

- worker: T consists only of the cell that is closest to the agent while being adjacent to the dispenser if it is not occupied (i.e. another agent, entity, or block attached to an agent of the group is on it) or all cells which have a distance of exactly two to the dispenser are also occupied. Otherwise, T consists only of the cell that is closest to the agent while having a distance of exactly two to the dispenser and not being occupied.

If the agent is a constructor or digger and reaches one of its target positions, it starts working on the task (i.e. its state changes from GO_TO_GOAL_ZONE to WORK_ON_GOAL_ZONE). The same happens when the agent is a worker and it reaches a position which has a distance of at most four to its target position to avoid blocking the dispenser. The behaviour of the agents which have the state WORK_ON_GOAL_ZONE is discussed in Subsect. 6.2.

5.4 Computing the Constructor Position

The following steps are performed to determine the constructor position for a goal zone that has a task assigned to it when forming a new unit, or when constructor cells of an existing unit are blocked for a long time (which is discussed in the next subsection), or when the tasks assigned to a unit changed:

Let the *constructor cells* be the cells on which blocks have to be in order to submit a task, given a constructor position and a task. If a constructor agent is already assigned to the goal zone, goal cells of the goal zone which the constructor agent cannot reach (i.e. there is no shortest path) are discarded as candidates for the constructor position first. Then, candidates on which there is a dispenser, an entity, an agent other than the constructor agent (if one has already been assigned to the goal zone), or a block attached to an agent of the current group are discarded, as are candidates for which any of these things is on any constructor cell (if the given goal cell is treated as the constructor position).

If any candidates remain, a candidate that has the lowest number of blocks and obstacles positioned on it or its constructor cells (which have to be cleared) is chosen as the constructor position. If no candidates remain, but a constructor agent is already assigned to the goal zone, the current constructor position remains unchanged, otherwise a random goal cell is chosen.

5.5   Changing the Constructor Position

To avoid that no task can be fulfilled because an opponent is positioned on a constructor cell, each unit stores for each constructor cell the number of the last consecutive steps an entity that is not part of the current group has been on that cell. If an entity has been on the same constructor cell for at least the last 8 steps, a new constructor position is determined as described in the previous subsection. If the new constructor position is different from the current position, the constructor agent has to go to it (changing its state to DETACH_THINGS, if necessary, and then GO_TO_GOAL_ZONE).

The constructor position is also updated in each step in which the constructor agent goes to the constructor position (i.e. while its state is GO_TO_GOAL_ZONE), but cannot reach it.

5.6   New Tasks

When a task disappears, the following procedure is applied to each unit to which this task had been assigned: First, an attempt is made to choose a new task as described in Sect. 3. If this does not succeed, or it does but there is a block type required for the new task which no agent is assigned to, all agents assigned to the unit are removed from it (and a new unit is potentially built as described in Subsect. 5.1). Otherwise, only the agents whose assigned block type is no longer needed are removed from the goal zone. Additionally, a new constructor position is determined (as described in Subsect. 5.4) if the current constructor position is not suitable: the constructor agent cannot reach the current constructor position or a dispenser, entity, agent other than the constructor agent, or a block attached to an agent of the current group is on a constructor cell with respect to the new task.

6   Collaboration Using Optimization Problems

For each group, there are two different goals which a subset of agents of the group try to achieve together by collaborating: exploring the world and submitting tasks.

It is important for the agents to explore the world and thereby extend their knowledge about it, e.g. to find role cells, goal zones, and dispensers, so that the agents can change their roles and start working on goal zones. Therefore, all agents of the group which are in state SEARCH_ROLE_ZONE or SEARCH_MAP try to explore the world, which is realized through an optimization problem that is executed in each step of the game and formally defined in Subsect. 6.1.

Based on the knowledge gained through exploration, the main goal of the game is to work on goal zones and thereby collect as much money as possible by submitting tasks, which poses several challenges: For example, the actions around the constructor need to be coordinated so that the blocks needed for the task are placed on the correct cells to submit the task. In general, it is important that agents do not block each other, especially close to constructors or dispensers. To meet these challenges, each group uses another optimization problem for all agents which are in state WORK_ON_GOAL_ZONE, which is executed in each step of the game and discussed textually in Subsect. 6.2.

6.1 Exploring the World

The optimization problem for exploring the world simulates a few future steps of the game, where each step is subdivided into *sub-steps*. The number of sub-steps is equal to the speed of the agent (to allow for actions such as move(["s", "e", "s"]) if the speed is 3). The potential actions of the agents are realized as corresponding variables for each simulated step, while the constraints ensure that the agents can only perform valid actions. Within the optimization problem, the assumption is made that agents which are not simulated (because they do not belong to the same group or are not exploring the world) do not move and that any agent exploring the world has no things attached to it. The goal of this optimization problem is to discover as many unseen cells as possible while staying on already seen cells, which is expressed by the objective function. To implement and solve this problem, the Java version of the CP-SAT solver from Google OR-Tools [3] was used, a constraint programming solver that is limited to integer variables. It has won in various categories of the MiniZinc challenge [4] in each year since 2013 and therefore seemed like a good choice for this project.

The optimization problem is formally defined next.

Definitions. The following symbols are used in the constraints and the objective function, where cells are represented as their positions in $\mathbb{Z}^2$:

- $T \in \mathbb{N}$ is the number of steps which are simulated. The last step represents the end state of the simulation, i.e. no actions are simulated in the last step.
- $M \in \mathbb{N}$ is the maximal *amount* of an obstacle that can be on a cell, i.e. each obstacle that has not been subject to a *clear* action has the amount M, which drops below M once *clear* actions have been applied to it. Here, M is used to represent the clear probabilities of the agents as integers by multiplying them by M (rounding them naturally).
- A is the set of agents.

- *MaxStepCells*: $A \to \mathbb{N}$ is the speed of the agent, i.e. the maximum number of cells that a given agent can traverse in one step.
- *ClearAmount*: $A \to \{0, \ldots, M\}$ is the amount of an obstacle the agent removes when clearing, which is its clear probability multiplied with M (rounded naturally).
- *ViewDist*: $A \to \mathbb{N}$ is the maximum distance a cell can have from a given agent for that agent to see it.
- $Ts := \{1, \ldots, T\}$, $TsR := \{1, \ldots, T-1\}$ are sets of all steps and of all but the last step, respectively.
- $Ss(a) := \{n \in \mathbb{N} : 1 \leq n \leq MaxStepCells(a)\}$ is the set of all sub-steps for $a \in A$.
- $MS(a) := TsR \times Ss(a) \cup \{(T,1)\}$ is the set of all *move steps* for $a \in A$, which are tuples composed of a step and a sub-step. For the last step, only the tuple consisting of itself and the first sub-step is part of this set, as it represents the final state of the simulation.
- $MSR(a) := TsR \times Ss(a)$ is the set of all move steps excluding the last step for $a \in A$.
- $NSTS_a$ is the next move step for $a \in A$ and $(t, s) \in MSR$:

$$NSTS_a(t,s) := \begin{cases} (t, s+1) & \text{if } s < MaxStepCells(a) \\ (t+1, 1) & \text{else} \end{cases}$$

- $N_{\leq}(c, d) := \{\gamma \in \mathbb{Z}^2 : ||c - \gamma||_1 \leq d\}$ is the set of neighbours of $c \in \mathbb{Z}^2$ with a distance of at most $d \in \mathbb{N}$.
- *Seen* $\subset \mathbb{Z}^2$ is the set of cells that have already been seen at the beginning of the simulation.
- $V \subset$ *Seen* is the set of seen cells excluding dispensers and agents that are not simulated, i.e. cells that an agent could potentially visit in the simulation.
- *Clearable* $\subset V$ is the set of seen cells which the agent is permitted to clear (i.e. obstacles and blocks which are not attached to an agent of the group and are not on a dispenser).
- $C = \{c \in \mathbb{Z}^2 : \min_{\gamma \in V} ||c - \gamma||_1 \leq \max_{a \in A} ViewDist(a)\} \setminus$ *Seen* is the set of cells that have not been seen yet but could be discovered by visiting cells in V.

The Variables. This problem has two main variables:

- $AgOn_{(c,a,t,s)} \in \{0, 1\}$ is true if and only if $a \in A$ is on $c \in V$ in $(t, s) \in MS(a)$.
- $Clear_{(c,a,t)} \in \{0, 1\}$ is true if and only if $a \in A$ clears $c \in V$ in $t \in TsR$.

The remaining variables are then defined based on these variables:

- $New_c \in \{0, 1\}$ is true if and only if $c \in C$ has become visible due to the movement of the agents.
- $Move_{(a,t,s)} \in \{0, 1\}$ is true if and only if $a \in A$ moved in $(t, s) \in MSR(a)$.
- $ClearAny_{(a,t)} \in \{0, 1\}$ is true if and only if $a \in A$ cleared a cell in $t \in TsR$.

- $ClearedAmount_{(c,t)} \in \{0, \ldots, 2M - 1\}$ is the amount of $c \in V$ that has been cleared before $t \in Ts$. It can be at most $2M - 1$, which is reached e.g. if an agent with a clear probability of $M - 1$ clears the cell in the first step and an agent with a clear probability of M clears the same cell in next step. It is not allowed to exceed this limit, as the constraints prevent clearing a cell that has been fully cleared already, i.e. if $ClearedAmount \geq M$.

The Constraints. $AgOn_{(c,a,1,1)}$ is set to the state of the world at the beginning of the simulation. Additionally, $AgOn_{(c,a,t,s)}$ is set to false for all $(t, s) \in MS$ and all marker positions c if $a \in A$ is not on a marker position at the beginning of the simulation, i.e. in move step $(1, 1)$, which prevents agents from going from unmarked onto marked cells and potentially being deactivated. Furthermore, there are the following constraints:

- Define New_c to be true if and only if any agent is on a visitable cell from which it can see the cell c in any step:

$$\forall c \in C : New_c \leftrightarrow \bigvee_{\tau \in Q} AgOn_\tau$$

with $Q := \{(\gamma, a, t, 1) : a \in A, \gamma \in N_{\leq}(c, ViewDist(a)) \cap V, t \in Ts\}$

- Define $Move_{(a,\tau_1)}$ to be true if and only if there is a visitable cell on which a is in move step τ_1, but not in the next move step τ_2:

$$\forall a \in A, \tau_1 \in MSR(a) : Move_{(a,\tau_1)} \leftrightarrow \bigvee_{c \in V} \left(AgOn_{(c,a,\tau_1)} \wedge \neg AgOn_{(c,a,\tau_2)} \right)$$

with $\tau_2 = NSTS_a(\tau_1)$

- Define $ClearAny_{(a,t)}$ to be true if and only if a clears exactly one cell (the sum cannot exceed one because $ClearAny$ is a Boolean variable) in step t:

$$\forall a \in A, t \in TsR : ClearAny_{(a,t)} = \sum_{c \in Clearable} Clear_{(c,a,t)}$$

- Define $ClearedAmount_{(c,t)}$ to be the amount of c that has been cleared before step t:

$$\forall c \in Clearable, t \in Ts :$$

$$ClearedAmount_{(c,t)} = \sum_{\tau=1}^{t-1} \sum_{a \in A} ClearAmount(a) \cdot Clear_{(c,a,\tau)}$$

- Each agent is on exactly one cell in all move steps:

$$\forall a \in A, (t, s) \in MS(a) : \sum_{c \in V} AgOn_{(c,a,t,s)} = 1$$

– At most one agent can be positioned on each visitable cell in each step:

$$\forall c \in V, t \in Ts : \sum_{a \in A} AgOn_{(c,a,t,1)} \leq 1$$

– An agent can only be positioned on an obstacle in a given move step if it is expected to be fully cleared in the previous step, i.e. its clear amount is at least M:

$$\forall c \in Clearable, a \in A, (t,s) \in \{(t,s) \in MS(a) : t > 1\} :$$
$$M \cdot AgOn_{(c,a,t,s)} \leq ClearedAmount_{(c,t-1)}$$

– Each agent can only move to an adjacent cell (or not at all) in each sub-step:

$$\forall c \in V, a \in A, \tau_1 \in MSR(a) : AgOn_{(c,a,\tau_1)} \rightarrow \bigvee_{\gamma \in C} AgOn_{(\gamma,a,\tau_2)}$$
$$\text{with } \tau_2 = (t_2, s_2) = NSTS_a(\tau_1) \text{ and } C := N_{\leq}(c,1) \cap V$$

– Each agent does not move once it stopped within a given step, which reduces the number of otherwise equivalent solutions with respect to the objective function:

$$\forall a \in A, t \in TsR, s \in SSR(a) : \neg Move_{(a,t,s)} \rightarrow \neg Move_{(a,t,s+1)}$$
$$\text{with } SSR(a) := \{n \in \mathbb{N} : 1 \leq n < MaxStepCells(a)\}$$

– If an agent clears anything in a given step, it cannot move in that step:

$$\forall a \in A, t \in TsR : ClearAny_{(a,t)} \rightarrow \neg Move_{(a,t,1)}$$

– An agent a can only clear a cell if it is close enough, where $MaxClearDist(a)$ is the maximum distance that a cell can have for a to clear it:

$$\forall c \in Clearable, a \in A, t \in TsR : Clear_{(c,a,t)} \rightarrow \bigvee_{\gamma \in C} AgOn_{(\gamma,a,t,1)}$$
$$\text{with } C := N_{\leq}(c, MaxClearDist(a)) \cap V$$

– An agent can clear a cell in a given step if it has not been fully cleared already through actions in earlier steps or actions of other agents in the given step:

$$\forall c \in Clearable, a \in A, t \in TsR : M \cdot Clear_{(c,a,t)} < 2M - Cleared$$
$$\text{with } Cleared := ClearedAmount_{(c,t)} + \sum_{b \in A \setminus \{a\}} ClearAmount(b) \cdot Clear_{(c,b,t)}$$

The Objective Function. The objective function is defined as follows, where $MSI(a, (t,s)) := MaxStepCells(a) \cdot (t-1) + s$ is the index of move step $(t,s) \in MS$

for $a \in A$:

$$\text{maximize } F \cdot \sum_{c \in C} New_c + S_1 + S_2$$

$$\text{with } S_1 := \sum_{a \in A} \sum_{\tau \in MSR(a)} MSI(a, \tau) \cdot (1 - Move_{(a,\tau)}),$$

$$S_2 := \sum_{a \in A} \sum_{t \in TsR} t \cdot (1 - ClearAny), F := \sum_{a \in A} \sum_{\tau \in MSR(a)} MSI(a, \tau) + |A| \sum_{t \in TsR} t$$

The first sum maximizes the number of newly discovered cells, the second maximizes the number of move steps in which the agent does not move, and the third maximizes the number of steps in which nothing is cleared. In the latter two cases, later (sub-)steps have a higher weight than earlier ones through the use of the index of the (move) step as the weighting factor, which incentivizes actions at the start of the simulation, since the first simulated step determines the actual action of the agent. This also disincentivizes move and clear actions that do not lead to newly discovered cells and thus reduces the number of equivalent solutions. F is an upper bound for the latter two sums, which results in the first sum always having precedence over the latter ones.

Determining the Next Actions. To determine the action of each agent a, it is investigated whether there is a cell $c \in V$ such that $Clear_{(c,a,1)}$ is true in the solution of the optimization problem. If this is the case, clearing this c is a's next action. Otherwise, it is examined whether there are sub-steps $s \in Ss(a)$ such that $Move_{(a,1,s)}$ is true. If there are such s, a will move over the corresponding cells as the next action.

If neither of the two cases is given, the set of all cells in the group's map for which an adjacent unseen cell exists is determined. If this set is not empty, the agent follows the shortest path to any of these cells, as described in Sect. 4, by setting the set T of target positions to this set. If this set is empty, the set of seen cells for which "old" information is stored are determined. A cell fulfils this property if it has been seen for the last time in a step not greater than $t_o = \max\{t_m, t - 30\}$, where t_m is the step in which the cell that has been seen the longest time ago has been seen and t is the current step. If this second set is not empty, each agent follows the shortest path to any cell from this set, as described in Sect. 4 (where T is set to the second set). Otherwise, the agent performs the *skip* action.

Changing the Role. If an agent has the *default* role while exploring the world and at least one role cell has been found by the group, it suspends its exploration and is therefore no longer part of the optimization problem. Instead, it goes to a role cell to adopt the *explorer* role to increase its speed. To do this, the agent follows the shortest path to any known role cell, as described in Sect. 4 (where T is set to the set of all role cells found by the agent's group).

6.2 Working on Tasks

To determine the actions of all agents of a group that work on a goal zone, another optimization problem simulating some future steps of the game is used. This problem is essentially an extension of the optimization problem used for exploring the world (see Subsect. 6.1), but far more expansive and complex: Multiple different jobs with different associated actions as well as attached blocks (each occupying a cell) are taken into account. Therefore, a formal definition of the problem is omitted for brevity's sake and an outline of the problem is presented instead.

In this optimization problem, the *worker* job is divided into two separate *statuses*: the *gatherer* and *deliverer* status. These statuses are updated outside the optimization problem and do not change within it. When a worker carries no blocks, it gets the *gatherer* status, whose purpose it is to attach two blocks of the type assigned to it (unless there is a norm that permits only one) from a dispenser. A gatherer can only attach blocks that are adjacent to itself and positioned on a dispenser, i.e. it is not able to attach blocks lying around somewhere else. Once a gatherer has the desired number of blocks attached to itself, it gets the *deliverer* status to deliver its attached blocks to its constructor. Only when a deliverer carries no more blocks, it gets the *gatherer* status again. The agent's job/status (constructor, digger, deliverer, or gatherer) is considered in the variables, constraints, and the objective function, which are discussed next.

The Variables. The variables are based on the variables of the optimization problem for exploring the world, but take into account the additional jobs/statuses of the agents: On the one hand, there are additional variables that describe the state of the world, such as unattached blocks on a dispenser or the attached blocks of the agents. On the other hand, the additional potential actions of the agents are represented through additional variables, such as rotating, requesting or attaching a block from a dispenser, attaching or connecting a block as a constructor, connecting or detaching a block as a deliverer, or submitting.

The Constraints. The constraints ensure that the agents can only perform valid actions and that these actions have the corresponding effects on the simulated world. Most of the constraints defined in Subsect. 6.1 are also used here, but slightly modified to take the different jobs of the agents and their attached blocks into account. Additionally, further constraint are added to incorporate the actions that have been introduced for this optimization problem: For example, the constraints ensure that a worker with attached blocks can only rotate in a given direction if the new positions of the attached blocks are (expected to be) free.

The Objective Function. The objective function reflects the goals and purposes of the agents' jobs by summing up different components for each agent depending on its job and status.

The most important component of each constructor serves to maximize the number of submissions, which are weighted more highly than all other components combined, while the only other component exists to maximize the number of clears. For each agent apart from the constructor, the two least important components are designed to maximize the number of move steps without movement and the number of steps without an action other than moving, respectively, especially at the end (analogously to S_1 and S_2 in the objective function from Subsect. 6.1). Both of these do not apply to constructors, as these cannot move and are forced to submit as soon as possible.

The remaining components reflecting the purpose of each digger are the following, ordered by their importance:

1. Maximize the number of *clear* actions that apply to blocks from the flock of the digger.
2. Minimize the distance from the closest obstacle in the digger's flock (up to its clear distance).
3. Maximize the number of *clear* actions that apply to blocks outside the flock.

The following components that apply to workers are weighted so that they should have a higher weight than any component of the digger in most cases. This incentivizes the diggers to perform actions that help the workers to fulfil their purpose.

The components (again ordered by importance) that express the purpose of each gatherer are the following:

1. Maximize the number of gatherers which carry as many blocks as they are allowed to.
2. Maximize the number of attached blocks.
3. Maximize the number of requests.
4. Minimize the distance from the dispenser assigned to the gatherer (up to a distance of 1).

The components (ordered as before) expressing the purpose of each deliverer are the following:

1. Maximize the number of attached blocks that a constructor attaches or connects.
2. Maximize the number of deliverers that deliver all their blocks.
3. Maximize the number of directions in which no block is attached.
4. Minimize the weight of a shortest path from the deliverer to a constructor cell of the same type. The graph for the shortest path is constructed to incentivize the deliverers to move towards the constructor cells even if they are blocked (but preferably free one), assuming that the other simulated agents move out of the way.

Determining the Next Actions. The action of each agent a in the next step is determined based on the solution of the optimization problem by investigating whether there is a variable v which is true in the first step and represents an action that is allowed to the job of a. If this is the case, the action that the variable v represents is the next action of a. Otherwise, if the agent a is not a constructor (which is not allowed to move) and there are sub-steps of the first step in which the agent moves, a's next action is to move over the corresponding cells. If neither of these two cases applies to the solution, the agent performs the *skip* action.

7 Analysing the Matches

BLUP played against each of the five teams taking part in the 16th Multi-Agent Programming Contest (FIT BUT, GOAL-DTU, GOALdigger, LI(A)RA, and MMD) outside the competition to avoid the appearance of collusion. The games served as warm-up matches for the teams participating in the competition, giving them the opportunity to play a game shortly before the competition and, thereby, to find bugs when playing against the agents of another team. The games against FIT BUT, GOAL-DTU, and GOALdigger took place two days before the start of the tournament, the game against LI(A)RA the day before. However, the game against MMD was played on the second day of the tournament, as it was not possible for MMD to play the game earlier.

As in the tournament, each game consisted of 3 simulations: In the first two simulations, the world had a size of 70×70 and each team had 20 agents at its disposal, where the first simulation consisted of 400 and the second of 600 steps. The third simulation consisted of 800 steps with a world size of 100×100 and 40 agents per team. Additionally, there were only two different block types in the first simulation, whereas there were three different block types in the other two. The amount of money collected in each simulation and the corresponding score of each game can be seen in Table 1—BLUP won 11 out of 15 simulations and won at least one simulation against each opponent, sometimes by large margins. This is the second-best result achieved by any team in the contest when including the games played in the contest.

Each team had a timeout of 4 s for sending the action of each of its agents to the server in each simulation. To comply with this time limit, an appropriate number of steps to simulate was determined experimentally for both optimization problems: If the team consists of 20 agents, 3 steps are simulated in the optimization problem for exploring (i.e. $Ts = \{1, 2, 3\}$) and 5 steps in the optimization problem for working on tasks, otherwise one step less for either optimization problem. Additionally, a timeout is set for solving the optimization problems for each group: If the solver is able to find a feasible solution (optimal or not) in time, the best solution found up to the timeout is used. Otherwise, in the case of the optimization problem for exploring, each agent performs the same action as if the agent performs the *skip* action in the solution (see Subsect. 6.1); in the case of the optimization problem for working on tasks, constructors perform the *skip* action, while the other agents move to the adjacent cell to the north if it is empty and not a dispenser (so that dispensers are not blocked for other workers

Table 1. The results of the games played outside the competition. The first value is always the result achieved by BLUP, the second value is the result of the corresponding opponent.

Opponent	Simulation 1	Simulation 2	Simulation 3	Score
FIT BUT	480 : 0	360 : 330	250 : 60	9 : 0
GOAL-DTU	710 : 320	610 : 280	570 : 0	9 : 0
GOALdigger	160 : 330	220 : 700	1270 : 320	3 : 6
LI(A)RA	600 : 110	120 : 60	1000 : 90	9 : 0
MMD	770 : 580	500 : 790	450 : 1690	3 : 6

of the team), or clear it if this cell is an obstacle or block unattached to an agent of the group, or skip otherwise.

When solving the optimization problem for exploring, the timeout was set to $1.75\frac{n}{o}$ s, while a timeout of $3\frac{n}{o}$ s was used when solving the problem for working on tasks, where n is the number of agents simulated in the corresponding optimization problem and o the number of agents which are part of any optimization problem of the team. The code was executed on the laptop of the author, which runs Manjaro Linux and contains an Intel Core i7-9750H CPU (6 cores à 2 threads) as well as 16 GB of RAM.

Subsection 7.1 discusses the strengths and weaknesses of BLUP which the analysis of the games it played revealed and which should lay a foundation to understand the games whose replays can be watched on the official website[4]. The appearance of all figures in this section is based on the appearance of the replays, where BLUP is always the second team and therefore coloured green. After this, a summary of the games played by BLUP is given in Subsect. 7.2. It is important to note that the first four games were played using an older version of the code, which contained some questionable behaviour and bugs that were fixed for the game against MMD. As the latest version of the code has been described in the previous sections, the changes in behaviour will be discussed where they had a significant impact.

7.1 Strengths and Weaknesses of the Approach

The Optimization Problem for Exploring the World. This optimization problem worked well in all simulations and no anomalies were found in the analysis of the games. To estimate how well the optimization problem worked, the first step in which there were no agents with the *default* role can be examined, since each agent of a group immediately goes to the next role cell, as soon as at least one has been found by exploring, and changes its role from default to something else and never chooses the *default* role again. In the first and second simulation, there were no agents with the *default* role after an average of 82

---

[4] https://multiagentcontest.org/2022/#replays.

and 85 steps, respectively. Therefore, the approach seems to have worked well, as the world consisted of $70 \times 70 = 4900$ cells with only 5 role zones (each one consisting of at most 61 cells) in the first two simulations. The same holds for the third simulation, in which there were no agents with the *default* role after an average of 133 steps (ignoring the third simulation against FIT BUT, where a bug caused the program to crash in the beginning) in a world consisting of $100 \times 100 = 10000$ cells (again with only 5 role zones with at most 61 cells).

The Optimization Problem for Working on Tasks. This optimization problem worked well in many situations, as it is the part which is responsible for submitting tasks and BLUP collected more money than the opponent in 11 of 15 simulations. An example in which the agents submitted two tasks consisting of three blocks in a short time can be seen in Fig. 5.

But this optimization problem also has some room for improvement. The biggest limitation was the small number of simulated steps to avoid exceeding the timeout of 4 s. If far more steps had been simulated, most problems should not have occurred in the optimization problem, as submitting tasks is the most important aim due to having the largest weight in the objective function. But as this is not the case, components and heuristics that incentivize desirable behaviour in the short term to submit tasks later are part of the optimization problem. However, these were not free of bugs, did not lead to the desired behaviour in all situations, or did not cover all possibles scenarios:

Deliverers were not allowed to clear cells in the optimization problem, although an agent carrying blocks can still clear adjacent cells. This resulted in deliverers waiting for a digger to clear a path, although they could have done it themselves (e.g. agent 13, a deliverer, in step 115 of the first simulation against FIT BUT).

In the optimization problem, a digger is allowed to clear blocks attached to an agent of the opposing team, which is useless, as an attached block cannot be cleared. In rare cases, this erroneous ability led to situations in which a digger tried to clear a block attached to an opponent to enable a deliverer to go onto the corresponding cell. As this was never successful, but the optimization problem continued to give this solution, the deliverer froze (i.e. skipped) until the task changed or the unit was removed. An example for this behaviour can be seen in Fig. 6.

In addition, there were diggers which did not clear cells that prevented a deliverer from moving towards its constructor or did not make room for a deliverer, instead clearing something (else). An example can be seen in Fig. 7. This problem, which occurred very rarely, was only fixed before the game against MMD by assigning higher weights to the components of the objective function that apply to the workers than to any component applying to the digger in most cases. This change resulted in the diggers helping the deliverers if that was possible within the simulated steps: In the aforementioned figure, the digger would move south and clear the obstacles blocking the deliverer. However, there were still situations in which the number of simulated steps was too low for a digger

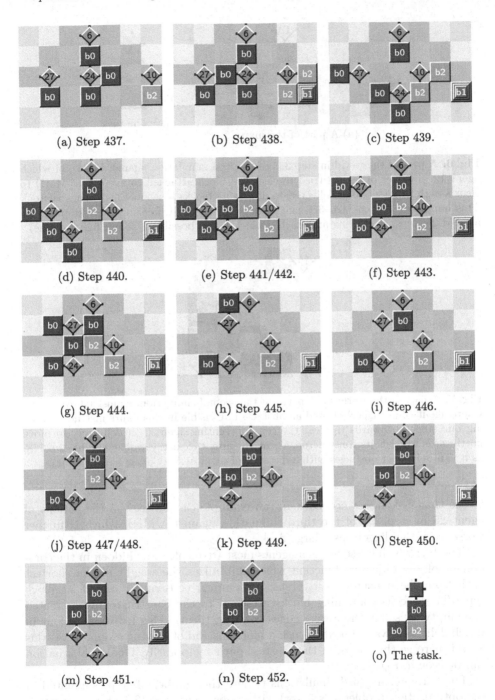

(a) Step 437.

(b) Step 438.

(c) Step 439.

(d) Step 440.

(e) Step 441/442.

(f) Step 443.

(g) Step 444.

(h) Step 445.

(i) Step 446.

(j) Step 447/448.

(k) Step 449.

(l) Step 450.

(m) Step 451.

(n) Step 452.

(o) The task.

Fig. 5. Steps 437–453 of the third simulation against GOALdigger, during which agent 6 (the constructor) submitted the task visualized in Subfig. (o) twice. (Colour figure online)

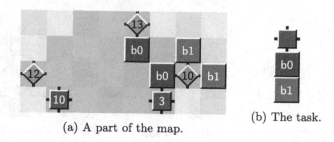

(a) A part of the map.

(b) The task.

Fig. 6. A part of the world in step 333 of the first simulation against MMD, in which agent 12 (a digger of BLUP) tried to clear the block attached to agent 3 of MMD to clear a path for agent 10 (a deliverer) to deliver its blocks to agent 13 (the constructor). This happened in steps 326–356 and resulted in agent 10 freezing (i.e. skipping) for around 25 steps, as clearing an attached block is not possible. (Colour figure online)

Fig. 7. A part of the world in step 178 of the second simulation against GOAL-DTU, where agent 16 (a digger) cleared an obstacle not visible in this figure instead of moving one step southwards to clear the cells preventing agent 6 (a deliverer) to move northwards towards its constructor. Agent 16 cannot clear these obstacles in step 178, as it can only clear obstacles with a distance of at most 5. (Colour figure online)

to see that a deliverer needed help (an example can be seen in the actions of agent 25 in step 295 of the third simulation against MMD), which is further worsened if the digger has a large flock.

The bug which caused frozen agents most frequently was hidden in the component of the objective function which minimizes the weight of the shortest path from the deliverer to a (preferably empty) constructor cell of its block type: There, cells containing blocks attached to the constructor were treated like empty cells (i.e. there were edges entering them). This led to situations in which deliverers waited next to such a block instead of moving around it, as this would increase the length of the shortest path temporarily. One such situation can be seen in Fig. 8.

Furthermore, in third simulations (where the number of steps simulated in the optimization problems is lower), situations where insufficient collaboration occurred close to the constructor occurred very occasionally, not because of a previously mentioned problem, but because no heuristic was added for such a

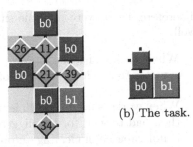

(b) The task.

(a) Part of the map.   (b) The task.

(a) Part of the map.

Fig. 8. A part of the world in step 171 of the first simulation against GOAL-DTU in which agent 2 (a deliverer with only the block to its north attached to it) skipped instead of moving around the attached blocks of agent 19 (the constructor) to deliver its block. This happened in steps 167–175 until the task vanished. (Colour figure online)

Fig. 9. A part of the world in step 314 of the third simulation against LI(A)RA where agent 39 (a deliverer) remained on the same cell instead of delivering its block to agent 26 (the constructor), because agent 21 (a deliverer) did not make room. This resulted in the goal zone being blocked for around 15 steps. (Colour figure online)

case. This is mainly due to deliverers that do not make room for other deliverers, as this would increase their length of the shortest path temporarily and the number of simulated steps is too low to see the future benefits. An example for this problem can be seen in Fig. 9. Additionally, it is disadvantageous to carry two blocks instead of one in this example: If only one block had been carried, agent 21 would have moved away already and agent 39 could deliver its attached blocks.

However, there were multiple situations in which carrying two blocks was beneficial: For example, a task consisting of three blocks was submitted in step 178 and 186 on the same goal zone during the first simulation against GOAL DTU because each of the three deliverers was carrying two blocks.

Gathering Shared Knowledge. The approach described in Sect. 3, in which all agents of the group gather shared knowledge together by storing e.g. a map of the world as well as merging two groups of agents when agents of different groups meet, worked well.

Managing Units. The approach for assigning agents to jobs to start working on a goal zone is the component that needs the most improvement. As described in Subsect. 5.1, the agents that are closest to the goal zone with respect to the L_1 norm are assigned to a unit of a goal zone, but this does not take into account that an agent might have to change its role first, which takes additional time. Furthermore, agents are assigned to jobs and block types in an arbitrary order.

Therefore, there were multiple situations in which the approach did not work well:

- When workers needed much fewer steps to reach the dispenser than the constructor to reach its constructor position and therefore had to wait to deliver blocks.
- When workers needed much fewer steps than the diggers to start working, but then had to wait for the diggers to clear a path for many steps, as a worker is not capable of clearing an obstacle when carrying more than one block.
- When the unit had far more agents for one block type than for another, although the task did not need more blocks of this type, so that the deliverers of one block type had to wait close to the constructor for the other deliverers. An example is the unit with agent 12 as its constructor around step 219 in the second simulation against GOAL-DTU, which had only one worker for block type b_2, but four for block type b_0, although the task required two blocks of each type.

Additionally, there was also a bug which made it possible that a digger had a flock assigned to it that was much larger than intended, which was fixed before playing against MMD. All these problems when assigning agents to a job were very noticeable and severe in some simulations and will later be referred to as the *Assignment Problem* when giving examples in the summary of a simulation.

There were also situations in which the distance between the dispenser and the goal zone was large, but only one digger per block type was assigned to the unit, which worked poorly. This was a consequence of requiring only one digger per block type and unit, but not assigning further ones in these situations. An example can be seen in the second simulation against MMD where agent 10, a digger, had a large flock around step 170. Furthermore, it can be observed (e.g. in step 160 of the first simulation against FIT BUT) that the approach of removing a unit when the goal zone is assigned a new task with a new block type (see Subsect. 5.6) could be improved. This is especially problematic, as the agents of the unit to be removed are only assigned to a unit again when they do not carry any block and therefore have to detach their blocks first, which can waste many steps for gathering new blocks. How advantageous it is to reuse a unit is evident in the situations in which the task assigned to a goal zone vanished, but the newly chosen task needed no additional block types compared to the previous one, as the unit is reused under these circumstances. An example can be seen in third simulation against GOALdigger, where there was a new task in step 596 and the unit with agent 6 as the constructor was reused. This made it possible to submit the new task, which consisted of three blocks, in step 604 for the first time.

A bug appears to be present when changing the constructor position, as described in Subsect. 5.5, since it worked in some situations (e.g. in step 122 of the first simulation against MMD, where agent 19 changed its position), but did not work in others (e.g. in step 272 of the third simulation against GOALdigger, where agent 33 did not change its position).

Removing a Unit. Another problem of BLUP, which will later be called the *Digger Bug*, was a bug that caused some diggers not to be removed from a goal zone properly when their unit was removed because of a new task. Instead, these diggers remained assigned to the same goal zone, retained their flock, and were never assigned to another goal zone. Therefore, these diggers became unnecessary once removed from a goal zone but continued to clear the world, which became very free of obstacles towards the end of most simulations. This bug, which had a small impact on some simulations (e.g. the first simulation against FIT BUT) and a large impact on others (e.g. the second simulation against FIT BUT), was only fixed for the game against MMD.

7.2   A Summary of the Matches

In this subsection, the games BLUP played are summarized and only problems which had a big negative influence on a simulation are mentioned again. The approach of every opponent differed from that of BLUP in that the opponent's agents almost always carried at most one block and were able to clear a path in more situations than the deliverers of BLUP, as well as having no constructor agents remaining and waiting in the goal zone for all required blocks. Some benefits and downsides of these differences are discussed in Sect. 8.

The Game Against FIT But. BLUP won all simulations against FIT BUT, which must have had a severe bug in the first simulation, as none of its agents ever attached a block (unlike in the later simulations), and was therefore unable to submit tasks. In the other two simulations, FIT BUT submitted tasks, but there were multiple occasions in which agents of FIT BUT carried all blocks required for a task (very close) to the goal zone, but were not capable of connecting the blocks properly or to submit. This happened on goal zones on which a unit of BLUP was working, but the teams were not blocking each other (e.g. in steps 160 and 448 of the second simulation), as well as on goal zones on which no unit of BLUP was working, but a digger of BLUP was on or very close to the goal zone (e.g. in steps 275 and 475 of the second simulation).

Additionally, FIT BUT had a few agents for which no action was sent to the server in some steps of the third simulation, which suggests that FIT BUT's program was sometimes too slow to send all actions before the timeout was reached. FIT BUT also blocked a dispenser in some steps of the third simulation by keeping a block on a dispenser for around 20 steps after attaching it to an agent (agent 29 in steps 542–560) or keeping an agent on the dispenser itself for around 70 steps (agent 29 in steps 725–799).

For BLUP, the Digger Bug was the most severe problem in the second simulation: This bug resulted in 17 agents having the *digger* and only 3 agents having the *worker* role from step 216 onwards, which resulted in the existence of only one unit with two workers and one constructor working on a task and contributed to the simulation being the closest BLUP played. Nevertheless, three tasks consisting of three blocks were submitted after step 216, which shows all the more how well the optimization problem can work.

While the Digger Bug had a negative impact on the third simulation too, although less severe than in the previous simulation (there were at least 31 diggers starting in step 623), the third simulation was the first and only simulation in which a catastrophic bug appeared that led to an eventual crash of the program: Only few actions were sent until step 120, in which the entire program crashed. The program was restarted in step 132, but the bug was not fixed, which resulted in actions not being sent to the server from step 262 onwards and the program crashing in step 280. After the first crash of the program, an attempt was made to fix the bug, which was part of computing the shortest path (see Sect. 4), and a "try-catch block" was added around the corresponding function, which makes the agent perform the *skip* action if an exception is thrown. The program was restarted successfully in step 374 and has not crashed since then. However, the agents had to explore the world again, as all earlier knowledge was lost, so that the first task was submitted in step 492. Furthermore, there were four agents which had blocks already attached to them when restarting the program, but three of them (agents 7, 8, and 19) were not aware of this, as the procedure to detach blocks when the program is restarted did not work correctly. This led to strange behaviour such as unsuccessful moves.

The Game Against GOAL-DTU. BLUP also won all simulations against GOAL-DTU, collecting more than twice as much money in each simulation, while the third simulation was the only simulation in which GOAL-DTU did not make any money in spite of its agents carrying blocks around.

The problems and bugs of BLUP described in Subsect. 7.1 had a relatively small impact in the first simulation, resulting in the amount of money collected by BLUP being the second-highest collected by a team in a first simulation of a warm-up game.

The money collected in the second simulation was the highest amount of money collected by BLUP in a second simulation and the first time that BLUP submitted a task consisting of four blocks. Among other things, the Digger Bug is again to blame for the fact that more money was not collected in the second simulation, because it caused the team to have 18 digger from step 410 onwards. This problem was even worse in the third simulation, as there were 40 diggers from step 469 onwards, so that the last task was submitted in step 446.

The Game Against GOALdigger. GOALdigger was the only opponent of BLUP which targeted the agents of BLUP on or close to a goal zone with clear actions. Through those clear actions, an agent looses energy and finally becomes deactivated, which makes it lose its attached blocks. The difficulty that arises when a digger tries to clear an opponent is that the digger, from now on called *saboteur*, cannot be sure that the agent of the opponent remains on the same position and therefore has to predict the future position of the opponent. The approach of BLUP to have a constructor agent waiting on the same position for the blocks to be delivered mitigates this difficulty for the opponent's agents.

Therefore, there were multiple situations in which the saboteurs of GOALdigger prevented attempts of BLUP to deliver blocks or submit tasks by deactivating a constructor or deliverer, and the first two simulations were the first simulations in which BLUP lost.

The tasks submitted by BLUP were either submitted on goal zones where no saboteur was active (e.g. the first task submitted in step 39 of the first simulation or all tasks submitted in the second simulation, apart from the last task) or on goal zones where saboteurs were trying to attack the agents of BLUP, but the deliverers were fast enough not to be deactivated. For example, saboteurs regularly attacked the unit of constructor agent 12 in steps 127–239 in the first simulation so that only one task consisting of three blocks and 4 tasks consisting of one block were submitted on this goal zone by BLUP.

In addition, the Digger Bug had a noticeable negative influence on BLUP in the first simulation, where it had at least 18 diggers from step 291 onwards, and in the second simulation, where it had at least 19 diggers from step 462 onwards, so that it was not capable of submitting any task since then. In the second simulation, the Assignment Problem also weighed heavily: Agent 7 waited during steps 147–201, agent 15 during steps 88–100, and agents 8 and 9 during steps 134–215, for a digger to clear a path to deliver their blocks.

However, BLUP won the third simulation against GOALdigger by collecting $1270, which was the highest amount of money collected by BLUP in any simulation. GOALdigger did not send an action for some agents in step 542 and sent no action at all between steps 543 and 550. Until step 542, BLUP had already collected $610 by submitting tasks on goal zones with no active saboteurs (which were active on other goal zones), whereas GOALdigger had only collected $320. From step 551 onwards, actions were sent for all agents of GOALdigger, except for six diggers, in each step and the agents of BLUP were not attacked by saboteurs since then. The biggest problem of BLUP in this simulation were the problems of the optimization problem for working on tasks, which resulted in agents that were frozen for up to around 65 steps.

The Game Against LI(A)RA. Against LI(A)RA, BLUP won all simulations with at least twice as much money as LI(A)RA in each simulation.

While the Digger Bug was very noticeable in the second simulation, resulting in at least 18 diggers from step 390 onwards, the Assignment Problem bears a lot of blame for not getting more money in the first and second simulation. In the first simulation, this was evident when a block of one type was requested in step 36 and the other one only in step 73 for a task needing two types of blocks or when agent 8 (a deliverer) waited for a digger to help in steps 126–238. The second simulation contained some situations in which this problem was significant as well, e.g. in steps 125–185 in which agents 10 and 5 (deliverers) waited for a digger to help. Because of these problems, the amount of money BLUP collected in the second simulation was the lowest amount BLUP collected in any simulation, but still more than the opponent.

In the third simulation, the Digger Bug (which resulted in 30 diggers from step 655 onwards) had a relatively small influence as well as the Assignment Problem.

The Game Against MMD. BLUP won the first simulation against MMD, the future winner of the Multi-Agent Programming Contest of 2022, collecting the highest amount of money in any first simulation of a warm-up match: The only very noticeable problem of BLUP was the problem visualized in Fig. 6 resulting in a frozen deliverer for around 25 steps. This simulation shows how successful the approach of BLUP can be.

However, BLUP lost the second and third simulation against MMD. The Assignment Problem was severe in both simulations: In the second simulation, agent 12 (a deliverer) waited for around 65 steps (starting in step 144) for a digger, agent 10 (a constructor) waited for a worker to request a block for around 60 steps (starting in step 404). In the third simulation, agent 26 waited as a constructor on its goal zone from step 147 onwards, but the first block was requested by a worker of the corresponding unit only after approximately 50 steps. In another situation in the third simulation, agent 17 (a worker) requested a block in step 598, but had to wait until step 648 for the constructor (agent 8) to reach its constructor position—only then could it begin to carry the blocks to the constructor. Furthermore, the problems of the optimization problem for working on tasks resulted in frozen deliverers in three different situations (for up to around 40 steps) in the third simulation. This makes the third simulation a good example for the strong negative influence the problems of both the optimization problem for submitting tasks and the Assignment Problem can have.

8   Possible Improvements

To improve the approach presented in earlier sections, the bugs and problems discussed in Subsect. 7.1 should be resolved. Bugs are not mentioned again in this section, as solving them is straightforward given their description. However, changes to the design of BLUP which can alleviate or solve the problems are proposed:

Since at least half of the agents had the *digger* job for the majority of the time—even after solving the Digger Bug—and the deliverers are dependent on diggers (as they cannot always clear a path themselves when carrying two blocks), it seems reasonable to remove the *digger* job, use those diggers as additional workers, and let workers carry at most one block. This way, each worker carries less (making it easier to clear a path), but there are at least twice as many workers and the workers are no longer dependent on diggers, so that a significant part of the Assignment Problem should be solved.

Based on this change, assigning agents to a unit could be improved as well by assigning those agents whose approximate number of steps before reaching the goal zone—including the number of steps needed to change the role and, if it is a worker, to go to the dispenser between adopting the role and going to the goal zone—is the lowest, instead of choosing agents that are closest to the goal zone with respect to the L_1 norm. Additionally, the block types should not be iterated over in an arbitrary order when assigning workers to a unit that already has the minimal amount of agents. Instead, it is more sensible to try assigning a worker to the block type whose quotient of already assigned workers and the maximal number of workers for this block type is the lowest. Here, only workers can be assigned whose approximate number of steps to reach the goal zone (as just described) is smaller than the number of steps before the deadline of the task. Furthermore, agents with an attached block but no unit should be candidates for joining a unit without detaching the block. The approximate number of steps when assigning such an agent to the same block type should only be the approximate number of steps to reach the goal zone (as it can deliver its attached block). Otherwise, detaching the block and going to the dispenser must be included in this number.

Moreover, when iterating over the goal zones to assign agents to them, it seems more reasonable to order the goal zones based on a measure of their quality instead of an arbitrary order. For example, the goal zones could be iterated over in ascending order with regard to the maximal distance between the goal zone and its closest dispenser of any block type needed for its task. In addition, assigning a task to a goal zone could be improved by also taking the reward of the task into account and by reconsidering the chosen task if a new task appears.

Lastly, the *constructor* job could be removed, as the constructor skips most of the time in most cases. Instead, all agents that work on a goal zone could be workers, and an agent carrying a block of the type that is needed first when building the task could fulfil the function of the constructor agent when it reaches the goal zone (if there is no such agent already).

9   Conclusion

In this paper we have presented BLUP, the first system to take part in the MAPC that utilizes constraint optimization techniques (to the best of our knowledge), which BLUP uses to explore the world and to complete tasks by simulating a few future steps. The solutions to these optimization problems made it possible to find role and goal zones quickly and to coordinate the agents close to dispensers and constructors. This allowed BLUP to build units of agents working together on a task quite early in each simulation and to occasionally fulfil even very large tasks.

However, the limited number of simulated steps hampered the effectiveness of BLUP when working on tasks, as long-term benefits were sometimes ignored when making decisions. Some issues and bugs—most importantly when computing shortest paths for the agents—were not resolved in time for the warm-up matches that BLUP played, and some design decisions and further implementation errors affected the assignment of agents to the goal zones. In spite of these limitations, BLUP won 11 out of 15 simulations against the participants of the contest (which BLUP did not participate in) and won at least one simulation against each contestant. This demonstrates the effectiveness of the approach and makes it a promising choice for participants in future iterations of the MAPC.

10   Team Overview: Short Answers

10.1   Participants and Their Background

Who is part of your team?
  Paula Böhm, who was a master student at TU Clausthal during the 16th MAPC, was the only member of the team.
What was your motivation to participate in the contest?
  To write my Master thesis.
What is the history of your group? (course project, thesis, . . .)
  I was in the last semester of my Master's degree during the development of BLUP and during the 16th MAPC.
What is your field of research? Which work therein is related?
  I have mainly used machine learning and mathematical optimization (which is related to my approach here) and worked on mobile app development in projects and for my Bachelor thesis.

10.2   Statistics

Did you start your agent team from scratch, or did you build on existing agents (from yourself or another previous participant)?
  I started my team from scratch.
How much time did you invest in the contest (for programming, organizing your group, other)?
  About 200–300 h for programming.
How was the time (roughly) distributed over the months before the contest?
  The work was distributed over the last two months before the contest.
How many lines of code did you produce for your final agent team?
  Around 5000 lines of code.

10.3   Technology and Techniques

Did you use any of these agent technology/AOSE methods or tools? What were your experiences?

Agent programming languages and/or frameworks?
  No.
Methodologies (e.g. Prometheus)?
  No.
Notation (e.g. Agent UML)?
  No.

Coordination mechanisms (e.g. protocols, games, ...)?
A centralized agent manager processes the percepts of the agents, tries to combine their knowledge, and coordinates their collaboration.
Other (methods/concepts/tools)?
Constraint optimization.

What hardware did you use during the contest?
My laptop, which contains an Intel Core i7-9750H CPU (6 cores à 2 threads) as well as 16 GB of RAM.

10.4 Agent System Details

Would you say your system is decentralized? Why?
No, as the centralized agent manager plans the actions for groups of agents.
Do your agents use the following features: Planning, Learning, Organizations, Norms? If so, please elaborate briefly.
The agents organize into groups of agents, in which units of agents working on the same goal zone are formed.
How do your agents cooperate?
Sharing knowledge and planning actions together in groups, especially based on constraint optimization problems.
Can your agents change their general behaviour during run time? If so, what triggers the changes?
Each agent has different states which entail different behaviour, e.g. searching the map or working on a goal zone. The state changes e.g. when a role zone is found or when a task vanishes.
Did you have to make changes to the team (e.g. fix critical bugs) during the contest?
Yes.
How did you go about debugging your system? What kinds of measures could improve your debugging experience?
Printing lots of information into log files and visualizing parts of the collected information as image files.
During the contest, you were not allowed to watch the matches. How did you track what was going on? Was it helpful?
Printing some basic information to the command line (e.g. the score), but this was not helpful for analysing the development of the score.
Did you invest time in making your agents more robust/fault-tolerant? How?
Yes, by catching exceptions and finding appropriate fallback actions.

10.5 Scenario and Strategy

How would you describe your intended agent behaviour? Did the actual behaviour deviate from that?
Agents search the map, form groups of agents they know, and form units

working on goal zones to fulfil tasks. The approach used to form groups and the approach used to work on tasks deviated from the intended behaviour in some situations, as they contained some deficiencies and bugs.

Why did your team perform as it did? Why did the other teams perform better/worse than you did?

Exploring the world worked very well, working on tasks worked well (apart from some noticeable bugs), while the approach used to form units had some significant issues.

Did you implement any strategy that tries to interfere with your opponents?

No.

How do your agents coordinate assembling and delivering a structure for a task?

Each unit working on a goal zone has an agent that waits on the goal zone, attaches/connects blocks delivered by other agents, and submits the fulfilled task. All of this was handled by one of the optimization problems.

Which aspect(s) of the scenario did you find particularly challenging?

Determining how much of a partially successful action was successful.

What would you improve (wrt. your agents) if you wanted to participate in the same contest a week from now (or next year)?

Fix bugs, make all agents that work on a goal zone carry blocks, and carry only one block per agent.

What can be improved regarding the scenario for next year? What would you remove? What would you add?

Add information about the blocks attached to an agent to its percepts. Consider removing or punishing agents that sit on dispensers for many steps.

10.6   And the Moral of it is . . .

What did you learn from participating in the contest?

Using optimization problems can be very effective, but requires a lot of fine-tuning if the runtime is very limited.

What advice would you give to yourself before the contest/another team wanting to participate in the next?

When the deadline comes closer, do not add more elaborate functionality, but focus on fixing existing components.

Where did you benefit from your chosen programming language, methodology, tools, and algorithms?

A lot of existing tools are written in Java and can therefore be used in Kotlin. Without CP-SAT (or something similar) this approach would not have been feasible, since solving these optimization problems efficiently is very challenging.

Which problems did you encounter because of your chosen technologies?

Kotlin is not particularly fast and the Java version of CP-SAT adds overhead.

Which aspect of your team cost you the most time?

Implementing and debugging the optimization problems.

10.7   Looking into the Future

Did the warm-up match help improve your team of agents? How useful do you think it is?
They were very useful for me;)

What are your thoughts on changing how the contest is run, so that the participants' agents are executed on the same infrastructure by the organizers? What do you see as positive or negative about this approach?
That depends on the performance of the infrastructure (better hardware would have been useful for CP-SAT). This approach would be fairer, but make bug fixes during a simulation a lot harder. Additionally, participants would need to test their agents on the hardware to comply with the timeout.

Do you think a match containing more than two teams should be mandatory?
I am unsure: With the current number and sizes of the goal zones, agents blocking each other would become more common.

What else can be improved regarding the MAPC for next year?
See the suggestions for the scenario mentioned earlier, but the contest was well-organized already.

References

1. Bresenham, J.E.: Algorithm for computer control of a digital plotter. IBM Syst. J. **4**(1), 25–30 (1965). https://doi.org/10.1147/sj.41.0025
2. Michail, D., Kinable, J., Naveh, B., Sichi, J.V.: JGraphT–a Java library for graph data structures and algorithms. ACM Trans. Math. Softw. **46**(2), 1–29 (2020). https://doi.org/10.1145/3381449
3. Perron, L., Furnon, V.: OR-Tools. https://developers.google.com/optimization/
4. Stuckey, P.J., Becket, R., Fischer, J.: Philosophy of the MiniZinc challenge. Constraints **15**(3), 307–316 (2010). https://doi.org/10.1007/s10601-010-9093-0

MMD: The Block Building Agent Team with Explainable Intentions

Miklós Miskolczi and László Z. Varga(✉)

Faculty of Informatics, ELTE Eötvös Loránd University, Budapest 1117, Hungary
{psbdho,lzvarga}@inf.elte.hu

Abstract. The Multi-Agent Programming Contest (MAPC) is an excellent test ground to stimulate research on the development and programming of multi-agent systems. The current Agents Assemble III scenario is a nice example for cooperative distributed problem solving in a highly dynamic environment, and it requires that the agents are normative agents. For MAPC 2022, we have implemented the MMD multi-agent system from scratch in the Python programming language to find out if a multi-agent system can be developed efficiently in a general programming language using multi-agent concepts. We describe the implementation details, including the coordination and the optimisation algorithms of the MMD multi-agent system to solve the complex and dynamic tasks, and also including the testing aspects that use explainable intentions as well. The performance indicators of the implementation are the development time, the development efforts, and the quality of the job done by the implemented multi-agent system. The development time of the MMD system is not more than any other system at MAPC 2022, including those that were implemented with agent-oriented programming. The comparison of the development efforts of the contest participants is difficult because the performance of the systems are also different, but the development effort is more likely to be independent from the implementation language used. The first position of the MMD system at MAPC 2022 seems to indicate that the implemented MMD multi-agent system is competitive with the systems developed with agent-oriented software engineering methods.

Keywords: Practical reasoning architecture · Blackboard architecture · Explainable intention

The work of L.Z. Varga was supported by the "Application Domain Specific Highly Reliable IT Solutions" project which has been implemented with the support provided from the National Research, Development and Innovation Fund of Hungary, financed under the Thematic Excellence Programme TKP2020-NKA-06 (National Challenges Subprogramme) funding scheme.

T. Ahlbrecht et al. (Eds.): MAPC 2022, LNAI 13997, pp. 54–97, 2023.
https://doi.org/10.1007/978-3-031-38712-8_3

1   Introduction

The Multi-Agent Programming Contest[1] (MAPC) is an excellent test ground to stimulate research on the development and programming of multi-agent systems. In the current Agents Assemble III scenario the agents explore a grid world and execute dynamically announced tasks. The goal of a task is to create a structure of blocks in goal areas, which requires that the blocks are collected, delivered and assembled by a group of agents. This is a nice example for cooperative distributed problem solving [5]. The Agents Assemble III scenario requires that the agents are normative agents [16]. The capabilities of the agents depend on their current role. Roles can be adopted at specific role areas. The agents have to adopt roles that are better suited for their specific goals, but they also have to take into account the norms that regulate the adoptable roles. The norms are dynamically created.

According to the previous experiences of MAPC, the systems that were developed with multi-agent programming languages usually performed better than those that were developed in a general programming language [2]. On the other hand, the history of multi-agent system research seems to show that the theoretically crafted platforms seldom lead to practical applications. The prime examples of agent systems are like Siri, Alexa, Cortana, high frequency algorithmic traders [17], massive fleet of warehouse robots [18], and the IT giants have their own implementations of multi-agent technologies like negotiation mechanisms [6].

When preparing for MAPC 2022, we thought that the agent-oriented software engineering methods and the related planning systems would involve restrictions for us. In addition, an experimental Python communication client for the 2020/21 edition of the Multi-Agent Programming Contest, used in the WESAAC 2021 short course [1], became available[2]. Therefore we decided to implement the MMD multi-agent system from scratch in the Python programming language to find out if a multi-agent system can be developed efficiently in a general programming language using multi-agent concepts.

We present our work in the following order. Section 2 describes the logical agent team architecture and how it is mapped to the software architecture of the implementation. Section 3 describes how the agents represent their beliefs of their environment, and how they find their way. Section 4 describes how the team is coordinated. Section 5 describes the building blocks of the individual agent behaviours. Section 6 describes the debugging of the system and how the agents helped this by explaining their intentions. In Sect. 7 we analyse the matches at the contest. Finally, in Sect. 8 we conclude our work.

---

[1] https://multiagentcontest.org/2022/.
[2] https://github.com/agentcontest/python-mapc2020.

2 Architecture

2.1 Agent Team Architecture

The architecture of the MMD multi-agent system is based on two architectural concepts: the blackboard architecture [7] and the practical reasoning agent architecture [3] as shown in Fig. 1. This is a reasonable architecture, because the MAPC requires cooperative distributed problem solving [5]. The team level problem solving is done on the blackboard, while the individual problem solving is done in the agents.

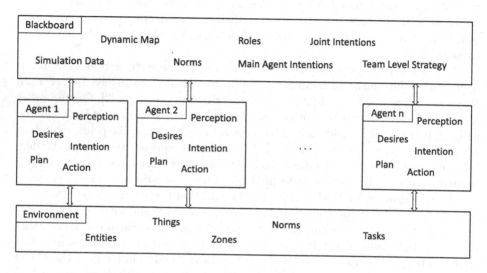

Fig. 1. The architecture of the MMD multi-agent system.

The agents have their own perceptions, desires and intentions. The perception is immediately submitted to the blackboard, where the perceptions from all the agents are processed, and the agents use this processed perceptions in their reasoning. The blackboard is not just a passive data store, because it has active reasoning capabilities as well, like reasoning on the team level strategy, and making decisions on the individual and the joint intentions [10] for the agents. This way, the blackboard is a coordinator similar to the general deSouches of the FIT BUT solution in 2019 [15]. The individual intentions on the team level are called main agent intentions in the MMD system. The main agent intentions are assigned to the agents, and the agents execute their own plan to achieve the goal of their main agent intention. The plans may involve other intentions which are managed on the agent level. When the agent executes its plan for the intention, it submits the agent actions of the plan to the MAPC simulation server.

Due to the highly dynamic nature of the MAPC environment, the main operation cycle of each MMD agent is the following:

- Check if there is a team mate in the perception area. If yes, then try to identify the agent. If the identification is successful, then handle map merging and map size determination.
- Generate desires.
- Filter the desires and commit to the best desire which becomes the current main intention.
- If execution of the main agent intention requires, then commit to another agent level intention as part of the main agent intention. Compute the next action of the current intention.
- Execute the action and process the dynamic perception from the action.

The agents basically communicate via the blackboard. If there are agents involved in the same joint intention, then they communicate via their intentions, which are directly connected to each other. The direct connection between the intentions is because of implementation considerations.

The blackboard contains all the information shared among the agents. In the beginning, the agents do not know each other, and each agent stores its perceptions in its own dynamic map on the blackboard. When the agents perceive other team members, then they try to identify each other, using an identification algorithm similar to the one in the LFC solution in 2019 [4]. If the identification is successful, then the blackboard merges the dynamic maps of the involved agents into a single dynamic map, which becomes the own dynamic map for each involved agent. In the beginning, the dynamic maps are infinite. If the map size determination algorithm described in Sect. 3.5 is able to determine the height or width of the map, then the dynamic map becomes finite in the respective direction. If both the height and the width of the dynamic map are determined, then the dynamic map becomes finite. The looping of the coordinates on the map is handled by the dynamic map.

The blackboard reasons on the team level strategy by considering the dynamic maps on the blackboard. If there is not enough information on a dynamic map, then the blackboard assigns exploration intentions to the agents of the dynamic map.

If the blackboard finds that enough information is gathered on a dynamic map for a task of the MAPC competition, then it may ask further information from the agents, for example the current desires of the agents or the bidding of the agents for given tasks. Based on the information on the blackboard and the information gathered from the agents, the blackboard decides the team level strategy. It selects the tasks of the MAPC competition to be achieved for each shared dynamic map, and selects one or more agents for each task. If the task requires only one block, then the best single agent is selected, and the agent receives the corresponding main agent intention. If the task requires several blocks, then the best group of agents is selected, and the agents receive the main agent intentions of the joint intention of the group. The joint intention is initiated by the blackboard. The execution and the termination of the joint intention is managed by the coordinator of the joint intention.

In order to keep to the rules of the MAPC competition rules, the agents have to manage their roles both individually and on the team level. The current roles of the agents are also shared on the blackboard. When a main agent intention is assigned to an agent, then the blackboard checks if the agent has the suitable role for the given intention. If not, then the blackboard posts a "role reservation" for the given agent on the blackboard. The "role reservation" is needed to facilitate the team level management of the role of the agents. When the agent creates its plan and finds that it needs another role, then the agent takes the role reservation from the blackboard and modifies its plan to adopt the role. The blackboard keeps track of the current norms of the MAPC competition, and reasons on the norms. If the norm is not considered to be "harmful", then it is just ignored. If the norm is considered to be "serious", then the blackboard changes the role reservations on the blackboard, or if it is necessary, then directly modifies the intentions of the agents to switch role or drop blocks.

This agent team architecture allowed a flexible intention management of the agents both on individual and on team level to achieve good results at the competition. In the beginning of a match, the agents know only their local perception area, so they start to explore the environment and their team mates. They do this, because their exploring desire does not have any pre-requisite, so they can commit to it by default. Once enough agents meet each other, and they share their map to be able to work on a task of the competition, they generate task execution desires, and then they commit to a joint intention to work on a task which is the most promising for the team. At any time, if an explosion event threatens an agent, then the agent generates a desire to escape from the threat. The escape is an important thing, therefore the agent drops its current intention and commits to the escape. If the agent with the escape desire is involved in a joint intention, then it first releases the other agents from the joint intention. The agents have open-minded intention management strategy, so they keep their desires during the escape, and when they get to a safe area, they continue with their normal operation. The normal operation means that they commit to task execution as soon as possible.

2.2   Software Architecture

Architecture. The system uses a unique combination of the repository and the layered architecture, which is shown in Fig. 2.

In the architecture, one client and two server layers can be found. One of the latter is the MAPC server, which is an independent service. The other is the MMD server, which can be divided into two parts: the blackboard and the scheduler. The client layer communicates with both of the servers in a bidirectional way.

The system's logical architecture is decentralized, each agent can be interpreted as an independent process, although it is implemented in a centralized way. The reason behind it is the simplicity: this way it was easy to design the communication and the synchronization, although parallelization could not be exploited.

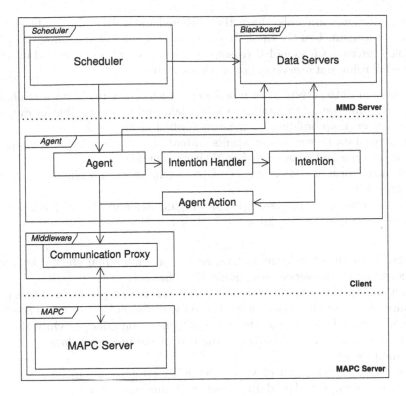

Fig. 2. System architecture.

Due to the centralized implementation, there is an individual component, the scheduler, which controls the system's operations.

Another effect of this decision is that there is no need for a separate communication layer between the MMD servers and the client. We needed a communication layer only between the MAPC server and the client due to abstraction.

Scheduler. The scheduler is a component, which controls the operation of the *data servers* and the *agents*. It does not persist any data and provides no functionality. Its only responsibility is to initialize the system and to initiate communication between the other components in every step.

Data Servers. The blackboard consists of data servers. The data servers are repositories and services, which gather information about a specific data category and provide business logic services on it.

Each data server collects its relevant type of input from the agents. The accumulated data are transformed, stored and can be accessed by any system component without any restrictions.

Some of them not only share the gathered data, but also build complex functions on them. Usually these functions are the ones that require data from multiple sources, such as global reasoning and coordination of several agents.

The following data servers exist in the blackboard.

- Simulation data server: basic repository, which stores raw data and parameters. It's functionality is similar to a data lake and it is accessible for everyone.
- Map server: map building manager, described in Sect. 3.2.
- Intention data server: stores agents' *intention* related information, such as their job type and data related to their current job.
- Role and Norm server: manager of the agent roles and simulation norms, described in Sect. 4.2.
- Task coordination server: service which organizes simulation task related jobs. Its functionalities are explained in Sect. 4.1.

Agents. In architectural perspective, agents are individual clients, that work together using the servers as communication channels.

They can directly communicate with the blackboard repositories, but a proxy is required to accomplish the communication with the MAPC server. Their business logic is mainly located at the *agent intention* components. Only the state of their intentions is stored by them, the rest of the incoming data is persisted at the data servers.

From a functional point of view, agents are standalone entities, that work together to accomplish shared goals, but individual ones, too.

Agents have intentions, which represent a complete job. The desires are optional intentions which may be selected for execution. At any given moment, an individual agent can have multiple desires. The selection of the best desire is based on the priority value of the desire. The priority value expresses the urgency of the desire. At every step, the desire with the highest priority is selected for the agent's current intention, and the agent commits to the intention.

The desires are either generated by the agent itself or by a data server. When an intention is finished, then it's removed from the agent's current desires.

Some jobs, like task achieving, require the involvement of multiple other agents. Agents can not directly communicate with each other, but it can be done through the specific data server.

Agent Intentions. This is the business logic layer of the agent component. This layer contains only those functionalities, whose results directly affect only the agent itself.

Each intention is a representation of a specific job related behaviour. Every one of them has its own purpose and an algorithm that leads closer to its goal.

Agent intentions define an interface, shown in Fig. 3, which must be implemented.

- Determine the next *agent action*, which leads closer to its purpose. The calculation is performed by the job related algorithm.

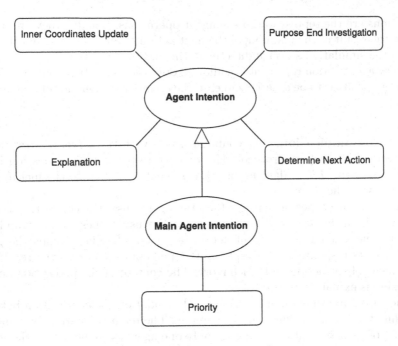

Fig. 3. Agent intention interface.

- Investigate if its purpose is reached, in that case the intention is finished.
- Update inner coordinate in case of coordinate system change (Sect. 3.4 and Sect. 3.5).
- Write explanation, which purpose is described in Sect. 6.

By implementing this interface, complex behaviours can be built easily by integrating separate intentions. The benefit of this property is that intentions can be structured hierarchically and they can be reused in other intentions.

Main agent intentions are a special type of intention. From an abstract point of view, they can be interpreted as the standalone, complete agent jobs. They can be prioritized, which defines an order if multiple top main agent intentions are active at the same time.[3] The execution of main agent intentions may invoke one or more agent intentions.

Agent Actions. The agent actions are simple data transfer objects used between the agent component and the middleware layer. The transfer is uni-directional from the agent component. The middleware layer transforms the object, so it can be sent to the MAPC server.

---

[3] The implementation used constant priorities for the main agent intentions, however, they could have depended on the current environment for better performance.

Actions are the representations of agent operations. Usually, they are initialized as the result of the planning of the next action of an intention, and they are sent to the simulation server indirectly at the end of each step.

Every agent action represents an allowed operation and its parameters. Their only prerequisite is to be deserializable, so the communication module can handle them.

Server Communication. The communication with the server is arranged by a bidirectional transport protocol. The request/response communication mode is used, using the *JSON* data format. Each agent uses its own channel to communicate with the server.

There are two types of requests that the agents use: the connection related ones and the agent actions. The former are the usual ones: connect and disconnect. The latter are the agent action requests. The client sends the given action and its response is a *perception*. The perception contains the result and the impacts of the action and much more. The content of the perception and its processing is explained in Sect. 3.1.

Due to the multiple different team sized simulations, the transition between the simulations must be handled in some way. The team sizes are only known at the start of each simulation, so always only one agent is connected to the server in the first simulation step. The single connected agent sends the information contained in the initial static percept to the scheduler. The rest of the team is created and connected to the server in the second simulation step.

3   Orientation

3.1   Perceptions and Observations

Perceptions. Information about the simulation and the environment is gathered through *static* and *dynamic perceptions*. Both of them are raw, unprocessed data sent by the MAPC server.

Static perception is invariable information, that is valid for the entire simulations. It is agent and state independent data and accessible by everything. It is uploaded to the simulation data server, by the first connected agent, without any transformation.

On the other hand, dynamic perceptions are based on the simulation's actual state. Some of them are agent independent, their content is equal to all agents. The rest of them are heavily agent dependent. These are narrow environment data from the receiver agent's point of view and only the receiver has access to it. The dynamic perception includes information about the agent itself and the things which are visible by the agent. The positions of the latter are relative to the agent, which means agents are not aware of their position of the actual map.

Dynamic perceptions are uploaded in raw format to a *dynamic map*, which is defined in Sect. 3.2, using the map server. In the beginning of every step, these are gathered from all agents.

Observation. The data which is required for the intentions to determine the next agent action, is all wrapped up in *observations*. These contain processed data, generated by data servers and the agents from the perceptions. Also access to several data server is granted by them, so not every data server related information must be stored in these objects.

Observations are generated from the data gathered from different sources at every simulation step by the agents. The agents use the observations to determine their next action. The observations provide an accurate view of the simulation, so that the intention calculations are as effective as possible.

For example, the perceptions only contain that a thing is attached to anything or not, but it does not tell where the thing is attached. Agents must be aware of their attached things, especially the blocks they are carrying. Therefore attached things must be tracked, which is done with the observations. Observations track every gain and loss of attached things. In agent oriented terms, we can say that the observations are the beliefs of the agents.

Observations are introduced into the software design, because of the architectural design. Intentions are the agent's business logic layer, therefore the intentions are not aware of the agent itself. Basically, observations are a combination of data transfer objects and proxies.

These objects are suitable for every type of intention, although not every intention requires all its data.

3.2 Map Building and the Dynamic Map

Dynamic maps are collections of data structures, which store things and their coordinates. At the same time, they provide different services, which are built on the stored data. Dynamic maps serve as repositories and services, too.

In the beginning, each agent orientates with its own map. The agents are not aware of their global location, so each of them builds its own map, using its own coordinate system: the agent starting position is the origo. The map is built using the data received from the perceptions, which is adjusted to the origo and to the agent position, too.

The following data is stored in the dynamic maps:

- Dynamic things, like agents, obstacles and blocks
- Dispensers
- Role and goal zones
- Marker zones

Dispensers and role zones are static, none of them are changed during the simulation. They are simply stored and managed separately due to their latter property.

On the other hand, dynamic things, goal and marker zones are stored and managed in a different way. A time stamp is associated to these data, so later it can be decided which information is more up to date compared to another one coming from a different source. The time stamp is needed when two agents merge their maps and they have to decide which one of them has the most recent information.

When the map is built, whether a coordinate from a perception is undiscovered or not, the coordinate and the thing associated to it are added to the map, because the current perception is the most up to date data source.

The dynamic maps are managed by a data server, called the map server. The map server's only purpose is to associate maps to agents, ensuring that the agents coordinate their activities via the map which is associated to them.

3.3   Agent Identifications

Agents of the same team are not aware of the positions of other team members by default. To work together efficiently, they must know the location of each other.

When more than one agent observe in their perception an other agent from the same team, then the identification process is initiated. An algorithm similar to the LFC solution in [4] is performed for the identification. The idea is that, if an agent notices another one, then asks the others if there is an agent in their perception in a reversed point of view. If this condition is met, then the common viewable things are checked if they match, filtering out non possible candidates. At the end, if there are more than one candidates, then the identification is unambiguous and fails. The identification is only accepted if the number of candidates equals to one.

After a successful identification, the result is used for map merging (Sect. 3.4) and map size detection (Sect. 3.5). Both have a positive impact on efficiency, so agent identifications are always performed at the start of every step.

3.4   Map Merging

Only those agents can work together, that share a common map. The goal is to use as few maps as possible, so more agents can cooperate and the map's shared resources, like dispensers and goal zones, can be managed more efficiently.

In the beginning, none of the maps are shared. When an agent identification is performed successfully and the participating agents belong to different maps, then the map merge process begins.

Map merge is done by integrating a map into another. Only two maps are merged at the same time, but more can be done at the same time step. The maps use different coordinate systems, so one of them is kept, while the other is shifted to the other one. The shift value is calculated by the participating agents.

The shift value can be calculated by the difference of the coordinates of the agents, which merge their maps. The calculation is performed by Eq. 1.

$$
\begin{aligned}
shiftValue &= ac_1 - ac_2 \\
ac_1 &= agent\ coordinate\ in\ own\ map \\
ac_2 &= other\ agent\ coordinate\ in\ own\ map
\end{aligned}
\tag{1}
$$

Those map elements that only exists in one map, are instantly added to the merged map. The elements that exists in both maps, are chosen by their time stamp: the more up to date value is stored, the other is discarded. The result is an union of the maps, which is shown in Fig. 4.

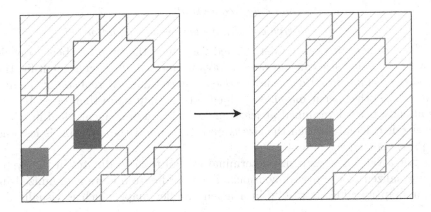

Fig. 4. Map merge result.

The map server guarantees, that all affected coordinates are shifted. It is done by the map merge and also by alerting the agents whose map has been integrated. The shift value is sent to all affected agents and it is their responsibility to update their coordinates inside the intentions.

After a map merge is completed, the involved agents belong to the same map, which ensured by the map server. From now on, these agents build the same map. They are able to manage the shared resources of the map to reduce possible conflicts and to work together to accomplish a given job.

In the beginning, the agents try to explore the world to build and merge maps. Task achievement is always preferred to map building. Often, there is no need to explore the whole map to complete tasks effectively.

3.5 Looping Grid and Map Size Detection

The end of the map cannot be detected directly, because the map repeats itself. For efficiency benefits, it is important that the dimensions of the map are known, if it is possible to calculate them. If it is not determined, then it can lead to performance decreases and to inefficient path findings. Because of the previous consequences, this must be dealt with.

The result of the agent identification process (Sect. 3.3) is used in map size detection as well. When an agent identification is performed successfully, and it turns out that the newly identified agent already belongs to the same map, but its map coordinate differs from the newly identified coordinate, then it means that the agent looped at least once on the map. Note that it is required, that the agent coordinates are always maintained correctly. In this case, the dimensions are determined by Eq. 2 using the agents map and relative locations.

$$(width, \ height) \ = \ | \ ac_1 - ac_2 + rc \ |$$
$$ac_1 \ = first \ agent \ coordinate$$
$$ac_2 \ = second \ agent \ coordinate \tag{2}$$
$$rc \ = \ relative \ coordinate \ between \ ac_1 \ and \ ac_2$$

Those dimensions can be determined for which the map has been travelled through. The map size calculation is always performed after agent identification. The size, calculated by Eq. 2, may be one or more times the real size of the map, because the other agent may have looped on the map more than once. If a size has already been determined at least once, and in a new agent identification a new size is calculated, then the size is updated only if the new size is less than the previous one.

After a valid new map size determination, all the coordinates in the system are normalized to the new dimensions. The coordinate update is organized just like at map merging. It results in a much smaller map, which is visualized in Fig. 5.

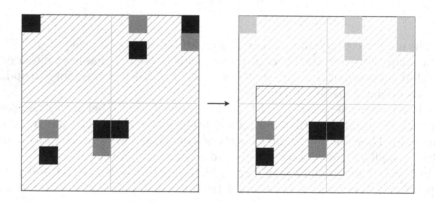

Fig. 5. Map size detection result.

Map size detection has a lower priority than merging all the maps and exploring every part of it. This does not necessarily mean that the latter precedes the former. According to our experiences, the dimension detection usually occurs earlier than the full map discovery, but not earlier than the merge of all maps.[4]

Map size detection has many advantages, but our agents may start task achievements even before the map sizes are determined, because it has proven to be more effective. Maybe it would be different at longer simulations.

---

[4] Despite of not prioritizing complete map exploration, our experience shows that usually all maps are merged into a single one by the half of the simulation, while the dimension detection occurs some time later. The full map discovery happens late in the simulation, although, it is exceptional.

3.6   Pathfinder

Modified A* Algorithm. The main idea of our pathfinding is based on the A* algorithm [9] and the anytime search algorithm [8]. Agents have limited time to find an optimal path, therefore a constant node visit iteration threshold has been introduced to meet the anytime requirement. If the threshold is reached, then the closest estimated coordinate to the end is treated as the end coordinate. The heuristic estimation for the distance to the end node in the A* algorithm is the euclidean distance to the end node. The found path may be not be optimal, because the pathfinding may be terminated before the full path is discovered. However, the non optimality of the found path is not critical, because the MAPC environment is highly dynamic, and the agents create a new plan for their intentions in every simulation step. Therefore only the first elements of the found path matter, and the starting direction will be approximately right in every simulation step.[5]

The first elements of the found path is an agent action, which can be either a move or a clear action. Agents can travel multiple coordinates, depending on their role and carried entities. Always the maximum possible movement is applied, until a clear or rotate action is needed, or maximum movement limit is reached.

However, we limited the maximum number of move actions per simulation step to two. When more than two move actions are performed in a single step, and they are only partially successful, then the agents may lose tracking of their absolute position, because the count of the successful movements are not known. The loss of the absolute position completely confuses our maps and consequently all our algorithms. This is why we had to introduce this limit.

Pathfinding with Attached Blocks. In order to support pathfinding while carrying attached entities, the algorithm had to be further improved. The basic principle is that agents pull the blocks behind them, so upcoming obstacles can be cleared under any circumstances. Complexity and various edge-case scenarios are introduced by this idea, so a simplification had to be applied. The simplification prescribes that only one block may be carried, per agent, at all times. This principle ensures that agents find a route under any circumstances, without clearing large sections. This is achieved because, regardless of the role, the agent can always clear the obstacles in front of it.

In order to ensure that blocks are pulled, agents have to rotate in certain situations. The basic idea is that if an agent moves to a direction, which causes the attached block not to be behind the agent, then a rotation is needed before that. However, this causes lot of unnecessary rotations, which slows down the agent's travel time. To avoid unnecessary rotations, an optimization has been

---

[5] Restarting the A* algorithm in every simulation step may not be efficient in terms of computation time. The D* Lite algorithm [11] would have been more efficient. On the other hand, the D* Lite algorithm uses more memory, especially if there are many agents.

introduced, that weakens the previous principle. Rotation is only required, if it is not possible to proceed without it: the attached block can not be moved due to blocking obstacles.

4 Team Coordination

4.1 Task Achievement

Task Completion Prerequisites. Task achievement has several essential prerequisites, which is visualized in Fig. 6. In order to begin a task, a group of agents must share a map, and a given set of conditions must be met on their shared dynamic map. This is because there is no sharing of resources between maps.

Fig. 6. Task prerequisites.

Regardless of the task itself, the location of at least one role and one goal zone must be known. The agents need to adopt the right role for the task, and they need a location where the submission can be done. If either of the previous conditions are not fulfilled, then the task cannot be started.

The same rule applies to dispensers, but it is task dependent. There must be at least one dispenser for each block type required for the task.

In order to begin a task, a goal zone location must be provided to the agents, where the blocks can be assembled and submitted. Therefore, the coordinates, where the assembly and submission are performed, should be reserved to avoid possible conflicts. The neighbouring coordinates are also included in this area, so agents have enough space to hand over blocks. The reservation makes sure, that other agents from the same team on the same map do not assemble blocks at the same location.

A reservation is made, when a task is started, and its lifecycle needs to be managed. The reservation needs to be ended when the task is finished. The task may be finished either because it is submitted or because it is dropped due to some critical reason. Another possible event is when multiple maps are merged, and the reservations are conflicting with each other. In this case, only the reservation that belongs to the team closest to the reserved target zones is kept. The rest of them are cancelled, therefore the tasks associated with them are dropped.

Dropping a task is not a serious problem, because the agents involved in the task will be freed, and they will bid for task execution in the next simulation step. If the same task is the best candidate next time, and these agents are in the best position for the same task, then these agents will continue with the task execution, but with a different goal zone which is not occupied by other team members. If the same task is not the best candidate next time, or these agents are not in the best position for the task, then the team will select a better task and/or group of agents for task achievement.

The size of the group of agents needed for each task is equal to the number of block requirement of the task plus one. The extra agent is the coordinator which organizes the rest of team which are the block providers. The coordination process is similar to the *Contract Net Protocol* [12,13]. The coordinator divides the task into sub-tasks, and the generated sub-tasks are allocated among the group. It is the block provider agents' responsibility to supply the correct amount and type of blocks. Meanwhile, the coordinator clears the assembly area, then acquires the blocks from the block providers, and submits the task at the end. The contract ends, when a task is finished either because it is submitted or dropped.

If the task requires a single block, then only one agent is needed, which performs the block provision and the coordination too.

Task Options. Task options are generated in each simulation step for each dynamic map. This is an agent and resource reservation independent pre-filtration. For each map, the available tasks are stored as possible options. The availability of a task is defined by a subset of the task prerequisites listed above (Fig. 6) with some additions.

- If there are no known role or goal zones for the given map, then no task can be started.
- A task cannot be started on the map, if no dispensers are known on the map for the type of blocks required by the task.
- If the block count of a task violates a norm, then it is ignored and skipped.
- A task should not be started, if surely there is not enough time to complete it. A simple lower estimation was used to calculate the minimum completion

time, which assumed that every agent required at least four simulation step to finish their part.[6]

Task Selection and Bidding. The generated task options are filtered by the available resources for each map. From here on, the beginning of a task depends on resource management: agent, role and goal zone availabilities.

For resource management a simple, local optimization algorithm was used. The algorithm always selects and starts only one task, and it is repeated until none of the tasks can be started. One task can be selected multiple times, there is no upper limit for that. Although, there should be some kind of limitation, because once a task is submitted a certain number of times, then it can not be submitted again. Therefore, the teams, which are still working on that task, have to change to another.

In each task selection iteration, the following conditions must be valid.

- There is at least one goal zone area free for reservation. The size of the area depends on the required block formation.
- There must be at least the given number of free[7] or explorer agents described in the prerequisites sub-section above.
- The required roles for the task can be reserved, i.e. they comply with the norm management of the team, which is described in Sect. 4.2.

After the filtering, the remaining tasks are sorted based on a value function. The value function defines a ranking, that determines which tasks worth the most in terms of rewards and efforts. The value of a task is calculated by Eq. 3.

$$value = \frac{\frac{reward}{agents} \cdot remainingTime}{1 + crowdednes} \tag{3}$$

where the variables are the following.

- *reward*: The reward points for the task.
- *agents*: The number of agents needed for the task completion.
- *remaining Time*: A quotient of the remaining time until the task deadline and a constant.
- *crowdedness*: Agent density estimation at goal zones. It is a rough constant multiplier based on how much space is needed for the block assembly, how many agents are performing task related jobs and how many goal zone coordinates are known on the actual dynamic map. The multiplier is calculated by Eq. 4. The *crowdedness* value is positive, if the number of agents already working on task achievement (*busyAgents*) plus a space proportional to the block requirements of the given task (*blocks*) increases three quarter of the goal zones. In this case, if there are more busy agents and there are more requirements of the task, then the crowdedness is higher.

$$crowdedness = max(busyAgents + 2 * blocks - goalZones * 0.75, 0) \tag{4}$$

---

[6] It was a very simple estimation, which have not been improved due to lack of time.
[7] An agent is free if it is not involved in task achievement.

The value of a task (Eq. 3) is higher if the team can produce more rewards per agent. The value is also higher, if it is more likely that the task can actually be submitted, because there is more time until the deadline. If the available free goal zones drop below one quarter of the known goal zones, then the value of the tasks with less block requirements will be higher, because these tasks need less space for submission. The one quarter limit for the goal zones is just a ballpark value that takes into account that the other team also occupies a part of the goal zones.[8]

The task with the highest value is started. The required amount of agents are assigned to the task to form a task achievement group. The members of the group are selected on the basis of the bids of the agents, which is described in the next subsection. For the selected agents, the right roles are reserved, if needed, and their intentions are inserted into their desires. The required goal zone coordinates are reserved for the team, which is selected by the coordinator. This is the end of the algorithm, and the agents start their task in the simulation next step.

Agent Task Bidding. When agents are considered to be part of a group for a given task, they are ranked by their bids. The bid of an agent estimates how much step is required for the agent to accomplish a given job. Agents that require the least amount of time are selected for the given sub-task.

A job can be a coordination, block provision or single block provision. Therefore, for each job, the agents bid differently.

Bid calculations consist of several different parts, where one depends on the other. For example, when the agent bids for a coordination, and does not have the right role for that, then the bid contains the cost of travelling to the nearest role zone, plus going from the role zone to the goal zone that is closest to the role zone.

Each bid calculation has a common part, the role adopt time. In the beginning, if the agent's actual role is not suitable for the given job, then the time to adopt the right role is included. It may occur, that a job requires more than one role. In this case, the calculation takes into account that more than one role is needed.

The jobs require that the following calculations must be made.

– *Coordination*: the time to get to the goal zone which is closest to the agent. The chosen agent's closest goal zone is reserved for the team.
– *Block provision*: the sum of time required to get to a right type of dispenser and then to the reserved goal zone.
– *Single block provision*: the sum of coordination and block providing costs.

---

[8] Although we had this complex task evaluation function, we are not sure that it really played an important role in the MAPC 2022 contest, because there were always only 2 active tasks at the contest, and there were not many options to choose from.

4.2 Role and Norm Management

The MAPC competition rules define the roles and the norms. The norms regulate the type of the roles and the number of the agents with given roles during the competition. Role and norm management is needed to keep to the rules of the competition, which may require team level coordination.

Role Categorization. The possible roles of the simulation are not known in advance, their available actions and other parameters are only known at runtime. Proper management of agent roles is key to effective operation. Choosing the wrong role for a given job can disable the agent from doing it or significantly reduce its performance.

At the beginning of the simulation, the agent roles provided by the MAPC simulation are categorized according to the job they are suitable for. This is needed, because for example, if an MMD agent wants to do the coordination job, then it needs to adopt a MAPC role which has the capabilities to attach a block, to connect two blocks and to submit a task. The role categories are determined by the possible agent jobs that are used in the MMD system:

– Coordination
– Block provision
– Single block provision
– Explorer or inter task role

In the future, the role categories might be extended with saboteur and surveyor categories.

The current design assumes that, that these roles exist as single roles, not as combination of more. Only the single block provision is excluded from that assumption.

Each role category has mandatory conditions, without them, the role is not suitable for the given job. Examples of such conditions are the permitted actions and the ability to move with attached things. There are optional conditions. The optional conditions can be used to rank the roles which one can perform better in the given job, usually determined by skill parameters.

Coordination roles require submit, attach and connect action options. The coordinator must be able to get blocks from others, using the attach and connect action. For task submission the submit action is mandatory. The coordinator should able to protect itself from saboteur agents, so a role, which has more promising clearing parameters, should be preferred.

The essential capabilities of the block provision are the request, attach and connect actions. The reasons for the attach and connect actions are the same as in the previous case. The request is used for block acquisition.

Single block providers require request, attach and submit actions for reasons similar to the previous ones. Should there be no single role for single block provision in the simulation, then the coordinator and block providing roles substitute the single block provider role. Only one role is allowed at the same time, therefore in this case at some point, the role must be changed.

There is no separate explorer category, but there is a so called *inter task role* category instead. Agents are optimized to complete tasks as soon as they appear. During exploration, a role from one of the previous three categories is chosen, so agents are always ready for a task job.

Usually the roles with higher speed are preferred, but because of role distribution balance, it was not included in the selection. The vision of a role could have been used at exploring, however, it has been treated just like the agent speed. The reasons behind the role distribution balance are described in the next subsection.

The importance of the role's attributes is visualized in Fig. 7.

Fig. 7. Role property prioritization.

Role Assignment and Reservation. The management of role assignments and reservations are controlled by the *role server*. Agents use the role server to obtain a role of a specified category, usually for a specific job. However, agents do not choose the specific role within the category themselves, they choose from the options offered, because norms must be handled on team level. Team level coordination of roles is facilitated by first reserving the role for future use by the team, and then assigning the role to a given agent when needed.

When the roles of a given category are requested, the role server filters them by their availability. The availability of a role depends on the norms, which limits the role usage at team level. If the sum of the count of assigned and reserved roles reaches a limit defined by a norm, then the role is not offered in any category, making the role unobtainable for the agents. The count of both assigned and reserved roles matters, because even if not at the given moment, but in the worst case, in the near future, the limit of the norm might be exceeded.

The role server service requires the tracking of the assigned and the reserved roles. When an agent requests a role of a given category, then the role server offers the agent the available options. The agent selects one of them, then reserves it. This indicates that the agent will take on the chosen role in the near future and it must be guaranteed to it. The role is removed from the reservations after either adoption or resignation. In the former case, the role is assigned to the agent.

When multiple roles are offered in a given category, then the agent chooses randomly. In this way, it is less likely that every agent adopts the same role, thus the team of agents is in a better position for upcoming role limits.

Norm Filter and Consideration. Norms are limitations, which can regulate agents at individual or team level. Violating them causes the agents to lose energy, which is a critical threat to them. Some norms are even extremely harmful, so they must be dealt with.

Norms are handled serially: only the upcoming ones consecutively. This is by no means the most optimal approach, but based on our experience, it solved the problem relatively efficiently and correctly.

Norms can be classified as ignorable and considerable ones.

The ignorable norms are those that do not require direct major intervention. An example is the limitation of the default role, because it is usually not needed. This experience is based on the test simulations prior to the contest. Another example is that a two-block limit norm does not really matter for two-block tasks, because in the case of two-block tasks, the time when the agent has two blocks is negligible.

The norms must be considered by their energy loss effect. A norm must be complied with, if the average agent energy drops below a certain level due to the energy loss caused by it and other norms that are not complied with during its duration. The constant energy recovery is included in this calculation, which is not known in advance, it is discovered by the agents, using simple energy comparison between steps. Once the energy recovery is discovered, then it is stored in the simulation data server. The energy threshold is a constant percentage of maximum energy. The calculation is an estimation and the threshold tries to mitigate its inaccuracy. While block norm violation only punishes an individual agent, it is treated as a team-level energy loss, as not even a single agent is allowed to drop out.

Norms are complied with by their category, which can be either block or role regulation.

If a block norm has to be complied with, than any task is stopped where the block count of the task exceeds the limit. In this case, only the coordinator is affected, however it stops the whole group of agents involved in the task.

Role norms are managed using the role server. First, the role server provides the count of the task performing agents of the affected role, which indicates how many roles have to be dropped. Then, the task performing agent group, which has the most given role reservations discards the task and the role reservations. This continues until the given role reservations drop below the limit of the norm or until the norm goes out of effect. If the norm is still in effect and all role reservations are discarded, then the algorithm is continued, but with the adopted roles. The algorithm starts with the reservations, because the reservations indicate that those agents are far from finishing the task, while the agents that have their proper roles are already working on tasks. The agents that do not participate in task jobs automatically change to available roles.

If more than one norm of a given type is active at the same time, the strictest one will always be taken into account.

5   Intentions

Intentions represent agent jobs, which can be either standalone or part of another intention. Every intention has a unique purpose, and when it is reached, then it is considered finished. Because the MAPC 2022 scenario is highly dynamic, the intentions determine the next action leading closer to its purpose in each simulation step using their observations.

Intentions are structured hierarchically. There are simpler and more complex ones, usually the latter include the former. Main agent intentions are at the top of this hierarchy, they can be interpreted as standalone jobs. Each main agent intention is associated with a priority, so it can be decided which of them is more important at the actual step.

In the following sections, intentions are categorized by their usage and explained in detail.

5.1   Common Intentions

The intentions listed here can be categorized as supporter intentions, they are usually included as building blocks in other intentions.

Idle. This is a placeholder intention, which never finishes and does nothing. Its only purpose is to make the agent's intention queue (described in Sect. 5.4) non-empty.

Skip. This simple intention is used for skipping the current simulation step. Has no purpose, never finishes.

It has an optional flag, which triggers that, if one of the agent's attached things blocks a dispenser, then it rotates to avoid to free the dispenser. This behaviour ensures that it does not hinder other agent's work. The flag is enabled only, if the attached blocks do not have to maintain a specified format for task achievement.

When an agent skips, it uses this intention to perform the skip action.

Travel. This intention wraps the pathfinder component. Its goal is to travel to a given destination with the invocation of the pathfinder.

If the given destination is reachable, i.e. the destination is not blocked by another agent, then it returns an action to get closer to it. The action can be either move, rotate or clear action. If the destination is not reachable, then it skips, because there is another intention to handle this case.

Wait. This is an extension of the travel intention. When the given destination is reached, then the skip intention is initiated. The wait condition is determined by another intention.

It has a simple defensive behaviour: after its destination is reached, it attempts to shoot at agents from the other team in the perception range to protect itself and to keep them away. This defensive behaviour is always active at the destination, but it can have a real effect only if the role of the agent allows that the clear action damages the other agent.

Agitated Travel. This is an improved version of the travel intention to handle the case when the target destination is unreachable. It applies the basic travel and wait intentions to achieve that.

It has two improvements. Firstly, it allows multiple destinations next to the target destination. When one of them is reached, then its purpose is considered reached. Second, if all of the destinations are unreachable, then it searches and travels to the closest reachable location between its current location and the destinations. By this behaviour, it is ensured that the agent is getting closer to the goal area at every step.

Agitated Wait. This is a combination of the agitated travel and the wait intentions.

After one of the goal locations are reached, it behaves just like the end of the wait intention. It waits unconditionally and attempts to shoot at hostile agents.

Distant Agitated Travel. This is a distance keeper version of the agitated travel intention.

It has only one destination, however, its purpose is not to reach it, rather to be in a given distance to it. It ensures, that the agent is near to a given destination, but not close enough, so the area around the destination is not crowded.

Detach Blocks. This intention detaches all the things which are attached to the agent. Terminates when nothing is attached to the agent.

Reset. This is a main intention, which is only initiated after the agent team got reconnected to the MAPC server.

Its only purpose is to drop every attached thing, by applying the detach block intention. This is because the individual agents can not remember their previous intentions and their task group. Therefore, the groups have to be recreated, but until then, the attached blocks unnecessarily hinder the agents.

Escape. When the agents notice that they are in a clear event area, then they start to flee. The flee process is handled by the escape main intention.

It uses the path finding component's calculations to find the shortest route to a destination, that is not affected by the clear event. Then the travel intention takes care of moving there. Before it tries to escape, it applies the detach block intention, which helps the agent to get to the destination as soon as possible. This may require some extra time, but the agent can reach its goal more flexibly and faster, and also, the pathfinder does not work correctly if more than one block is attached to the agent.

Clear Target. This is a simple intention to clear the given coordinate, if a block or obstacle is located at it. First of all, it moves to a coordinate adjacent to the target coordinate by the travel intention, and then clears the given target. If the target is unreachable then it skips, and this case will be handled in the intention from where the clear target intention is invoked.

Clear Zone. This is an extended version of the clear target intention, which allows the clearing of multiple targets, while preserving a minimal amount of energy. It chooses its current target as the closest one, making the clear process optimal.

If the agent's current energy is low, then it just skips to gain energy. The energy limit is defined by a constant parameter. By this, it is ensured, that not all of its energy is consumed and even preserves some, if suddenly an escape is needed.

At random occasions it rather shoots at hostile agents to keep them away from the given area the same way as in the wait intention.

Adopt Role. The purpose of this intention is to adopt the given role. It uses the agitated travel intention to get to the closest role zone area. After that, the intention adopts the given role.

5.2 Explorer Intentions

Explorer intentions ensure that the map is discovered and kept up to date as much as possible.

Explore. In the beginning, most of the map is completely unknown. The task of the explore intention is to discover as much parts of the map as possible, in the least time possible.

It begins to explore the agent's environment in a spiral like shape. It moves with the basic travel intention towards an unknown location, which is closest to the starting point of the agent and also to its current position. If there are more than one locations like this, then a random one is chosen, which may cause the agent to start exploring in another direction. The selected destination is a little bit further than the selected unknown location, in order to move the whole perception range of the agent out from the already explored area. Because of this exploration algorithm, the shape of the exploration is like a spiral. The shape is visualized in Fig. 8.

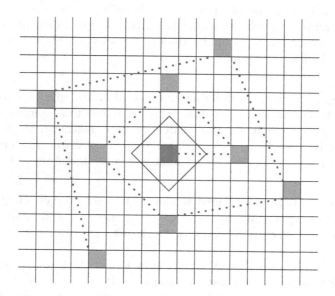

Fig. 8. Direction of the exploration.

This movement assists the agents to find each other as soon as possible, and also explore unknown areas with minimal effort. The explore algorithm is compatible with the map merges. The behaviour does not change, although the exploration does not keep the spiral like shape, but it still wanders around the edge of the already explored area.

The intention is finished, when the map dimension is calculated and all the points are known. These conditions are rarely fulfilled.

If there is a reserved role for the agent, then the adopt role intention is performed to adopt it during the exploration. Usually this scenario happens only, when the agent has to change a role due to a norm violation.

This main intention has lower priority than the task related ones, therefore the map is rarely explored completely.

Map Update. The map update main intention takes the explore intention's place, after the map is fully discovered.

It explores coordinates, which were discovered the earliest. The closer ones to the agents are always preferred. The exploration is performed by the basic travel intention.

This intention has the same role handling behaviour like the explore intention. Their priorities are also equal.

This main intention is never finished, because there is always a point to explore again, but a task related intention may make this intention inactive for a while.

5.3   Task Achieving Intentions

In this category, all the intentions are part of the task achieving process. Only the coordinators and block providers use the intentions listed here.

Block Collection. The responsibility of the block collection intention is to acquire a given type of block, that can be consumed in a task submission. It is used by single or regular block provider agents.

The intention searches for dispensers, from where the given type of block can be gathered. It uses the agitated travel intention to travel next to the dispenser. While going to the dispenser, if the agent perceives an abandoned block of the correct type, and the abandoned block is closer than the dispenser, then it targets the abandoned block.

However, not all the dispensers and abandoned blocks are measured the same way. The dispensers, that are not completely occupied by other agents, have always greater priority. There is a high chance at dispensers surrounded by agents, that there will be a conflict for the requested block. The conflict can be either waiting for other agents or suffering damage from hostile agents.

The abandoned blocks are not prioritized, rather they are filtered by their surroundings. If there is any agent or block besides them, then they are ignored, because the abandoned block may be attached to the agent or the block. We allow to hold more than one thing only for coordinator agents, because it would hurt the "maximum one attached thing per agent while moving" principle. The coordinator agents do not move if they have at least one attached block.

The "maximum one attached thing per agent while moving" principle can also be hurt when attaching a block from a dispenser. This may happen if more than one agent attach the block at the same time from the same team. When the agents belong to the same map, then an attach order is defined by themselves. However, if they do not belong to the same map, the previous scenario might happen. When this scenario is recognised by the agents, then the agent either detaches the attached block with 50% chance or skips with the same chance. Basically, the conflict resolution is random based, because after a while at least one agent detaches the block. If both agents detach the block, then they attach it again in the next step. Sooner or later, only one of the agents holds the block and it is free to go with it.

The intention is finished, when the agent has acquired the block and there is no other thing attached to it.

Connect. This intention hands over an attached block to another agent, usually to a coordinator. It is usually performed by a block provider agent to connect a block to a coordinator agent during the block delivery. The intention is initiated when the involved agents are close to each other.

The intention receives the exact location, where the block must be delivered. By the basic travel intention, the agent moves to one of the given destination's adjacent coordinates. After the travelling is finished, it rotates the attached block to the given location.

When the block is in the right location, then the agent either detaches the block or connects the block to one of the coordinator's attached blocks. The required action is determined by the block position. If the position is directly besides the coordinator, then a detach action is sufficient. If not, then a connection must be made, which must be closed immediately.

The intention is finished, when the block provision intention signals that the transmission was successful and the agent holds no longer the block.

Block Delivery. The block delivery intention ensures that an attached block is transported to a coordinator agent. It is only used by block provider agents.

The intention uses the agitated travel intention to go close to the coordinator agent and then to follow it.

When the block provider agent is close enough to the coordinator, then sooner or later, it receives a signal to exchange the requested block. The exchange process is managed by the connect intention.

The process ends, if the connection intention is finished and the coordinator agent approves the exchange, indicating it by a signal.

Block Providing. This main intention handles the block providing job by scheduling and managing the block collection and the block delivery intentions.

First of all, if the agent has the wrong role for the block providing, then it adopts the right one, using the adopt role intention.

If the agent has either no blocks or the wrong ones, then all the attached blocks are detached using the detach block intention. Then the block collection intention is initialized to acquire the right block.[9] If the agent has the right block, either because already having it or from the block collection intention, then the block delivery intention is initialized to deliver the block to the coordinator agent.

---

[9] There could have been an optimization, if the right block is included in the attachments, then only keep that one. It was not implemented due to lack of time.

The intention recognises if it loses its attached block, for example by a clear event. In this case, the process starts over by acquiring the right block.

The intention can be finished in several ways. The positive outcome is when the block is successfully delivered. The negative one is determined by the coordinator agent, usually when the task can not be completed in any way.

Assemble. This intention is used by a coordinator agent to acquire an attached block from another agent, usually from a block provider agent. The intention is started for each required block, when the corresponding block provider is close to the coordinator. The coordinator agent assigns a connect intention to its block provider agent to connect the delivered block at a given location. The intention is finished when the block is acquired, and if connection was required, then the connection is closed.

Coordination. This is the main intention of the coordination process. Its purpose is to accomplish a task submission flow, by its own logic, and to control the block provider agents of the task group.

It consists of the following steps:

1. If just initialized, the attached blocks are checked, and the wrong ones are detached.
2. Before determining the next step, the intention checks if the task can still be completed. If not, then the intention ends.
3. The current agent role is checked, if it has the wrong one, then the intention adopts the right one.
4. It travels to the chosen goal zone destination.
5. While none of the right block providers are ready for the block exchange, it clears the area from obstacles and abandoned blocks using the clear zone intention.
6. One by one, the blocks are exchanged from the providers when they are ready.
7. Once, it is in the possession of all required blocks, then it submits the task.

If the intention just got initialized, then it needs to make sure, that the agent has only the right type of blocks in the right positions. All the attached blocks that do not satisfy the condition must be detached, using the detach block intention.[10]

Before continuing, in each step, it must be determined, that the task can be still completed. The influencing factors, which can interrupt the flow, can be divided into two parts. The first part is the critical, which make the task completion impossible, like task expiration or a norm violation. The other part is the optional, which just set back the task completion. These hindering factors could be handled by the intention, however for simplicity purposes, they are handled like the critical ones: the intention is terminated, and if it is still relevant,

---

[10] Due to lack of time, wrong block selection algorithm was not implemented, therefore if there is at least one wrong block, then all the attached blocks are detached.

then it will be restarted in the next simulation steps anyway. The optional factors are the following: either when the goal zone disappears or when a clear event appears on the agent itself or one of its attached blocks.

If the intention has to be interrupted, then it releases the block provider agents from the task group. Then the detach block intention is initiated to drop all the attached blocks.

If the agent has the wrong role for the coordination, then the adopt role intention adopts the right one.

The goal zone area, where the blocks can be assembled are determined by the dynamic map associated to the agent. Until one of the coordinates of the goal zone area is not reached, the intention always chooses the closest one and travels there, using the basic travel intention.

After the arrival to a goal zone, if none of the right block provider agents are ready for block exchanging, then it starts to clear the area. Its purpose is to clear the area from obstacles and abandoned blocks, to make exchange easier for the block provider agents. It is performed by the clear zone intention.

The order of the block exchange is determined on the basis of the task block requirements and the block provider agents' readiness. Only one exchange at a time can be completed for simplicity purposes. From experience, there were usually no complex tasks where parallelization could be used. The task block requirements itself defines a non linear order of the possible options, which is filtered further, by the available blocks from the block provider agents, at the given moment. If there is any hand over opportunity, then one of them is chosen randomly. The exchange is performed by the assemble intention. The block exchange loops until all the required blocks are attached.

When all of the required blocks of the task attached to the right positions, and none of the block provider agents are connected to the coordinator, then the task is submitted, and the intention is finished.

Although we have a goal zone reservation scheme to prevent that two groups of our team block each other by trying to submit a task at the same place, the block reservation scheme cannot take into account the other team of the match. If the coordinator finds that an agent from the other team stays for a longer time at the reserved goal zone, then the coordinator drops the task and releases its block providers. If the same task and the same group of agents are still preferable, then the group will be recreated with a different goal zone in the next simulation step. If not, then a new group will be formed.

Single Block Submission. The purpose of this intention is to deliver a single block to a goal zone, and then to submit the task. A prerequisite of this intention is that the task requires only one block. Only the single block provider agents have this intention.

The intention determines the closest goal zone in each simulation step the same way as in the coordination intention. The goal zone determination in each simulation step is useful, because when a goal zone disappears, then the intention can go to another goal zone with the same block. If the goal zone is reached, then the intention rotates the block into the direction required by the task, and submits the task. If the location at the rotation target is blocked, then the intention either clears the location, if possible, or selects another location within the goal zone.

The intention ends, if the task is submitted successfully.

Single Block Providing. This main intention is a unique mix of the block collection and coordination intention. Just like the single block submission intention, only the single block providers can have it.

Its purpose is to accomplish a task submission flow, which requires only one block. It's the intention's responsibility, to collect the given type of block and to submit it in a goal zone, without the assistance of other agents.

First of all, if the agent has the wrong role for the block collection, then the adopt role intention adopts the right one.

Just like at the coordinator intention, if the agent has wrong blocks, then the detach block intention is performed. After that, the block collection intention is initiated to acquire the right block.

At this point, if the agent's role is not suitable for the task submission, then the adopt role intention is performed again, to change role.

Then the single block submission intention is executed to deliver the block and submit the task. If the agent loses the block, the algorithm starts over.

Just like at the coordination intention, the task completion can be interrupted by several factors. It is handled the same way, excluding the release of the block providers.

The intention is finished, when either the single block submission intention ends or if it had to be ended for some reason.

5.4   Agent Intention Management

Agents usually have more than one main agent intention at the same time, but only one is active at any given moment. Often these intentions are not performed sequentially. At every step, the most important one gets activated, which might be different than the one in the previous step.

The active intention is changed often, so all the agent intentions must be persisted with their actual state. Main agent intentions are stored in a priority queue. This priority queue is called *agent intention handler*, which stores and manages the main agent intentions. Each agent has its own intention handler.

In every step, the main agent intention with the highest priority gets activated. The priority is defined by the main agent intention itself.

The intention handler manages the insertion of the new intentions, and also the removals of the finished ones. Intention insertion is usually initiated from the outside, but the intention handler can also generate intentions from the inside. The inside generated intentions are usually the agent's individual intentions, like the escape and explore intention.

The transition from one intention to another one usually does not have to be handled specially, because they do not depend on other agents. The coordination intention is the exception, because if it must be cancelled immediately, then all the block providers must be released. This special transition is handled by the agent intention handler.

6   Debugging and Explanations

6.1   Challenges of the Debugging

Despite following the principle of simplicity, the multi-agent system had a lot of error sources. Fail-safe was a prerequisite for many algorithms, therefore the cause of all errors had to be spotted.

One of the most challenging factors in debugging was the randomness of the MAPC 2022 scenario. The agents have to operate in a random based dynamic environment. In this dynamic environment, the elements of the map, the norms, the opposing team and the success of the agent actions themselves vary. Even some intention algorithms contain randomness. The factors listed above all make the reproduction of the bug difficult.

Most of the times the reproduction of rare faults were the most challenging. It is almost impossible to start the MAPC server and our agent team from a given situation, because for example it is difficult to recreate dynamic maps and agent states. The server and the agents can only be started from the beginning of a match, and then the same situation may not occur due to randomness. Sometimes repeated execution was the only solution to find out more about the cause, due to the complexity of the error.

The occurring faults were also challenging to solve. Due to the system architecture, intention related fatal errors were difficult to associate with actual agents. Most of the times, the fault itself could not be perceived, only its consequences could be seen. For example, if two agents stick together, then their map becomes confused. Later when they are detached and everything seems fine, then they may identify the wrong size for the map, which may invalidate all the dynamic maps for the whole team. Therefore the pathfinding of the agents does not work correctly, and we see that the agents issue inexplicable actions.

6.2   Explanations

In order to help the debugging process, we created an option to make the agents explain their intentions. Explanations are brief strings that summarize the agent's current intentions. Due to their low level of detail, they are only usable with some kind of other debugging tool, such as visualization. Their level of simplicity is shown in Fig. 9.

In each step, all agents have an explanation, which is only shown for the given step. Explanations are not persisted, because their purpose is to provide brief information, so they can be read between the simulation steps, so the MAPC

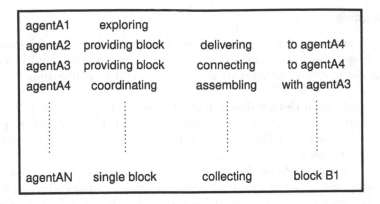

Fig. 9. Explanation strings.

simulation server has to be paused. Unfortunately, the MAPC simulation server cannot be operated step-by-step, so the "continue" and the "pause" commands have to be typed in quickly on the console to see the progress of the explanations.

An agent's explanation is equal to the agent's active intention's explanation string at the given time step. The explanation of an intention describes the actual state of the intention, such as its actual sub goal. These descriptions can be easily constructed, due to the hierarchic structure of the intentions. The explanation string is built by concatenating the embedded intention's description with explanation string of the given intention.

Although the explanation strings of Fig. 9 look like simple print-outs on a console, they are a little bit more than that. The print-outs on a console runs away, and they are hard to follow, while the explanation window stays and displays the current behaviour of the agents. They are really explanations, because they describe why the agent is doing what it is actually doing. If we just see that the agent is going to somewhere, then we do not know why. If the explanation says that the agent is going to fetch a block from a dispenser to deliver it to a given agent, then it explains us why it going on its way. The explanation string may contain more complex explanations as well. For example we can put into the explanation string, that the agent became block provider of block x, because its bid for block provision had a given value. Such explanations were not needed for debugging. However, this type of explanation needs the modification of the source code. A more flexible solution would be to make the explanation feature interactive.

The main benefit of this low level of information providing is that the presence of bugs can be easily found out. Also, simple bugs can be eliminated without effort. However, in case of complex errors, these are only beneficial to approximate the error. For the identification of complex errors, the explanation strings would have to be made more complex, but the available space is not enough for that.

6.3 Logging

Log entries are detailed information about anything which might be involved in possible bugs. The most common entries are about intentions and blackboard data, such as intention actual state and decision or the modification of common data.

Generated log entries are detailed and therefore persisted. Due to their high level of detail, they can not be read properly between the simulation steps. This information are independently useable, although, more details are provided when used with server logs.

There is no exact schema for the content of log entries. The only exceptions are time step and the agents involved, which are almost always relevant. The rest of the content usually depends on the actual fault, which can be very diverse.

Contrary to the explanations, the implementation of the logging infrastructure is quite a challenge. A proper logging infrastructure has never been implemented. There were several reasons behind this decision. The main challenge was the implementation of a logging, which level can be regulated by various parameters. Due to the diversity of the faults, a lot of parameters would have been required, which could not be known in advance. By logging everything in high detail would have made the debugging nearly impossible without the right infrastructure.

Instead, a simple ad-hoc logging was implemented. This logging infrastructure was implemented every time after a fault occurred, and it was highly specialized to the fault. In the long term, this solution was not effective, because it had to be developed almost every time after a new fault occurred.

The main benefit of the logging is that complex faults can be tracked down more easily. Blackboard data change and the behaviour of the agent intentions are more traceable with this method.

7 Match Analysis

In order to evaluate the quality of the jobs done by the implemented MMD system, we summarize the performance of all the teams at MAPC 2022 in Table 1. The table includes the warmup matches against master student Paula Böhm from TU Clausthal, outside of the competition. The columns of the table show the points collected by the teams against each team and each simulation run (or match with another word). The total amount of collected points by the team is at the bottom of the table, together with the scores and placements of the teams. The points are the rewards for the tasks completed in the matches. The winner of a match is the team that collects more points. The scores are given for the matches: 3 for a win, 1 for a draw and 0 for a loss. The placement at the contest is determined by the total scores.

There is randomness in the matches, therefore the points collected by a team may vary with each match even if all the conditions are the same. When the MMD system was tested against the MMD system before the contest, sometimes

Table 1. Summary of the points at the contest. The columns contain the points of the teams against the teams in the rows.

		LI(A)RA	GOALdigger	MMD	FIT BUT	GOAL-DTU	Paula
LI(A)RA	Sim1		350	760	60	120	600
	Sim2		410	750	540	160	120
	Sim3		310	1600	780	0	1000
GOALdigger	Sim1	130		500	220	0	160
	Sim2	0		200	320	0	220
	Sim3	80		840	490	520	1270
MMD	Sim1	120	370		80	480	770
	Sim2	10	300		760	150	500
	Sim3	150	720		170	0	450
FIT BUT	Sim1	220	120	770		230	480
	Sim2	60	320	680		630	360
	Sim3	120	520	1140		0	250
GOAL-DTU	Sim1	310	180	910	0		710
	Sim2	80	370	780	670		610
	Sim3	270	410	1520	1640		570
Paula	Sim1	110	330	580	0	320	
	Sim2	60	700	790	330	280	
	Sim3	90	320	1690	60	0	
Total points:		**1810**	**5730**	**13510**	**6120**	**2610**	**8070**
Total score		9	22	30	19	9	N/A
Placement		4	2	1	3	4	N/A

there were big differences in the points collected by the two MMD systems, although the two systems had the same capabilities. Nevertheless, we can see in the table, that the total points mainly correlate with the scores and the placements.

Each team played 15 matches in Table 1, which is not a big number statistically, but the points collected by the MMD team in the matches at the contest and against Paula are similar to the points collected during our test matches when the MMD system played against the MMD system. The points collected by the MMD system in every match are mainly in the range 600–1600. There is one exception, the MMD system collected observably less points in the matches against the GOALdigger system. This is because the GOALdigger team had "saboteur" agents to block the agents of the competitor.

The design of the MMD system focused on the task completions in order to complete as much tasks as possible, and to collect as much points as possible. Table 1 confirms that the design goal was mainly achieved in comparison with other teams.

GOALdigger-AIG-Hagen vs. MMD. At the match against the GOALdigger system we noticed that many of the agents of the MMD system lost their energy and got deactivated for a while. After the contest, we have learned that the deactivation was caused by the attack from the "saboteur" agents of the GOALdigger system. Figure 10 shows such a situation. The MMD agent is surrounded by three GOALdigger agents, all of them issuing a clear action against the MMD agent. Because the agents are next to each other, the MMD agent loses its energy quickly, and gets deactivated.

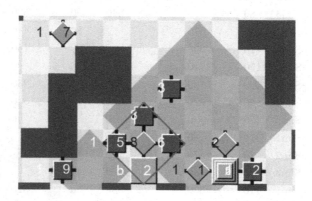

Fig. 10. Three blue GOALdigger agents attacking one green MMD agent. (Color figure online)

The MMD system delivers multiple-block tasks with agents that stay around a goal zone for a longer time, either because they coordinate task delivery and are waiting for block delivery, or because they are delivering blocks and wait for their turn to hand over the block. This kind of task delivery strategy makes the MMD agents vulnerable to "saboteur" agent attacks which obviously reduced the task completion capability of the MMD system when played against the GOALdigger system.

Other teams may have had different kind of task delivery strategy, or they did not spend too much time to deliver multiple-block tasks at the goal zone, because they did not have salient performance degradation against the GOALdigger system, as it can be seen in Table 1.

The "saboteur" agent concept seems to be efficient in reducing the task delivery capability of a competitor like the MMD. However, if a team has several dedicated "saboteur" agents, then the team has less number of agents to deliver tasks, therefore the "saboteur" agents reduce the task delivery capability of their own team as well. The "saboteur" agents not only block the agents of the other team, but they block the goal zones as well if the attacked agent is on the goal zone, thus they reduce the task delivery capability of both teams. Our experience was that one of the bottlenecks of task delivery at the contest was the lack of enough free goal zone. Because of the lack of goal zones, we introduced the goal zone reservation scheme, and we also took into account the availability of goal zones at the task selection.

The MMD agents also have the capability to attack other agents, but only while they are involved in task delivery, and they happen to have nothing important thing to do. Actually, in the configuration files of the contest, the roles that were able to deliver task had only maximum clear distance 1, which did not allow attacking other agents. On the other hand, the roles that were able to attack other agents did not have task delivery capabilities, so only dedicated "saboteur" agents could operate. Thus the MMD agents never attacked any other agent at the contest.

8 Conclusion

We have presented how we have implemented the MMD block building agents for the 2022 Multi-Agent Programming Contest (MAPC 2022). The system is implemented in a general programming language in order to compare the resulting system with other systems implemented in multi-agent programming languages. The key performance indicators of the implementation are the development time, the development efforts, and the quality of the job done by the implemented multi-agent system. The development time and the development efforts of the contest participants can be found in the introductory chapter of this book and in the answers to the questionnaire of each team. The quality of the job done by the MMD multi-agent system can be found in Sect. 7.

The development time of the MMD system is not more than any other system at MAPC 2022, because all the contest participants had the same deadline. In addition, the MMD team was formed only for the 2022 competition, while there were two other contestants who already had participated in the previous MAPC contest(s) with similar rules, so they could build on their previous implementation and experiences. Our experience showed that the implementation of our own version of the practical reasoning agent architecture for the individual agents and our own version of the blackboard architecture for the coordination of the agents could be done in time, and the use of a general programming language did not hinder us to meet the deadline.

The comparison of the development efforts of the teams is a bit difficult, because two teams already participated in the previous contests, and they only had to modify their systems. In addition, the declared development efforts are mainly rough estimates. Nevertheless, we can see that the modification of the already existing system required the least development efforts. The teams putting more effort into the development have achieved better placement. The teams using agent oriented programming languages had spent less effort for the development, but the less effort was reflected in their placement as well. We cannot conclude that the usage of a general programming language would require more development effort, because the more development effort resulted in better performance of the system. According to our experience, the biggest development challenge was the debugging of the system. The chosen debugging infrastructure made the debugging easier, but even so, it was still the most time-consuming part of the development.

The contest results seem to indicate that the implemented MMD multi-agent system is competitive with the systems developed with agent-oriented software engineering methods. There is randomness in the contest and we cannot say that a better team always wins against the other team. In spite of this, the first position of the MMD team is reaffirmed by the total points of the contestants in Table 1. This indicates that the quality of the job done by an implemented multi-agent system mostly depends on the knowledge implemented in the system rather than the programming language used.

We could have implemented further improvements into the MMD system if we had more time. The different estimation and cost calculations in the system are only approximate, and more precise calculations would probably give better results. More efficient resource management of roles, agents and tasks would be another improvement. We did not exploit the "saboteur" capability of the agents, and although we thought of "saboteur" agents in other teams, we have not prepared any defensive behaviour. A surveyor agent could make the exploration of the world faster in the beginning of the match. The pathfinder algorithm could be improved by multi-agent pathfinding algorithms [14]. These are future works for the contests of the next years.

We think that we have implemented a basic agent architecture and a basic blackboard architecture for the collaboration of the agents, and these architectures can be used in other MAPC scenarios as well. Of course, modifications are necessary if the scenario changes, but this holds for multi-agent programming language implementations as well. If the environment changes, then the interaction with the environment, as well as the internal model of the environment have to be changed in both approaches. If the logic of the scenario changes, then the logic implemented in the agent team has to be changed in both approaches. Because the implementation effort of the MMD system is comparable to the implementation efforts of the other teams, we think that the modification effort would be comparable as well.

16th Multi-agent Programming Contest: All Questions Answered

A   Team Overview: Short Answers

A.1   Participants and Their Background

Who is part of your team?
  Miklós Miskolczi, László Z. Varga
What was your motivation to participate in the contest?
  We wanted to do an experience with multi-agent systems, and of course we
  wanted to be the winner.
What is the history of your group? (course project, thesis, ...)
  The MSc diploma work of Miklós Miskolczi.

What is your field of research? Which work therein is related?
Multi-agent systems, online routing game model, multi-agent path finding.

A.2 Statistics

Did you start your agent team from scratch, or did you build on existing agents (from yourself or another previous participant)?
The agent team was started from scratch, but we used a modified version of the experimental Python client for 2020/21 edition of the Multi-Agent Programming Contest to communicate with the contest server.

How much time did you invest in the contest (for programming, organising your group, other)?
We started in February 2022 and worked on the program 28 h per week, a total of 896 h.

How was the time (roughly) distributed over the months before the contest?
Continuous development. The last two weeks mainly testing.

How many lines of code did you produce for your final agent team?
github.com/AlDanial/cloc v 1.94 T=0.13 s (649.6 files/s, 72314.5 lines/s)

Language	files	blank	comment	code
Python	83	1882	2050	4842
Text	1	121	0	553
Markdown	1	3	0	12
SUM:	85	2006	2050	5407

The above data include the modified experimental Python client, which is:
github.com/AlDanial/cloc v 1.94 T=0.05 s (20.9 files/s, 15498.5 lines/s)

Language	files	blank	comment	code
Python	1	115	102	526

A.3 Technology and Techniques

Did you use any of these agent technology/AOSE methods or tools? What were your experiences?

Agent programming languages and/or frameworks?
No.
Methodologies (e.g. Prometheus)?
No.

Notation (e.g. Agent UML)?
No.
Coordination mechanisms (e.g. protocols, games, ...)?
We used a simple (one level) Contract Net protocol, which includes a simplified auction mechanism.
Other (methods/concepts/tools)?
We used our own version of the practical reasoning agent architecture. We used our own version of the blackboard architecture for the coordination of the agents.
What hardware did you use during the contest?

Hardware	Specification
Processor	AMD Ryzen 5 3600 6-Core Processor
RAM	16 GB
OS	Windows 11 Pro

Only about 20% of the processing power of the computer was used by the agent team.

A.4   Agent System Details

Would you say your system is decentralised? Why?
Although the coordination of the agents is done by a central blackboard, and the implementation of the whole agent team is a single Python program, the system can be seen as a decentralised one in the sense that the planning and the activities of the agents are done individually. The agents were meant to be separate threads, but threading in Python is not fast enough, and we had to refactor the code to speed up the system. Python multiprocessing might be the solution for the next competition.
Do your agents use the following features: Planning, Learning, Organisations, Norms? If so, please elaborate briefly.
The actions needed to achieve a goal is basically hardcoded in the implementation. Simple learning is used to discover e.g. the cost of a clear action. In order to solve a multiple-block task, the agents are organised into a sub-team. The sub-team is connected through the intentions of the members. The intentions are assigned by the blackboard.
How do your agents cooperate?
Cooperation is done through the intentions of the agents (which is a simplified and direct communication between the agents) and the shared blackboard which includes the shared maps as well. The planning for the cooperation is hardcoded in the intentions.
Can your agents change their general behaviour during run time? If so, what triggers the changes?
Intentions are reconsidered in each simulation step. If there are changes in

the environment, then the agents may change their intention. The behaviour of the intentions may be different depending on the match configuration. The capabilities of the agents depend on the match configuration as well. The behaviour of the blackboard depends on the current state of the environment and the agents.

Did you have to make changes to the team (e.g. fix critical bugs) during the contest?

The code and the settings were not changed, but there was a problem with the connection to the server at the second and third simulation of each match, and the agent team had to be restarted manually after the first simulation steps. Interestingly, this problem did not occur during the warm-up match before the competition with the real competition server. Also, this problem did not occur with the localhost.

How did you go about debugging your system? What kinds of measures could improve your debugging experience?

The basic "debugging tool" was the printout on the console, but we also implemented an "explanation function". If the system is run with the explanation function, then the agents give information on what they are doing. The given information might be their believes, or their current intention and its details. The server logs and replays were also used to trace back various complex cases.

During the contest, you were not allowed to watch the matches. How did you track what was going on? Was it helpful?

The agents printed on the console the same information as those during the testing period before the contest. It was helpful in the sense that we could see that everything goes well.

Did you invest time in making your agents more robust/fault-tolerant? How?

Robustness and fault-tolerance was part of the development process.

A.5 Scenario and Strategy

How would you describe your intended agent behaviour? Did the actual behaviour deviate from that?

The agents mainly do what they are intended to do. Sometimes they produce strange behaviour, but we know that this may be due to the incompleteness of the solution. For example, individual route planning may produce deadlock like situation.

Why did your team perform as it did? Why did the other teams perform better/worse than you did?

The results at the competition were similar to those at the testing period, excluding the cases when the other teams were heavily agressive against opponent agents.

We do not know much about the other teams.

Did you implement any strategy that tries to interfere with your opponents?

Yes.

The tolerant way: If our agents notice that the other team stay in a goal zone for a long time at the place needed for our team, then our team go to another place.

The agressive way: When our agent is at the goal zone, then it tries to keep the agents of the other team away from the goal zone by shooting at other agents approaching the goal zone, assuming that the role capabilities of our agent allows this. This goal zone defendence behaviour was not possible with the match configuration of the competition, so our agents did not shoot at the other team during the competition.

How do your agents coordinate assembling and delivering a structure for a task?

Multi-block tasks are delivered by a single coordinator agent and block provider agents for each block. The coordinator goes to the selected goal zone. The coordinator clears the surrounding of the goal zone until the first block provider arrives. Block providers fetch the block from a dispenser and take it to the surrounding of the coordinator. The block provider waits until the call from the coordinator. When the call arrives, then the block provider takes the block to the place requested by the coordinator, and then the two agents connect the blocks.

Which aspect(s) of the scenario did you find particularly challenging?

Map building, map merging, map update, map size determination, path finding on the looping map. Shortly: dynamic map management.

Limited (and in our opinion, not realistic) perception of the agents, which means, among others, the following: When the agent moves and there is a failure, then the agent does not know which step failed. The agent does not know which blocks are attached to which agent.

What would you improve (wrt. your agents) if you wanted to participate in the same contest a week from now (or next year)?

We have ideas, but we keep them for the next competition. Surely we have to prepare to defend our agents from the potential saboteur agents of the other team.

What can be improved regarding the scenario for next year? What would you remove? What would you add?

Perception capabilities of the agents (see above).

There were only two active tasks in the current scenario, and often there was no big difference between the two tasks. Therefore a good task selection strategy was not so critical in the current scenario. Bigger choice of tasks would be more challenging.

A.6   And the Moral of it is . . .

What did you learn from participating in the contest?

Good programming and debugging exercise in a non-deterministic and hardly reproducible environment.

Building an agent architecture from scratch in a general programming language.

What advice would you give to yourself before the contest/another team wanting to participate in the next?

Now we have more knowledge to build a cleaner agent architecture.

Where did you benefit from your chosen programming language, methodology, tools, and algorithms?

The main benefits were the development speed and the simplicity. We followed the "keep it simple principle" to ensure fault-tolerance and make components open for extensions and optimizations.

Which problems did you encounter because of your chosen technologies?

Performance issues. Full parallel operation would need another implementation approach.

Programming errors are signalled in Python only when the actual line of code is executed. This way, it is easy to make errors.

Which aspect of your team cost you the most time?

Architecture building, safe map management, path finding and ensuring fault-tolerance.

A.7   Looking into the Future

Did the warm-up match help improve your team of agents? How useful do you think it is?

We did not change anything after the warm-up match, but it was good to know that the connection to the server works.

What are your thoughts on changing how the contest is run, so that the participants' agents are executed on the same infrastructure by the organisers? What do you see as positive or negative about this approach?

The positive aspect would be that all teams have the same conditions (for example network speed).

The negative aspect would be that we cannot correct any problem during the competition. For example we had to restart the team manually, because the connection to the server did not work the same way as at the warm-up match.

Do you think a match containing more than two teams should be mandatory?

This might be a possibility, but probably with not too big team sizes.

What else can be improved regarding the MAPC for next year?

Nothing more than those already mentioned above.

References

1. Ahlbrecht, T., Dix, J.: Multi-agent programming contest - Lecture 2 at 15th Workshop-School on Agents, Environments, and Applications. https://www.youtube.com/watch?v=HgNlfKm7YdQ&t=1417s. Accessed Nov 2022
2. Ahlbrecht, T., Dix, J., Fiekas, N., Krausburg, T.: The multi-agent programming contest: a Résumé. In: Ahlbrecht, T., Dix, J., Fiekas, N., Krausburg, T. (eds.) MAPC 2019. LNCS (LNAI), vol. 12381, pp. 3–27. Springer, Cham (2020). https://doi.org/10.1007/978-3-030-59299-8_1
3. Bratman, M.: Intention, Plans, and Practical Reason. Harvard University Press, Cambridge (1987)
4. Cardoso, R.C., Ferrando, A., Papacchini, F.: LFC: combining autonomous agents and automated planning in the multi-agent programming contest. In: Ahlbrecht, T., Dix, J., Fiekas, N., Krausburg, T. (eds.) MAPC 2019. LNCS (LNAI), vol. 12381, pp. 31–58. Springer, Cham (2020). https://doi.org/10.1007/978-3-030-59299-8_2
5. Durfee, E.H.: Cooperative distributed problem solving between (and within) intelligent agents. In: Rudomin, P., Arbib, M.A., Cervantes-Pérez, F., Romo, R. (eds.) Neuroscience: From Neural Networks to Artificial Intelligence. NEURALCOMPUTING, vol. 4, pp. 84–98. Springer, Heidelberg (1993). https://doi.org/10.1007/978-3-642-78102-5_5
6. Edelman, B., Ostrovsky, M., Schwarz, M.: Internet advertising and the generalized second-price auction: selling billions of dollars worth of keywords. Am. Econ. Rev. **97**(1), 242–259 (2007). https://doi.org/10.1257/aer.97.1.242
7. Englemore, R., Morgan, A.: Blackboard Systems; Edited by Robert Engelmore, Tony Morgan (the Insight Series in Artificial Intell, 1st edn. Addison-Wesley Longman Publishing Co., Inc., Boston (1988)
8. Hansen, E.A., Zhou, R.: Anytime heuristic search. J. Artif. Intell. Res. **28**, 267–297 (2007). https://doi.org/10.1613/jair.2096
9. Hart, P., Nilsson, N., Raphael, B.: A formal basis for the heuristic determination of minimum cost paths. IEEE Trans. Syst. Sci. Cybern. **4**(2), 100–107 (1968). https://doi.org/10.1109/tssc.1968.300136
10. Jennings, N.R.: Coordination through joint intentions in industrial multiagent systems. AI Mag. **14**(4), 79 (1993). https://doi.org/10.1609/aimag.v14i4.1071. https://ojs.aaai.org/index.php/aimagazine/article/view/1071
11. Koenig, S., Likhachev, M.: D*lite. In: Proceedings of the Eighteenth National Conference on Artificial Intelligence and Fourteenth Conference on Innovative Applications of Artificial Intelligence, Edmonton, Alberta, Canada, 28 July–1 August 2002, pp. 476–483 (2002). http://www.aaai.org/Library/AAAI/2002/aaai02-072.php
12. Sandholm, T., Lesser, V.R.: Issues in automated negotiation and electronic commerce: extending the contract net framework. In: Proceedings of the First International Conference on Multiagent Systems, San Francisco, California, USA, 12–14 June 1995, pp. 328–335 (1995)
13. Smith: The contract net protocol: high-level communication and control in a distributed problem solver. IEEE Trans. Comput. **C-29**(12), 1104–1113 (1980). https://doi.org/10.1109/tc.1980.1675516
14. Stern, R., et al.: Multi-agent pathfinding: definitions, variants, and benchmarks. In: Proceedings of the Twelfth International Symposium on Combinatorial Search, SOCS 2019, Napa, California, 16–17 July 2019, pp. 151–159. AAAI Press (2019)

15. Uhlir, V., Zboril, F., Vidensky, F.: Multi-agent programming contest 2019 FIT BUT team solution. In: Ahlbrecht, T., Dix, J., Fiekas, N., Krausburg, T. (eds.) MAPC 2019. LNCS (LNAI), vol. 12381, pp. 59–78. Springer, Cham (2020). https://doi.org/10.1007/978-3-030-59299-8_3
16. Vázquez-Salceda, J.: The Role of Norms and Electronic Institutions in Multi-agent Systems. Birkhäuser Basel (2004). https://doi.org/10.1007/978-3-0348-7955-2
17. Wooldridge, M.: Understanding equilibria in multi-agent systems. In: Keynote presentation at FTC 2021 - Future Technologies Conference 2021 (2021). https://youtu.be/Iqm8UTXUG24?t=411. Accessed Nov 2022
18. Wurman, P.R., D'Andrea, R., Mountz, M.: Coordinating hundreds of cooperative, autonomous vehicles in warehouses. AI Mag. **29**(1), 9 (2008)

GOALdigger-AIG-Hagen Multi-agent System: Team Description

Benjamin Geweke$^{(\boxtimes)}$, Marco Gromball, Julia Hübner, and Isaac Soriano Tapia

Artificial Intelligence Group, University of Hagen, Universitätsstraße 11,
58097 Hagen, Germany
info@fernuni-hagen.de, benjamin.geweke@studium.fernuni-hagen.de
https://www.fernuni-hagen.de/

Abstract. This paper reports the inception, planning and construction of the GOALdigger-AIG-Hagen multi-agent system, and how it achieved second place in the 16th edition of the Multi-Agent Programming Contest. GOALdigger-AIG-Hagen was programmed in the GOAL agent programming language. The aim of this paper was to improve on AI techniques for multi-agent systems, like machine learning in task selection and ant colony optimization algorithms in the optimisation of map exploration. Further, the use of agents to sabotage the rival team was researched. On the technical side, debugging and logging the states of agents with a custom mini-percept was explored. Saboteurs have been found to be very advantageous by reducing the score of the opposing team of agents. A repelling ant colony optimization algorithm has shown to reduce the time needed to explore the map, compared to a semi-random algorithm. Tournament data on task selection with machine learning could not be obtained due to a programming bug. The custom mini-percept was found to make debugging and learning about the state of agents faster and simpler than unordered log files.

Keywords: multi-agent system · MASSim · simulation

1 Introduction

This paper introduces GOALdigger-AIG-Hagen multi-agent system, which took part in the 16th edition of the Multi-Agent Programming Contest (16th MAPC) [16]. According to their stated aims and scopes, the competition is held to stimulate research in the area of multi-agent system development and programming by identifying key problems, collecting suitable benchmarks and gathering test cases which require and enforce coordinated action, that can serve as milestones for testing multi-agent programming languages, platforms and tools; they also expect that participating at the contest helps to debug existing systems and to identify their weak and strong aspects [14]. This multi-agent system was built with GOAL [11], an agent programming language and development framework tailored to multi-agent systems.

T. Ahlbrecht et al. (Eds.): MAPC 2022, LNAI 13997, pp. 98–119, 2023.
https://doi.org/10.1007/978-3-031-38712-8_4

GOAL was chosen because it is well documented [5] and its framework has an extensive feature set. We set out to improve on two survey results from the The 14th edition of the Multi-Agent Programming Contest [1]. First, many teams mentioned limited debugging capabilities in their chosen frameworks, resulting in using simple print statements. Our solution was to collect print statements in a module and print them all at once when needed, with a structure meant to help while debugging. Second, the survey showed a lack of advanced AI techniques in most participating teams. We addressed this by implementing the ant colony optimization algorithm (ACO) [3] for exploring the map as a team of agents and by using custom machine learning techniques for choosing tasks. Further, we set out to improve on the attack action for agents introduced in the 15th edition of the Multi-Agent Programming Contest [2] by focusing the attacks on rival agents carrying blocks near and inside goal zones. The implemented sabotage strategy had a major part in achieving second place in The 16th edition of the Multi-Agent Programming Contest.

The source code of GOALdigger-AIG-Hagen used in the 16th MAPC tournament is available for download at GitHub [4].

This work is organized as follows: Sect. 2 presents the methodology used for building the multi-agent system in the GOAL agent programming language. Section 3 covers the results in the tournament match-ups, in researching advanced AI techniques, the effectiveness of saboteurs and debugging. Section 4 describes the conclusions and Sect. 5 deals with future improvements.

2 Methodology

To participate in the 16th edition of the Multi-Agent Programming Contest (16th MAPC), with the simulated scenario Agents Assemble III [16] running on the MASSim (Multi-Agent Systems Simulation Platform) 2022 server [15], a multi-agent system was built. As this was the first entry for the GOALdigger-AIG-Hagen team, it was built from the ground up with the multi-agent system programming language and development framework GOAL. Multi-agent systems are a complex challenge that require agents to coordinate themselves to submit tasks in the simulated scenario, to get rewards and in the end score higher than the opposing team of agents. The tasks in the 16th MAPC require assembling block constructs and submitting them according to offered tasks in goal zones. The more blocks a structure contains, the more reward is given for the submitted task. Blocks can be acquired from dispensers. Agents are spawned in a 2d cell world, without knowledge about their surroundings and perceive their surroundings through percepts in every simulation step; normal perception range is 5 cells. The agents of a team build a shared map through messages and moving through the simulated world. This information is needed to coordinate the submission of complex tasks (tasks that require more than one block) by cooperating agents. Further complications arise in the simulated scenario from events, norms and opposing agents, that can punish agents by deactivating or hindering them.

2.1   GOAL Language and Framework

To implement the multi-agent system, the declarative language GOAL was used [11]. GOAL is an agent programming language specially designed for multi-agent systems with an associated development framework. It provides basic functions for an agent and integration with the Environment Interface Standard (EIS) [10] to connect to the simulation server. The programming framework is added as an add-on in Eclipse [12]. This provides an integrated development environment (IDE) for GOAL.

By using a framework, it was possible to go deeper into the logic of a multi-agent system than it would have been possible having to implement all necessary functions from scratch. A decisive point for choosing GOAL was its comprehensive and clear documentation [5,12]. In addition, a multi-agent system programmed with GOAL achieved second place in the Multi-Agent Programming Contest 2021 [8]. Within GOAL, Prolog functions were used for the knowledge base. However, the use of Prolog in relation to GOAL is limited to a section of the language [9]. In GOAL, the knowledge database could also be implemented in SQL or other languages.

Figure 1 shows the regulated program flow. First, a new percept with updated data arrives from the simulation server through EIS at every step of the simulation. Every agent gets a unique percept data set for their status and world surroundings. The percept data depends on the simulation, and in the 16th MAPC it contained simulation step, agent name, energy level, available tasks, neighbouring cell data (up a distance of 5 or 7 cells, depending on the role of the agent), result of last action sent to the server, and more. The arrival of a percept starts one execution loop of agent code. First, the event module gets executed consecutively to update the knowledge base depending on the information contained in the new percept and/or knowledge base. Percepts are transient and only available in their corresponding simulation step; to store percept data for later simulation steps, the information has to be written into the knowledge base of the agent. Each agent has its own knowledge base. The whole purpose of the event module is to update, delete and store data in the agent's knowledge base. The event module also handles messaging between agents. Like percepts, incoming messages are transient and can lead to updates, deletions and inclusion of data in the agent's knowledge base.

The main module gets executed automatically after the event module. The purpose of the main module is to choose one action per step and send it through EIS to the simulation server. The action is chosen based on the current percept, message and knowledge base data. Executing the event module before the main module keeps the knowledge base current. In the 16th MAPC simulations, there were 12 possible actions: move, skip, clear, request, adapt, rotate, attach, detach, submit, connect, disconnect and survey. Some actions have variables, move for example has variables for the movement direction. The actions can be classified in three different categories: movement actions move the agent around in the simulated grid world, environment manipulation actions change or get information about the status of the cells or agents around them and skip ends the agent code execution for this step. If no action is chosen in time (timeout set by EIS corresponding to the timeout set in the simulation server), the agent's code execution loop gets aborted and the agent must wait for the next percept to start a new code execution loop. Since one action has to be chosen in the main module, every branch in the code inside the main module ends with an action. After sending an action in time to the simulation server through EIS, the agent waits for the next percept.

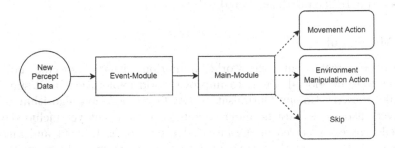

Fig. 1. Program sequence of GOAL framework.

2.2   Messaging Between Agents

The GOAL framework has an built-in messaging system with channels, broadcasting and targeted messages. In our multi-agent system, every agent broadcasts a status message to every other agent at every step. These messages contain important information such as name, position, availability, carried block, random seed, and more. From those messages, every agent learns the address corresponding to every agent name, enabling them to send targeted messages. The status message gets stored in the knowledge bases of the agents, information from a higher simulation step overwrites information from lower steps.

A kind of agent we call 'submitter leaders' look for agents who can support them in the stored status messages. First, they need agents that broadcast that they are available. Then, they need to know the offsets between their coordinate systems. When agents are available and the offsets are known, the submitter leader can send a targeted message to the closest fitting agent with a request for assistance in complex tasks. Messages arrive at the earliest in the next simulation step after they are sent, but this is not guaranteed and they could arrive a few steps later. Even if messages arrive on time, their information can be temporally inaccurate. Requested supporters can decline cooperation, for example if they recently already committed to supporting another submitter leader. The submitter leader will then redo its calculations and request support from another agent.

When an agent stores new map information from its percept, it broadcasts this information to all other agents. Agents can immediately store this information in their own world map if the relative offset between the two agents coordinate systems is known, or cache the message until they learn the offset to the sender needed to translate it into their own map coordinates. Every agent checks its cached messages at every step of the simulation and, when it finds cached data corresponding to stored offset values of another agent's world map data, it stores it in its world map in its own coordinate system. The corresponding cached data then is then deleted.

2.3   Movement

To move an agent around the world simulation, situation-specific movement patterns were developed. First, to improve world exploration until simulation step 100, the Ant Colony Optimisation (ACO) exploration algorithm is used. Perceived dispensers, targets and role zones that are not yet included in the knowledge base are stored in the knowledge base of each agent and messaged to other agents so that they can add it to their maps or cache them for later addition to their map. Later, the agents use Manhattan distance [3] to target a location and a semi-random exploration algorithm to avoid obstacles.

For the optimised exploration of the world map, the agents should find new paths more quickly, following the example of an ant colony. Unlike ants, which use pheromones to lead other ants in the colony along the same paths, agents perceive the pheromone trails of their fellow agents as repulsive and thus avoid the routes followed by their predecessors. Every agent stores the location of every other agent regularly, which leads to a growing data set of pheromone markers in each agent's knowledge base. For performance reasons, with this growing data set, this algorithm is only executed at the beginning of the simulation, until step 100. In addition, a good exploration algorithm is most important at the beginning of the simulation, when the world map is at least explored.

The semi-random exploration algorithm initialises each agent with an inclination to a cardinal direction (north, south, west or east). This exploration algorithm is used after simulation step 100. The agent tries to follow this direction; only in case of obstacles or other agents in its direct path can the agent turn away from the intended travel direction for one step by 90° and then resume the cardinal direction. The preferred travel direction changes randomly and regularly by 90° after n steps, where n is once initialised at agent creation with a random value between 10 and 20 steps. The 90° turn prevents moving backwards. An agent surrounded by obstacles both in its cardinal direction and both perpendicular directions can free itself by randomly changing the cardinal direction by its opposite direction after n steps. Compared to the ACO algorithm, this needs no stored pheromone markers in the knowledge base of the agents, which improves system performance.

The Manhattan Distance (MD) algorithm uses two types of movement: one is movement with one block attached to the agent, where agents carry only one block at a time into the target zone holding it behind them in the direction of movement. This makes agents more agile, since there are no obstacles or other agents in front of the block that can prevent movement, and allows agents to manoeuvre better in case of obstacles by clearing only the obstacles or blocks in front of them. The second type of movement is without a block. In this case, the shortest path is chosen; for equal Manhattan distance values, one option is chosen at random.

For special situations, modules regulating the movement around a dispenser or for supporters around the submitter leader were developed. At the dispenser, blocks can only be requested from the four cardinal directions; if the dispenser is at a diagonal position, the agent must move to a straight position. The supporter also uses an adjusted movement pattern to avoid the submitter leader, when the leader is in waiting position inside the goal zone for supporters, if the supporter is coming from the north. The supporter's trajectory looks like a rain drop moving down a window, avoiding obstacles in its path to change positions from north of the submitter leader to south of it. This is necessary because the MD movement to the delivery position may go around other agents or clear through obstacles and blocks. However, a submitter leader can also have blocks southwest or southeast of it which cannot be cleared (as is the rule for attached blocks) and cannot move (when they are connected to the submitter leader in the goal zone). If a supporter comes from the north it would get stuck on those blocks. Thus, switching to another set of movement rules enables the supporting agent to move around their submitter leader. From there, the supporter delivers the block for the multi-block task.

The various movement implementations of GOALdigger, like movement with Manhattan distance and nearly always removing obstacles in the agent's path worked very effectively, since there are no permanent obstacles requiring a more complex pathfinding solution. Although it can lead to deadlocks between agents from the own and the rival team, especially in goal zones, this is equally detrimental for both teams.

2.4   Map Construction

Each agent has its own coordinate system. The cell they start on at the beginning of the simulation start becomes their origin of coordinates. Each agent of the team starts on a different cell. If an agent sees an object, it saves its position in its world map. In addition, the agent broadcasts a message with the position of the object to all other agents. If a receiving agent knows the coordinate system offset to the sender, it can translate the map data into its own coordinate system and store it in its own world map. Else, it stores the message until it knows the offset and then adds the information to its world map. Agents store the positions of goal zones, role zones and dispensers. Agents also save the positions where other agents have been. With this data, they can explore parts of the map which have not been explored by their team yet, as explained in the Sect. 2.5 "Map Exploration".

2.5   Map Exploration

Each team has a limited time to reach a higher score than the rival team. It has to explore the map in an efficient way. The positions of dispensers and goal zones must be known to submit the given tasks. To achieve this in an efficient way, our agents used a variation from Sven König et al. [13] ants coverage method. During the first hundred steps, if an agent has no other goals, it explores the map. The exploration algorithm is like that of ants [13]. Ants leave marks (pheromones) where they find food or other needed resources for the colony and for building ant trails.

Each agent has its own coordinate system and stores its last position in its knowledge base. When two agents meet, they store an offset to each other. In subsequent rounds, each time one of the agents communicates its position, the other agent can convert it to match its own coordinate system. Each agent stores the other agent's positions as position markers in its own knowledge base. These position markers serve as pheromone markers. Thus, the agents know that a particular position has already been explored. Before moving, each agent checks to see if a marker is nearby. If a marker is found in a 5×5 quadrant, the agent does not move in that direction.

Figure 2 shows these markers around the agent. The red star symbolizes a position marker where another agent was and the yellow circle is the last position marker of the agent itself. Two markers block north and east. The circle blocks south. Therefore, the agent will choose to explore west. In addition, if the agent detects another agent of its team in its field of view, this direction is blocked, too. If all directions are blocked, the agent chooses one direction to explore at random. This way, the agent tries not to explore the same parts of the map twice.

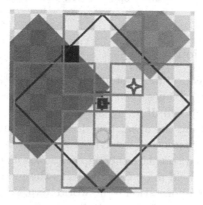

Fig. 2. ACO algorithm example

2.6   Agent Hierarchy and Roles

The agents receive a meta role at simulation step 24 and keep it until the end of the simulation. Their decision starts by acquiring one of three meta roles: submitter leader, saboteur or supporter. The submitter leader submits complex tasks, the saboteur attacks agents of the rival team to prevent them from scoring and the supporter submits 1-block-tasks or helps in complex tasks by bringing blocks to the submitter leader. Submitter leaders can command supporters to acquire and deliver them needed blocks for complex tasks. If the supporters don't have a command from a submitter leader, they submit 1-block tasks by themselves. Beside the meta roles, there are domain roles as given by the simulation. These roles define which actions an agent can perform. Submitter leader and supporter use the worker role, because it offers double moving speed actions without a block and the submit action. The saboteur uses the digger role, the only role that can attack other agents with the clear action; every agent can perform clear actions, but only in the digger role do they damage other agents by reducing their energy level. Agents keep their custom and corresponding domain roles throughout a simulation and even with role norms, that can punish the agents with deactivation, the punishment is accepted, instead of taking up the path to a role zone and change roles during norm activation. The time lost for changing into another role would just be another kind of punishment. The relations of the meta roles are shown in Fig. 3.

There is an automatic distribution of meta roles after simulation step 23 among all GOALdigger agents using the division algorithm and a random seed-based hierarchy. The division algorithm tests the position number in the hierarchy, if it can be divided without remainder by 6 for deciding on submitter leaders. All agents create a random number, that they broadcast every simulation step, after which they are numbered in descending order of size. Seed collisions are prevented by creating a new seed when a collision is detected, but only until step 24, which should be enough time to have no seed collisions over all agents. By using the number in hierarchy and doing a modulo 6 equals 0 on it, every sixth agent becomes a submitter leader. In groups of 20 agents, like for tournament simulations 1 and 2, the agents with hierarchy numbers between 1 and 5 become saboteurs. The remaining agents become supporters, so that 3 submitter leaders, 5 saboteurs and 12 supporters are active in simulations with 20 agents on a team. With teams of 40 agents, like in tournament simulation 3, agents with numbers between 7 and 9 become saboteurs too. All other agents turn into supporters. For the tournament simulation 3, that meant 6 submitter leaders and 8 saboteurs were active. Figure 2 shows the agent hierarchy.

2.7   Task Selection with Machine Learning

Another advanced AI technique that we explored is machine learning to help submitter leaders in choose complex tasks. GOALdigger uses a custom machine learning algorithm inspired by Q-learning techniques [7]. In Q-learning, Q-values represent a possible reward corresponding to an action, the Q-value can change

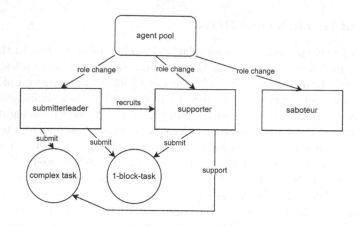

Fig. 3. Agent hierarchy.

through an algorithm, that gets executed on a trigger event(for example a submitted one-block task). Out of all possible actions, the one with the highest reward will be chosen. The actions here corresponds to choosing one of three possible complex tasks: two-block task, three-block task and four-block task. The Q values are stored in a variable:

```
qtable(q-value2blocktask,q-value3blocktask,q-value4blocktask)
qtable(33,34,33)
```

For the custom machine learning algorithm, the Q value represents the probability of selecting a complex task type. The first three Q-values represent, in order, the percentage chance of selecting two-block tasks, three-block tasks, and four-block tasks. They add up to 100%. Shown are the initial values, meaning that every complex task has (nearly) equal chances to be chosen.

When a complex task succeeds or fails, agents share this information through messages. Successful tasks effect a positive reinforcement learning, and failed tasks effect a negative reinforcement learning. With this information, every agent recalculates their Q-table. Through the shared messages, their knowledge is transferred between them, and every Q-table should be identical. When a task succeeds, the corresponding value of Q goes up and the others go down so they still add up to 100%. For successful two-block tasks, q-value2blocktask goes up by 16% and the other two Q-values go down by 8%. For successful three-block tasks, q-value3blocktask goes up by 24% and the other two Q-values go down by 12%. For successful three-block tasks, q-value3blocktask goes up by 32% and the other two Q-values go down by 16%. The amount of correction correlates to the amount of reward a task can give: a higher reward equals a higher shift in percentage.

When a task fails, its corresponding value and the values of more complex tasks go down, while the values of simpler tasks go up, except for the simplest complex task, that still goes up because there is no simpler task. For unsuccessful two-block tasks, q-value2blocktask goes up by 10%, and the other two Q-values go down by 5%. For unsuccessful three-block tasks q-value2blocktask goes up by 16% and the other two Q-values go down by 8%. For unsuccessful three-block tasks, q-value3blocktask goes down by 10% and the other two Q-values go down up 5%. The lower changes for failed tasks mean that failed tasks have a weaker learning effect than successful tasks. It is assumed that when a complex task fails and a simpler task is available, it would be advantageous and more successful to try the simpler task next time.

There is a further rule ensuring that all available task types can always be chosen. The value of Q cannot go below 10% or over 80%, so there is always a minimum chance of choosing any of the 3 available complex tasks first. When the sum of all three values of Q goes above 100, the biggest value of Q will be reduced until they sum up to 100 again. This ensures that the Q-table can develop in any direction without getting stuck with a particular task type on 100% for the whole game.

The actual task selection works by getting a random number between 0 and 100 and relating it to the percentages from the Q-table, and seeing if the preferred complex task type is available. Since it is not guaranteed the preferred complex task type is available it is assumed that the next simpler task with one less block in its structure is a good replacement. With 2 concurrent tasks in the MAPC simulations, there is only a 66% chance a preferred task is active in simulations limited to up to three-block tasks. With additional four-block tasks, the chance is 50%. The choosing of simpler tasks continues until all two-block tasks get evaluated and if that does not choose a task, complex tasks that have more blocks than the preferred task are tried. If no complex task gets chosen this way, a one-block task can be chosen. The agent changes a one-block task for any complex task if it becomes available. If a complex task is chosen, the agent does not change its task for other tasks but tries to submit the complex task. This ensures the agent chooses a task from the available ones, even if they are not preferred. When a tasks fails or succeeds, all Q-values will be recalculated. This information helps all agents choose the most rewarding task type in the simulation through machine learning.

2.8   Task Delivery

Submitter leader agents can submit complex tasks and prefer them over one-block tasks. After they have chosen a complex task, they calculate their closest available agents and order them to bring the desired block of the complex task to their own current position. This position gets updated when the submitter leader moves. When an agent declines the request, the submitter leader requests another of its closest agents. This is necessary because the request could have been made on the basis of obsolete information because of temporal data inconsistencies through message delay.

The submitter leader acquires the fitting block from the closest matching dispenser if it is not already carrying it. With the right block, the submitter leader goes to the nearest goal zone. Inside the goal zone, submitter leaders move away from each other to other cells in the same goal zone until they can't move further or the distance between them is 4 cells. This prevents deadlocking each other's delivery cells. Inside the goal zone, submitter leaders rotate their block south into the submitting position and wait for their recruited agents to bring the missing blocks as Fig. 4 shows for submitter leader agent 5. While waiting, they repeatedly try out all possible connecting actions for missing blocks in the block structure of the task.

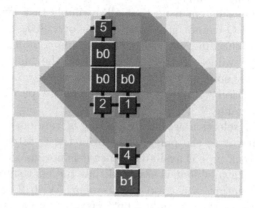

Fig. 4. Delivery pattern of complex tasks.

Supporting agents bring blocks for the complex task to a waiting position a few cells south of their intended position, as seen for agent 4 in Fig. 4, to prevent deadlocking of supporters. Blocks intended for the east, west and south position relative to the submitter leader's block can always be delivered and need no waiting position. Blocks intended for the first row below the submitter leader can be delivered immediately, too. Supporters deliver their block by moving and rotating it north onto the delivery position, as shown in Fig. 4 by agents 2 and 1. Supporters in a waiting position wait until they detect a connected block above their delivery position and then move and rotate the block into delivery position. Supporting agents send only one kind of connection action when in final position. They always send connect actions with the name of the submitter leader and the position of the block they brought, which is north.

The submitter leader tries out all logical and possible connect actions when in final position. It has to send connect actions with up to 3 possible agent names for 4-block tasks. Further it is possible for supporters to connect blocks to blocks that are already connected to the block south of their submitter leaders. This requires the submitter leader to find the right name and block position for the connect action. To reduce unnecessary connect actions, the submitter leader does not try connect actions with agent names who have already delivered blocks or with blocks that are not yet there. This system introduces some delay while the submitter leaders tries connect actions until finding the right one, but removes the need for message coordination between submitter leaders and supporters.

The blocks connect when matching connection actions of submitter leader and supporter happen at the same time in the simulation. Supporters become free agents again after a successful connection. The submitter leader tracks all blocks needed for a complex task and their connection status. When all blocks are connected, the task gets submitted if it is still active and the submitter leader is still on a goal zone.

2.9 Sabotage of Rival Agents

An agent in the meta role of saboteur attacks rival team agents in order to prevent them from scoring points. The meta role of the saboteur is performed by an agent with the digger role. An agent with this role can use its clearing actions to hit rival agents. In addition, its clearing actions have a longer reach and are not restricted to adjacent cells. When aimed at a rival agent, a clear action causes it to lose energy, deactivating it if its energy level is already low enough. Although it is a configurable setting, the energy loss is defaulted to decrease with increasing distance, making this kind of attack impractical at Manhattan distances greater than 2.

The strategy of the saboteur determines the agents being targeted by them and their way of moving through the map. Since workers carrying a block can only move one cell at a time, and it makes it easier to track and correctly identify those kind of agents are an obvious target. It was assumed that the rival team could be harmed the most by attacking their agents after they had gone through the trouble of picking a block from the dispenser and on approach to a goal zone. The nearer to its goal an agent would be attacked, the better. Deactivating them at that point and subsequently clearing the blocks they were carrying would force them to go back to the dispenser, thus making them lose more time. For this reason, the saboteurs were made to focus on goal zones, and target only agents while a goal zone is in sight, as is shown in Fig. 5, where agent 10 attacks (red rhombus) agent 9 and agent 16 attacks agent 3.

Since goal zones may get crowded easily, and with default energy and harm levels it would take several hits to deactivate a rival agent, the saboteur needed a way to prioritize its targets. The highest priority would be for rival agents standing still with a block in southern position, since they are good candidates for members of a multitask team awaiting for other members to submit their tasks. Deactivating those agents would harm the rival teams the most, since they would have scored big points otherwise. The second priority would be for rival agents carrying a block in any position and standing still, since they are easier to target. In the third place, agents carrying a block and moving would be targeted. Other than that, rival agents would be targeted by proximity, avoiding whenever possible to target a non-adjacent rival agent by getting closer to them first. Only when an agent at distance 2 (usually an agent standing still with a block on the southern side) cannot be reached in one step (because of some obstacle between saboteur and agent) is this agent targeted by the saboteur.

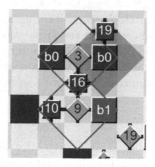

Fig. 5. Saboteering agents 10 and 16 attack agents 3 and 9 in and around the goal zone.

In order to keep records of their energy levels and predict their next movement, the saboteur keeps track of rival agents in its field of view. Since the information of the server only informs agents about whether a block is attached to some agent, but not to which agent precisely, it is not possible to determine with certainty who is carrying what and thus who is a suitable target for the next step. Before being a target, a rival agent in the field of view of the saboteur is processed as a "sighting". The saboteur keeps records of these sightings until they are no longer in its perceived cells. A rival agent is considered a sighting if it is adjacent to an attached block. To avoid confusion, only agents beside blocks without other adjacent agents are recorded as sightings. Those blocks are then implicitly assigned to the agent adjacent to them. A sighting has a position, an energy level estimate, a block position and a direction of movement. At first, rival agents are believed to have a full energy level. The block position of the sighting is what is considered while prioritizing the next target, as explained in the previous paragraph. In subsequent steps, the sighting data is updated according to the current observations: rotation of carried blocks and changes in direction. In case of crowded areas, guesses are made conservatively.

There is an important exception to the tracking of sightings: if a dispenser happens to be inside a goal zone, and an agent carrying a block of the same type as the dispenser is standing beside it, it is presumed to be performing simple tasks. Since such agents will be able to perform lots of simple tasks even during the attack, and the time an agent stays inactive is not that long, it was considered to be a futile endeavour to target them and prefer to keep the saboteur free to attack others. For this reason, such agents are only recorded as sightings if their blocks are already facing south. If the sighting persists in the next step (i.e., if the agent does not lose its block by submitting a simple task immediately), the agent is presumed to be a part of a task submitting team and it makes sense to target them.

The movements of the saboteurs depend on a certain set of rules. First, there are rules for when the saboteur is next to a goal zone. In that case, they will preferentially move towards potential targets according to the aforementioned priorities. If a goal zone has still not been declared empty (more on that later) and there is no better destination, the saboteur will move towards a rival agent without attached blocks, hoping to be led to some interesting spot. If no rival agent is available, the saboteur will select a distant point of the same goal zone and move there.

Then, there are rules aimed at finding suitable goal zones, those where rival agents try to submit their tasks. If a saboteur has already found a suitable goal zone, but has strayed away from it (e. g., by pursuing a rival agent), it will return there as soon as it stops perceiving it. In any other case, the saboteur will search for suitable goal zones following this order: first, go to a recommended goal zone; otherwise, go to a goal zone which is not believed to be empty or to any goal zone if no better information is available.

Goal zones get recommended by other GOALdigger agents: whenever they perceive block-carrying rival agents next to a goal zone, they send messages about their sightings, stating time, place and number of sighted rival agents. The saboteur receives these messages and caches one at a time according to the number of sighted agents and the distance.

Whether a goal zone is empty or not, depends on whether rival task submitters have been sighted there a certain time ago. For that, the saboteur sets timers to a certain cell of a goal zone which increase so long as no task submitter (i.e., rival agent carrying a block facing south) is sighted within a certain radius. As soon as one such agent is sighted, the timer is reset. If other rival agents carrying blocks are sighted, the timer is not reset, but also not increased during the current step.

2.10   Logging and Debugging

Each agent's percepts, messages and beliefs, as well as module executions and data changes, are logged in an unordered manner at each step of the simulation with some loss of performance. In order to be able to evaluate relevant data in an orderly, quicker and easier way, a custom "mini-percept" log with the most important information was created (see Fig. 6). Here, additional information about the saboteur as well as about task selection is collected. Some data is sent by messages so that the information shows up in every log. It is designed so that it is enough to debug the entire agent system on a team or individual agent level.

Figure 6 shows the mini-percept for step 24, seen in line 641 of the pictured log excerpt, which also shows that the agent acquired the worker domain role and the result of the last action the agent sent to the simulation server on the previous step 23. The last action partially failed and, instead of moving two cells north, the agent only moved north by one cell. Step 24 is also the step in which the agent determines its meta role from the hierarchy, it is the fifth agent in the hierarchy and every hierarchy number that divides by 5 becomes a submitter leader, also shown on line 639. The current position of the agent is shown in line 642, followed by the coordinates and type of a Manhattan Distance (MD) target. But the MD is not active as shown in line 647. Other targets are in line 645 and 646 with coordinates (70/70), block types (bx is a placeholder, a block type 1 would be b1) and distances for dispenser and goal zones. Both are filled with placeholders and are only used when needed for finding closest dispenser and goal zones. After line 649 (named MISC DATA for 'miscellaneous data'), information is output about how long the calculations of the last step took in milliseconds (shown here as 0, which means that this agent finished in less than 1 ms). This is followed by the current energy level of the agent and by information about whether the agent is currently deactivated (agents get deactivated when their energy level falls to 0). The next intention of the agent is to acquire a new task (see line 643), since it has already acquired a meta role (submitter leader) and a domain role (worker), which must happen before processing tasks as a submitter leader. After acquiring a task, the agent needs a block that matches the task, since it does not have a block at the moment (line 648).

```
638 ====== Our Mini Percept =====,
639 Agent hierarchy position: | 5 | submitterLeader,
640 This is simulation: + 1,
641 24 | worker + Agent: + partial_success + move | n | n,
642 This step AgentAt: | -2 | -3 + TargetMD: | -5 | -3 | rolezone,
643 MyTask: + noname + -1 + 999 | 1 | 1 + noBlock | needNewTask | needNewTask,
644 2-BLOCK: | placeholder | placeholder + 3-BLOCK: | placeholder | placeholder
645 TargetDispenser: | 70 | 70 + Block+Distance: | bx | 1234567,
646 TargetGoalZone: | 111 | 111 + Distance: | 123456,
647 Manhattan Switch Inactive,
648 HaveBlock: + false +  Direction:  + n + HaveDelivery: + false,
649 ++++++ MISC DATA ++++++++++++,
650 Calculated time for Step + 23 + in milliseconds:  + 0,
651 Energy: + 100 | Deactivated: + false +  Last deactivation on step:  + -10,
652 Affinity: + n | Change after: + 17 | Seed: + 1409,
653  Agent knows this world size: X + 54321 + , Y + 54321 + .",
654  Agent knows this world size: XList + [] + , YList + [] + .",
655 ====== End Mini Percept =====,
```

Fig. 6. Example of mini-percept custom logging. Extract of line 638 to 655 from agent's log file.

This curated logging makes the status and intentions of the agent more human-readable, and the recurring lines 638 and 655 enable the extraction of all mini-percepts from the logs of every agent and for all simulation steps. The complete logging requires about 30% of the computing power and had been turned off for the duration of the tournament. Simulation 3 with 40 agents led to crashes when not all resources where available.

2.11   Tournament Preparation

In preparation for the matches, a variety of debugging maps was used. Those maps reduced the complexity to the bare minimum needed to test one aspect of the agent system. For example, the one-block task carousel map, as seen in Fig. 7, has just three dispensers (b0, b1 and b2), one goal zone (red zone), one agent (blue 1) and one task, changing every 75 steps. A success condition would be the one agent constantly working on the current task by switching between steering to a dispenser, fetching a block and then delivering it to the goal zone. On task change, it would switch to the new required block type. From this constant driving around and submitting tasks comes the apt name "carousel".

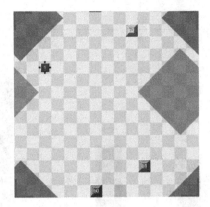

Fig. 7. Simplified test map for one block tasks. (Color figure online)

The GOALdigger team came from a practical course at University of Hagen and did 6 tournaments against 5 other teams before the MAPC. Every tournament was more advanced than the previous one until the last one nearly reached the difficulty of the MAPC qualification maps. GOALdigger achieved 3 first and 3 s places there.

3   Results

As mentioned earlier, the aim of this paper was to build on the survey and research results of the The 14th edition of the Multi-Agent Programming Contest [1]. The survey mentioned limited debugging capabilities and a lack of advanced AI techniques. Machine learning for task choosing and Ant Colony Optimisation were chosen as research objects for advanced AI techniques. Further, the implementation of saboteurs and the general behavior of GOALdigger in the The 16th MAPC tournament was researched.

3.1   Effectiveness of the Saboteurs

The saboteurs reduced the amount of reward other teams achieved. Figures 8, 9, 10 and 11 show the average score of each rival team in the tournament against all teams other than GOALdigger for all three simulations compared to their scores against GOALdigger. Over all games by GOALdigger with saboteurs, the rival teams only achieved 75% of their average scores against the other teams. Removing GOALdigger's first simulation against FIT BUT, where that team achieved a score 470% higher than in all other first simulations against other teams, this value gets down to 35%. Even in cases where a bug prevented sabo-teurs from adopting the role of digger enabling them to damage the opponent, and apart from simulation 3 against GOAL-DTU, at least one fully-functioning saboteur was always active.

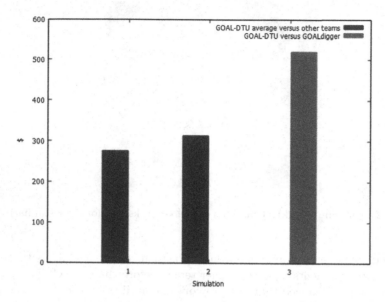

Fig. 8. GOAL-DTU's average scores against other teams and scores against GOALdig-ger

3.2   Logging with the Mini-Percept

The curated and collected logging of the current state and intentions of every agent for every simulation step in human-readable format helped find bugs and problems faster than raw logs that must be searched and interpreted first.

3.3   Tournament Matches

Matches Versus GOAL-DTU. The matches against GOAL-DTU (with two victories and one defeat for our team) showed how our team heavily favored one-block tasks, while GOAL-DTU preferred complex tasks, ignoring simple tasks altogether. This made both teams heavily reliant on the kind of tasks offered during each match, with GOAL-DTU not scoring any points when complex tasks were not available. During these matches, some yet unknown errors in the implementation of the saboteur meta-role assignment became evident, as saboteurs were not available in the expected quantities. In addition, some of the saboteurs seemed disoriented and could not find their way to the goal zones.

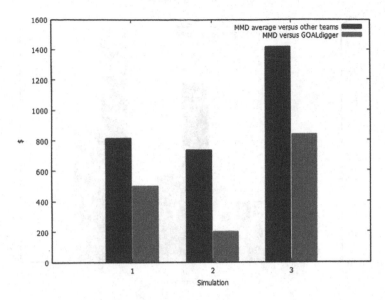

Fig. 9. MMD's average scores against other teams and scores against GOALdigger

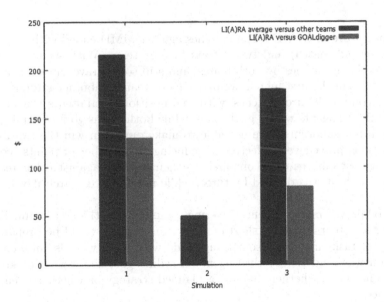

Fig. 10. LI(A)RA's average scores against other teams and scores against GOALdigger

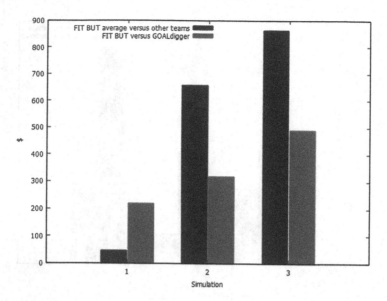

Fig. 11. FIT BUT's average scores against other teams and scores against GOALdigger

Matches Versus MMD. The matches against MMD ended with one victory (in the second match) and two defeats for our team. With seemingly similar task selection strategies by both teams, and still some grave saboteur availability problems in the first match, we first see our team's sabotage strategy pay off in the second and third matches, with well-positioned saboteurs efficiently disabling MMD's agents within goal zones, while both teams go for complex tasks. Although our saboteurs were not able to make our team win the third match, their actions proved very effective in reducing the number of points scored by MMD against our team as compared to their average against other teams: in second match, it was divided by three, while in the third match it was almost halved.

MMD proved more efficient delivering complex tasks than our team. The fact that our saboteurs made us short of some agents which could be preparing the delivery of tasks may have something to do with it. It was also observed that our team was hindered by rival agents crowding goal zones without attacking us. It is not clear whether this was a planned strategy or whether it happened by chance.

Matches Versus LI(A)RA. Our team won all matches against LI(A)RA. Like in previous matches, not all our intended saboteurs were available, but those available halved LI(A)RA's expected scores. Like in the matches against MMD, agents from both teams tended to deadlock with each other, thus being unable to score.

Matches Versus FIT BUT. In the matches against FIT-BUT (with one defeat, one tie and one narrow victory for our team), it was observed that the inability of some saboteurs to find the relevant goal zones in time affected their efficacy in shorter matches. In longer matches we would expect GOALdigger to profit from better saboteur maps and see it reflected in higher score differences with FIT-BUT. Expectedly, the efficacy of saboteurs was also reduced in cases where the number of goal zones was greater than their own number, thus preventing them to patrol all of them at the same time. It was observed that FIT-BUT was also using diggers as saboteurs, but shooting from further away, thus reducing the effectiveness of their attacks and showing that our strategy of closer-range attacks was more apt. During these matches, GOALdigger preferred simpler tasks, while more complex tasks gave FIT-BUT the upper hand in some occasions.

3.4   Effectiveness of the Ant Colony Optimisation

Compared to the semi-random exploring algorithm, it was observed that agents using an algorithm from Ant Colony Organisation's family of algorithms were prevented from exploring in directions that they themselves or agents of the team with known coordinate system offsets had already explored. This enables a faster exploration of the map details through coordination in the agent team. This can lead to a higher score based on more information gathered in a shorter period of time and on which to base the selection and delivery of a task.

3.5   Effectiveness of the Machine Learning in Task Choosing

After the tournament, it was discovered that a bug prevented changes in the Q-table. This led to only using the initial values in the Q-table during all 3 simulations. With these values, the selection algorithm is nearly identical to choosing complex tasks randomly, and no data was collected about the effectiveness of machine learning for task choosing in the tournament.

4   Conclusion

We have demonstrated the effectiveness of using saboteurs in the 16th MAPC. Five saboteurs were active in simulation 1 and 2, that had 20 agents on a team. In simulation 3, with 40 agents on a team, eight saboteurs were active. They became a big factor in achieving the second place by reducing the opponents' score. Averaged over all simulations, a reduction to 75% of the expected score was achieved. Removing GOALdigger's first simulation against FIT BUT, where that team achieved a score 470% higher than in all other first simulations against other teams, this value even gets down to 35%.

In setting out to improve debugging from simple print statements, we found that collecting print statements in a central module and curating them to improve their readability for humans helps in debugging and understanding the state and intentions of the agents.

Further, we had partial success in implementing advanced AI techniques like algorithms from the Ant Colony Optimisation algorithm family and machine learning. The Ant Colony Optimisation algorithm with repelling pheromones markers worked as intended: agents traveled into directions with the least amount of pheromones markers, helping in exploring the simulated world more effectively. Our attempt to use machine learning for task selection failed due to a programming error that was discovered after the tournament; therefore, no conclusions can be drawn.

The chosen agent programming language and framework GOAL also delivered a technically mature and beginner-friendly multi-agent system design experience and can only be encouraged for further use, research and development.

5   Future Improvements

Apart from group reinforcement learning, GOALdigger's task selection algorithm is very simple with just building a localized team around a leader calculating distances to dispensers by himself. Future versions should calculate distances for supporting agents as well in order to reduce delivery and acquisition times of blocks.

The saboteur was big part of the success of the GOALdigger multi-agent system. A coordinated effort between saboteurs was not implemented and could enhance their effectiveness by covering all goal zones equally and by using coordinated attacks.

To reduce limitations of the GOAL agent programming language, the integration of Java into the framework could be explored. Salvador Jacobi already demonstrated this possibility [6].

Some features of MASSim were not implemented. Using the explorer domain role and calculating the world size with it is one of them. Using the survey action was another one.

Finally, reinforcement learning could be applied to more parts of the multi-agent system. One option would be data points on how much time is left in a task or how the agent team distributes roles between themselves.

Acknowledgements. The GOALdigger-AIG-Hagen team likes to thank Professor Thimm and Lars Bengel from the AI group and our fellow 22 students from their practical AI course who helped us to prepare GOALdigger with their 5 teams in 6 tournaments for the MAPC. Finally, we would like to thank the organizers of the MAPC for their amazing tournament.

References

1. Ahlbrecht, T.: The Multi-Agent Programming Contest 2019: Agents Assemble - Block by Block to Victory. Lecture Notes in Computer Science Ser, vol. 12381. Springer, Cham (2020). https://doi.org/10.1007/978-3-030-59299-8, https://ebookcentral.proquest.com/lib/kxp/detail.action?docID=6355954
2. Ahlbrecht, T., Dix, J., Fiekas, N., Krausburg, T. (eds.): The Multi-Agent Programming Contest 2021: One-and-a-Half Decades of Exploring Multi-Agent Systems. Springer eBook Collection, 1st edn., vol. 12947. Springer, Cham (2021). https://doi.org/10.1007/978-3-030-88549-6
3. Blatt, F.A.: The multi-agent flood algorithm as an autonomous system for search and rescue applications: the multi-agent flood algorithm as an autonomous system for search and rescue applications. Ph.D. thesis, Gottfried Wilhelm Leibniz Universität Hannover, Hannover (2017). https://doi.org/10.15488/8943, https://www.repo.uni-hannover.de/handle/123456789/8996
4. Geweke, B., Gromball, M., Hübner, J., Soriano, I.: GOALdigger multi-agent system for MAPC repository (2022). https://github.com/BenPapple/ai-GOALdigger
5. Hindriks, K.V.: Programming cognitive agents in goal (2021). https://goalapl.dev/GOALProgrammingGuide.pdf
6. Jacobi, S.: Planning in multi-agent systems (2014). https://goalapl.atlassian.net/wiki/spaces/GOAL/pages/33137/Planning+Agents
7. Jang, B., Kim, M., Harerimana, G., Kim, J.W.: Q-learning algorithms: a comprehensive classification and applications. IEEE Access 7, 133653–133667 (2019). https://doi.org/10.1109/ACCESS.2019.2941229
8. Jensen, A.B., Villadsen, J., Weile, J., Gylling, E.K.: The 15th edition of the multi-agent programming contest - the GOAL-DTU team. In: Ahlbrecht, T., Dix, J., Fiekas, N., Krausburg, T. (eds.) MAPC 2021. LNCS (LNAI), vol. 12947, pp. 46–81. Springer, Cham (2021). https://doi.org/10.1007/978-3-030-88549-6_3
9. Koeman, V.: SWI prolog - supported predicates (2018). https://goalapl.atlassian.net/wiki/spaces/GOAL/pages/48594945/SWI+Prolog+-+Supported+Predicates
10. Koeman, V.: EISHub/EIS: the environment interface standard (EIS) (2022). https://github.com/eishub/eis
11. Koeman, V.J., Hindriks, K.V.: GOAL webpage (2022). https://goalapl.atlassian.net/wiki/spaces/GOAL/overview
12. Koeman, V.J., Pasman, W., Hindriks, K.V.: Goal-eclipse user manual (2021). https://goalapl.dev/GOALUserManual.pdf
13. Koenig, S., Szymanski, B., Liu, Y.: Efficient and inefficient ant coverage methods. Ann. Math. Artif. Intell. 31(1), 41–76 (2001). https://doi.org/10.1023/A:1016665115585
14. TU Clausthal Department of Informatics, Computational Intelligence: Multi-agent Programming Contest (15022023). https://multiagentcontest.org/
15. TU Clausthal Department of Informatics, Computational Intelligence: MASSim 2022 server (2022). https://github.com/agentcontest/massim_2022
16. TU Clausthal Department of Informatics, Computational Intelligence: The 16th edition of the Multi-agent Programming Contest webpage (2022). https://multiagentcontest.org/2022/

General deSouches Commands Multi-agent Army for Performing in Agents Assemble III Scenario: FIT-BUT at MAPC 2022

Frantisek Zboril$^{(\boxtimes)}$ ⓘ, Frantisek Vidensky ⓘ, Ladislav Dokoupil, and Jan Beran ⓘ

Department of Intelligent Systems, Faculty of Information Technology, Brno University of Technology, Brno, Czech Republic
{zborilf,ividensky,iberan}@fit.vutbr.cz
https://www.fit.vut.cz/.en

Abstract. The Multi-agent Programming Contest provides a good opportunity to compare different approaches to creating a multi-agent system for given scenarios. In this edition, the FIT-BUT team tested solutions based on their own design of a multi-agent system, both on its organisational levels and on the actual architectures of the agents used. The three-level organisation of our multi-agent system was based on the principle of central strategic planning, which results in strategic goals for some subset of agents. These agents execute the goals as their mission and are coordinated by the agent that lies between them and the central element in the hierarchy. The resulting system has stood up to competition and some aspects of it may inspire the design of other multi-agent systems.

Keywords: Artificial Intelligence · Multi-Agent Programming · Decision-making Planning · Self-organisation · Rational Agents

1 Introduction

The third participation of our team in the Multi-agent Programming Contest (MAPC 2022) was also the third opportunity to design a multi-agent system for the assignment called Agents Assemble. The scenario is based on composing specific patterns from blocks in a discrete 2D space. Agents move in a discrete environment with obstacles. Other objects there are places where blocks are dispensed (dispensers), zones where the role of the agent can be changed (role zones), zones where tasks are submitted (goal zones) and possibly assemble the patterns to be submitted. An agent does not know its absolute position, but it has a line of sight to a certain distance. If it sees another agent, it does not know which one it is specifically, but only whether it is an agent from its own team or from another team.

During the competition round, tasks appear randomly. Agents must assemble certain pattern from basic blocks and submit it within a limited time to complete

T. Ahlbrecht et al. (Eds.): MAPC 2022, LNAI 13997, pp. 120–150, 2023.
https://doi.org/10.1007/978-3-031-38712-8_5

the task. Blocks can be acquired at several positions and are of different types. A correctly composed pattern from the corresponding blocks can be submitted. Roles give the agents various abilities including the range of their oversight, the ability to carry multiple blocks, the ability to take multiple actions in one turn or perform actions to remove obstacles or attack other agents. The dynamics of the environment are due to the fact that so-called 'clear events' can occur in the environment. When a 'clear event' occurs in some area, obstacles are rearranged and agents near the location of the event can be paralysed and deprived of the blocks they are currently carrying. For a more detailed description of the scenario, we refer to the competition website.

In this text, we present a description of our solution and specifically the architecture and the implementation of the multi-agent system we developed for the competition. We have developed our own system which is not based on any existing agent or multi-agent system as part of this competition. We understand that the right technical work should use the best and most appropriate solutions that have been developed in the field, but the desire to try and build a system of our own based on our knowledge prevailed. We have done this for the following reasons:

- Practical experience to find out the pitfalls and problems not necessarily visible to the user when building a multi-agent system in the still widely used programming language.
- Some frameworks and platforms that are now popular for implementing multi-agent systems tend to be already used by other teams in this competition [2,5]. For reasons of diversity, we wanted to come up with a new approach and see if it can compete with those systems.
- We intended to discover new possible approaches in the design of multi-agent systems.
- We intended to use a generic, non-agent programming language for wider possibilities to implement some parts of the agent (planning, group reasoning, coordination).

We summarise how this approach has worked for us in the conclusion of this text.

Our system is named after General deSouches. He is a historical figure who is connected to the city of Brno, where the technical university from which our team comes is located. The hierarchical decomposition of the problem at hand into coalitions and individuals controlled by a central agent, which is used in this architecture, may resemble military organisations, and it is General deSouches who was chosen as the person connecting the military and our city.

The following text aims both to describe this architecture and to implement a concrete multi-agent system for deployment in MAPC competitions, more specifically for the tasks called Agents Assemble. In the second section, we provide a description of our architecture, and in the third section, we provide a concrete implementation of our system for the competition. We then discuss the results achieved in the competition and the advantages or disadvantages of the chosen solution.

2   deSouches Multi-agent Architecture

As in previous cases of our participation, we announced that Java will be our programming language. In the previous two editions [12,13], a system based on hierarchical planning was used, combining proactive planning on individual layers with their activation according to priorities in the hierarchy. This architecture was inspired by Brooks' system [3].

In this year's competition, we designed a new system architecture. In order to specify it, we will present its structure as the interconnection of the expected roles in the whole system. By roles in the system, we will mean general roles in the system architecture. Later the term 'roles' in a different sense will also be applied to agents at the lowest situated in the environment, so when we talk about roles in the system we will mean roles in the deSouches architecture. Next, we describe the different roles in the system and the interactions between them.

Our architecture is based on a hierarchical grouping of roles in a system of agents, where there is a control agent (deSouches) at the top level. At the second level, then there are coordinating agents, and the third level consists of agents that are situated in the environment and act to achieve specified goals in that environment. Agents at the lowest level interact with the environment they are in, perform actions in it and receive inputs. Agents at higher levels do not interact directly with the environment, they only interact with other agents in the system, as shown in Fig. 1.

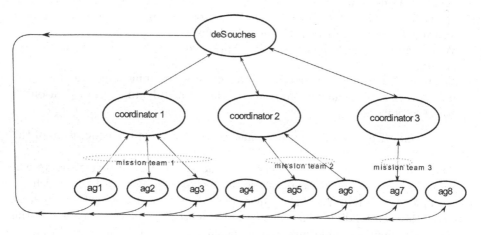

Fig. 1. Architecture of the deSouches Multi-agent System

Situated agents, as we will call third-level agents from now on, have their internal state defined by their mental states, including beliefs, goals or desires and intentions. This is common in agent systems; for example, in BDI [9] or 2APL [4] systems, beliefs, desires (as possible goals of the agent) and intentions are the basic elements. The system can also identify options and exceptions that can lead to changes in the mental states of one or more agents. Similar to the distinction we made between agent and organisational levels in the arrangement of individual agents, we will also distinguish beliefs, goals and options according to the purposes they serve within the multi-agent architecture. As for beliefs and goals, we will distinguish them according to whether they serve to make decisions at the situated agent level or to make organisational decisions. We will talk about strategic beliefs if they serve as practical reasoning about strategic goals, and strategic goals will be assignments for an organised group of agents. Next, at the organisational level, we will talk about options that can trigger reasoning and exceptions that can cause a revision of the currently specified goals. Situated agents at the lowest level will be driven by intentions, as persistent goals, that have been assigned to them from higher levels.

The meaning of options and exceptions as well as the meaning of the adjective 'strategic' for our system deserves further explanation. It will be presented in the following paragraphs, where we describe how goals are organised in the system and the plans that are used to achieve them. We then introduce the different organisational roles and their interactions.

2.1   Hierarchy of Goals and Missions

A common approach to representing the hierarchy of plans for artificial agents is the Goal-plan tree [11]. Such a model is based on BDI systems and is designed to explore the possible ordering of an agent's intentions. In our system, we have three levels of goals. Strategic goals are the top-level goals and are set by deSouches. A strategic goal can be atomic in the sense that it is given directly to an agent and if the agent achieves it, the goal is considered satisfied. Non-atomic goals can either be decomposed for processing by multiple agents, or into a sequence of goals for a single agent, or both. Similar to the JaCaMo system [6], we call a mission a group goal for agents acting coherently to achieve it. Then we first consider decomposition within an agent group and possibly subsequently into other subgoals. While the first decomposition can be described as an AND decomposition, in the case of the decomposition of the lowest-level goals, we have an OR decomposition of some sequence of agent mission goals that are to be (all) satisfied sequentially and is thus again an AND decomposition. In Fig. 2 we show these decompositions such that the sequences are words from a language.

Each mission has a goal, which is divided into subgoals for individual agents. If we assume that each agent must satisfy its subgoal to complete the mission, we can view such a decomposition as an AND decomposition. This goal need not be atomic but can be viewed as some sequence of lower-level subgoals whose successive execution achieves the agent mission goal. Specifically, it is represented by a finite state automaton, where states are subgoals and transitions are determined by the results of attempts to achieve these subgoals. These results are usually "succeeded"/"true" or "failed", but are not limited to them. Thus, an agent for executing a mission goal may execute different sequences of subgoals. Since the state automaton accepts regular language, we can think of such sequences as words of some language accepted by the automaton.

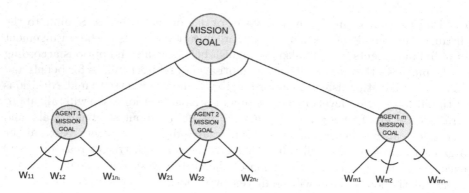

Fig. 2. Goal Hierarchy in deSouches Multi-agent System

Consider that $g1$ is the subgoal of the agent to reach the dispenser and pick up a block, $g2$ is the subgoal of getting to the goal area, $g3$ is the subgoal of waiting for other agents to arrive at their positions, and $g4$ represents the subgoal of connecting the block to other agents. If an agent sequentially executes all these subgoals, then their ascent is a success, which is represented by the terminal symbol t and the automaton should accept the word $t\ t\ t$. However, if the agent fails to execute goal $g2$, for example, due to a clear event, the agent must retry to get the block and execute the whole process from the beginning. Thus, the result is a sequence $t\ fce\ t\ t\ t$, where the terminal symbol fce denotes the failure to reach the goal due to a clear event. However, despite the failure in the subgoal, the mission goal was achieved and hence this sequence will be accepted by the automaton. In the goal decomposition shown in Fig. 2, we then represent the above as an OR decomposition into the individual words accepted by the automaton for a given subgoal, and the individual sequences must then be executed as a sequence of subgoals according to the states over which the automaton accepted the word.

We will mention how these goals are set and evaluated later in the section on coordinator agents. We now return to the hierarchical structure of system roles and describe these roles in turn, and in the case of situated agents, their architecture and operating principle. To better organise the description of the roles, we define the roles according to the GAIA methodology [14] using their responsibilities, activities, interaction protocols, and the permissions (access to data) they work with.

2.2 Top Level: deSouches/central Agent

As we mentioned earlier, we chose the name deSouches for the control-level agent which is at the top of the system management hierarchy. It is responsible for setting the strategies of the entire multi-agent team during its operation. Conceptually, deSouches creates missions and assigns agents to them from the population of situated agents at the third level. As a rational agent, it is tasked with assigning goals in a way that best fits the stated goals of the entire system. deSouches works with beliefs passed to him by the situated agents and also keeps the information about the current state of assigning agents to missions. It performs group reasoning in each cycle after it receives information from all the situated agents. This group reasoning results in options that can lead to the creation of missions. The creation of missions is also related to the creation of a mission coordinator, i.e., a second-level agent, and the assignment of initial goals to the agents assigned to the mission.

More specifically, the responsibilities of this role can be described as follows

- It creates a population of situated agents at the third level and assigns them primary goals. The population size is constant.
- It assigns goals to agents on request.
- It processes strategic information from lower level agents (as it comes in)
  • Based on this information, it identifies strategic options.
  • It processes mission termination information.
- It processes strategic options (after the barrier, which will be mentioned in more detail later)
  • It defines strategic goals.
  • It creates a mission coordinator and assigns situated agents to the strategic objectives. At the second level, agents are created and terminated as missions are created and terminated.
- It assigns a goal to a situated agent based on options, or when asked to do so by such an agent.

The activities are based on the responsibilities stated above:

- An agent must be able to process information provided by other agents, identify options in the system within which it operates, be able to rationally identify missions, and select appropriate goals for agents when requested. Related to this, it maintains a record of missions assigned to agents.
- In terms of data, it maintains information about the teams formed. It also manages aggregated data from each situated agent in the environment. It also creates strategic goals and objectives for individual agents based on the strategic decisions made.
- It receives synchronisation information (salut) from the agents and starts making strategic inference after receiving salutes from all agents in a given interpretation cycle.
- Is informed by the coordinators of the completion of missions, whether successful or unsuccessful.

Protocols determine how a role interacts with other roles in the system. deSouches is the bottleneck of the entire system. If deSouches fails, mission teams will stop forming. We have not addressed this issue in this version of the system, however, to guarantee the robustness of the multi-agent system, we will consider some possibility of decentralization or substitutability at the control level for the following competitions.

2.3   Second Level: Organisational Agents

We have already introduced agents at the organisational level in the section on organising goals in systems. They are created by the central agent after it has created a mission. Their task is to assign goals to the situated agents and to process information from them about the outcome of their actions. We have stated that we understand sequences of results of specified goals as words of some language. These words lead to the achievement of a goal to be accomplished by an agent within a mission. In our system, the language is accepted by finite state automata and thus is regular. Agents with behavioral models tend to be implemented as automata [7], and even in the case of this system, the automaton will receive as input the results of the agent's efforts to execute the mission subgoal, and the output will be the agent's new/next mission subgoal. If the automata reaches the goal state, the agent has also fulfilled its mission goal. Since a mission can be performed by multiple agents, the coordinator operates the automata for each of them. In addition, it can synchronise these automata. Thus, if an agent has finished processing a goal and is to be synchronised with one or more agents, the coordinator will only issue another goal to the agent when it can issue all other goals to other agents that are in a barrier.

The agent may report exceptions to the coordinator. These have already been mentioned above and are worth commenting on here. This is a situation that the agents discover that could lead to a change in mission control. They are not informed about the outcome of the agent's efforts, but they may lead to a change in the assigned goals of one or more agents in the mission team, or to the termination of the mission. Again, the exceptions are not specified and depend on the system implementation for the task.

The responsibilities of the agent coordinator are:

- Creating missions and informing assigned agents that they are assigned to a mission and assigning them primary objectives.
- In the event of mission termination, informing the assigned agents that they are released from the mission.
- Processing the results of the agents' efforts to accomplish the missions.
- Assigning goals to individual mission agents on an ongoing basis.
- In the event of mission termination (successful or unsuccessful), informing deSouches of this.
- Reacting to exception communicated by agents.

The data they are working with is just the reported output from the situated agents' efforts to meet the assigned goal and the reported exceptions from those agents as well. They produce data in the form of goals to these agents and a report on the outcome of the deSouches mission when it is completed. The activities and protocols associated with this are first initialising the agent team for the mission, processing the data from the agents, processing the mission completion, i.e., releasing the agents, and then informing deSouches.

2.4   Third Level: Situated Agents

The agents operating at the lowest level are the agents that actually work on specific tasks and operate in the environment in which the multi-agent system is situated. The architecture we use for these agents is inspired by current agent architectures, especially those of BDI, but we have retained the freedom to implement it and have omitted some specific constraints that are present elsewhere. For example, some parts that are specified in BDI systems, such as beliefs, events, or even the processes of selecting plans to selected goals, are not so constrained in our case and the implementation can use the resources provided by Java.

Below we present the control loop of our agent, which we describe in more detail later:

Algorithm 1: Agent's control loop

Loop
    Procedure *sensing*
        get information from environment;
        if *ordered by coordinator or deSouches* **then**
            adopt new goal;

        propagate last action result to intention pool;
        update belief base;
        send strategic information to deSouches;
        salut deSouches ;   `/* sending strategic information finished,`
        `synchronise */`
    Procedure *practical reasoning*
        select intention from intention pool;
        if *last action demanded a subgoal* **then**
            push the subgoal to the intention;

        get goal at the top of the intention;
        revise plans for that goal;
        execute one step of highest priority plan of that goal;

In general, however, an agent makes inferences based on data that represent the agent's perception of the state of the environment it is situated in. The types of data depend on the particular implementation of the system. They can be atomic elements of the types available in Java, as well as complex structures with their own reasoning mechanisms, for example for building a map of the environment they are in. Agents modify the beliefs in their belief base appropriately in each cycle. Agents also pass strategic information to deSouches. What is considered as strategic information depends once again on the specific implementation of the overall system. After sending all such information, they send the information that everything needed for this cycle has already been sent. We call this last message a salute.

The next stage in the agent's control cycle is practical reasoning about goals and the means to achieve them. The agent is supposed to work proactively towards its goals. These are persistent goals that the agent follows until it achieves them or finds that it is not possible. This is how we understand the agent's intention in our system as well. What differs from current BDI systems is that the goal for which the intention is formed is specified by deSouches or the mission coordinator, which we have already introduced in the previous sections. Thus, it is not created in response to an event but is set from outside.

The way to accomplish the goal, if accepted as an intention, is the execution of some relevant plan. This means that the goals in our system are procedural. This plan is a linear sequence of actions. The planning and re-evaluation of plans are performed during each cycle of the agent for the chosen goal in this cycle, thus guaranteeing its reactivity. This is an example of the difference from classical BDI systems, where reasoning is first performed to process events and find relevant and applicable plans to them. In our system, practical reasoning is performed by first selecting a goal and selecting plans for it. Of course, a change of plan does not have to take place every time, as long as the previously constructed plan for the goal is suitable. After the plan re-evaluation phase, the agent uses the plan and executes one step from it.

An agent can create multiple plans for a single goal with different priorities. For example, if an agent is following a path according to a plan and sees an enemy agent, it can create a short plan with a higher priority to attack the enemy. Once this is completed, the agent will move on to the lower priority plan. Based on this example, we introduce one more attribute of a plan, namely the one that determines whether its execution will result in the goal being met or not. The goal is then satisfied only when the plan that is set to be final is fully executed.

The agent may also set subgoals during the re-evaluation of plans. We introduced this capability into the system despite the fact that goals are primarily set by agents at higher levels, and the ability to create a priority hierarchy of plans may mimic the way goals are hierarchically created in BDI systems, where plans may include declared subgoals. In the case of our system, subgoals are rather considered as procedures that are executed by agents for different goals. For example, a 'block pick up' goal may have as a subgoal to get to a given position (near the dispenser) and a goal for 'approaching goal area' may use the same subgoal to approach a given position.

Since an agent can have multiple intentions at the same time, and since we have not limited the possibility of an agent being in multiple teams at the same time, the agent's intention pool will be part of the situated agents. Figure 3 shows an example of an intention pool with two intentions. Each intention has a goal and one or two subgoals, where these goals or subgoals have one to three plans with given priorities (to the right of the plan name) at any given time, some are final and some are not (green or red box). In addition, the intention pool stores a reference to the most recently processed intention and a reference to the most recently executed plan for each goal or subgoal. This is in order to

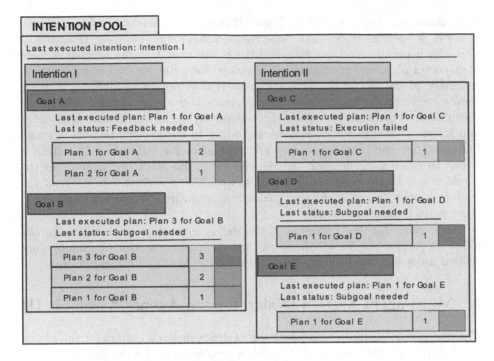

Fig. 3. Structure of Intention Pool (Color figure online)

properly propagate the result of the last executed plan action. In the example above, *Goal A* is subgoal of *Goal B*, *Goal C* is subgoal of *Goal C* and *Goal D* is subgoal of *Goal E*. *Goal A* can be achieved by executing *Plan* 2 for *Goal A*. However, *Plan* 1 for *Goal A* should be executed first at that point in time because it has a higher priority. This can be changed during the re-evaluation of the plan. If *Goal A* was achieved, *Plan* 3 for *Goal B* which triggered it may continue. If this plan succeeds, *Goal B* would still need to be achieved for Intention I to be fulfilled. This is because *Plan* 3 for *Goal B* is not final. It can be achieved by executing plans 1 or 2 for this goal.

The structure of the intention pool is re-evaluated twice during the control loop. Firstly, after the agent receives the results of an action execution and secondly, when a goal is to be followed. The reason why both do not occur at the same time is that there may be some additional cycles between the processing of the action result and the execution of the intention again. Because of this, the result must be processed immediately in the next cycle by the currently selected intention, while another intention can be executed later in the same cycle.

The result of an action can be interpreted in different ways. The actions and plans themselves are some objects, and an object may have as property information about how to handle the failure of execution. An action may cause the plan to fail and be removed, or conversely, the action may be retained and be repeated, or retained for a given number of repetitions or with a given probability.

Following a goal can end in failure if no plan is available after the plan revision. If agent's mission goal fails, the coordinator is informed. If a subgoal fails, this is then treated as a failure of the action of setting the subgoal in some higher-level plan, and treated as we described for failures of actions as such. A summary of the role of the situated agent is that the responsibilities of these agents are to try to achieve the specified goals and to report the result to the coordinator. Furthermore, agents must share strategic beliefs with deSouches and inform it also about exceptions according to the specific implementation. On the other hand, an agent may ask deSouches for strategic information if it has to make some decision that should be in line with the strategy of the whole team. Thus, while communication with the coordinator is given in the form of success/failure of the goals, communication with deSouches depends on the specific implementation.

This concludes the discussion of the deSouches agent architecture. In the following paragraphs, we will discuss a concrete implementation of a multi-agent system using this architecture, specifically for the MAPC 2022 competition.

3 Multi-agent System Design for the Agents Assemble III

The first and so far only implementation of deSouches is a system for the Multi-agent Programming Contest and Agent Assemble tasks. In the following paragraphs, we describe the concrete implementation of this system at the control, organisational, and situated agent levels. First, however, we will present our approach to the implementation of the situated agents in Agent Assemble III.

3.1 Strategy and Mission of the FIT-BUT Team for Agent Assemble III

The idea behind Agent Assemble scenarios is to get as many points as possible within a given number of steps. Points are earned by the agent (from now on, unless we use the term agent with further specification, we will mean situated agents) submitting an object of a specified pattern at one of the designated locations. The pattern can be a single block but it can also be more complex patterns that can be assembled from multiple blocks. We have identified all possible constructions for two to four blocks. From experience in previous years, we have estimated the maximum number of blocks to be just four since more complex patterns have not appeared before and the probability of successful delivery of a pattern decreases with the number of blocks needed. In total, we considered 42 possible patterns for these numbers of blocks.

Our solution was based on the execution of a task by a group of agents to deliver every single block of the desired pattern to a goal area. If all the agents in the group successfully transport their block to the goal area, they interconnect them together and one of them then submits the pattern to agents. It is therefore necessary that such agents have knowledge of where the pattern will be constructed and where each agent should bring its block. To do this, however, the agents must know each other's position. Therefore, in the first phase of the run, the agents try to coordinate with each other and achieve a shared coordination system. After their mutual positions are known for a group of agents, as well as their positions with respect to the dispensers and the goal area, such agents can be used for a mission during which they accomplish the task. The next question is what capabilities such agents must have. Although the roles of agents can be defined in any way, the teams were informed that the set of roles would be given in advance and there would be no need for a special reasoning mechanism to analyse offered roles. In our case, in addition to the default role that was assigned to the agents at the beginning, we limited ourselves to the worker and digger roles. The worker role gave the agents the ability to request blocks from the dispenser, assemble them, and submit the required constructs. The digger role had better skills for removing obstacles in space and possibly attacking other teams' agents.

This year, norms were added to the scenario. In multi-agent systems, a norm is a collective commitment by members of the organisation to follow certain rules, and penalties are a way of enforcing compliance with such norms. Norms here took the form of specifications, for example, which roles agents could not take on or how many blocks they could carry at most. Since we assumed, according to the provided settings, what the penalties for violating them were, and took into account what agents would have to perform to not violate these norms, for example, to reach a role zone and change their temporarily forbidden roles, we decided to ignore the norms and accept the penalties. Without analysing this in detail, this seems to us to be a rational solution and our system was still able to compete in the competition with its rivals.

From what we have now outlined, some of the activities and responsibilities that the various system roles in our solution are expected to perform. We will again make a description of each of these system roles in our solution.

3.2   deSouches in MAPC

If we are to specify the control agent's/deSouches' responsibilities, activities, protocols and permissions, let us start with the primary responsibility of creating a multi-agent population. Our system uses JADE but only to a limited extent. We do not make use of the more complex behaviors of these agents, the means of communication between agents, or the other functionality that JADE [1] provides. Basically, we have used this system to create agents as threads that can execute a method in cycles (i.e., we use the cyclic behavior of the JADE agent). deSouches itself is a JADE agent, and so are all situated agents created as the first activity of deSouches. Next, it connects these agents to the competition server, and from then the system runs with these agents until termination (i.e. when the agents receive information from the server that the game is over). The primary goals of situated agents follow the described behavior of our system. Agents must be able to cooperate with other agents of their team, and to do so they must synchronise with others. However, the very first goal that the situated agents receive is different, for purely practical reasons. During the previous years, the whole multi-agent system had to be restarted if there were some undetected errors or when the communication with the organisers' server collapsed. We solved the problem of possible connected blocks to agents by first instructing all agents to try to get rid of any connected blocks. Then, even after a restart, they can proceed as if the game has just started and the agents have no connected blocks. After the agents have performed actions in accordance with the initial 'DetachAll' goal, they will use their permissions against deSouches and ask it to assign a goal or mission. At this point, deSouches assigns the agents a 'DivideAndExplore' mission, which we will present in more detail later.

In the following paragraphs, we describe deSouches responsibilities. We will start with those related to setting up coordinated agent groups and managing their maps.

Assigns Roles to Situated Agents. The first of the responsibilities deSouches has to its situated agents is making decisions about what roles these agents should take on. Now, if we talk about roles, we will refer to the roles in the competition scenario. In our system, when situated agents find themselves in a role zone, they try to take the opportunity to change their role and ask deSouches what role would be appropriate for them. This decision is straightforward in our current implementation; deSouches responds with either the worker or digger roles in some ratio that we set to 5:1.

Establish and Coordinate Groups of Agents. The idea for coordinating individual agents is to group them together in a way that they can unify their coordinate systems. Initially, there are groups of agents corresponding to the number of situated agents, and each group contains just one agent. Thus, for some population of agents A, we have a set of groups $G = \{g_1, g_2...g_n\} = \{\{a_1\}, \{a_2\}...\{a_n\}\}, |A| = n$ and each agent is in one group. deSouches works with strategic information, including what distance vectors individual agents see other agents in their team. We can synchronise the groups g_i and g_j of agents if there are agents from these groups that can unify the coordinates and thus merge the two groups into one. We can write that $\exists a_i, a_j, a_i \in g_i \wedge a_j \in g_j \wedge g_i \neq g_j : d(a_i, a_j) + d(a_j, a_i) = (0, 0)$ where $d(a_i, a_j) = (x, y)$ is the distance on the axes x and y and a_i, a_j are the only pair of agents in A for which this holds. The $d(a_j, a_i)$ represents a vector that gives the distance between these agents in the horizontal and vertical directions. New group of agents is created, the two groups' maps are merged into one, and the coordinates of the elements on the two maps are aligned. For example, if two agents at distance $d(a_i, a_j) = (3, 2)$ from the perspective of agent a_i who sees another agent of his team three positions away from it in the horizontal direction and two positions away in the vertical direction, for example east and south of each other, then $d(a_j, a_i) = (-3, -2)$ because the second agent sees the first agent west and north at the same absolute distance values.

We could synchronise multiple groups in a single cycle if the pairwise distances were different, i.e., one pair of agents would see each other at some distance and these distances would be different for one and the other pair, but in our solution we synchronise groups only when there is only one such pair. Since we have done this in the same way in the previous two editions of the contest, we refer to our first publications on MAPC for a closer look at this algorithm [12].

Maintain Group Maps. Agents act based on the map, just as deSouches makes decisions based on the map. In the case of agents, they work with the map of their group, which we understand as strategic information provided by deSouches. It is in fact responsible for keeping information about which group the agent belongs to and what information this group shares. In each cycle, agents transmit information about what they see, and based on this information, their group maps are updated. In addition to the actual objects recorded on the map, the map provides methods for finding nearby objects of a given type (objects, friendly or hostile agents, dispensers, obstacles...). The map also indicates each position when the agent last saw it. This serves as a pheromone and can be used by agents to better search the area. Furthermore, the map can provide an agent with information about where an object is located that can or cannot be traversed or destroyed, what objects appear to be attached to an agent, and so on. Thus, a group map is some object shared by a group with appropriate methods that allow agents to make better reasoning. When merging groups, deSouches also merges the maps of both groups into one, which is then the group map for the newly created group.

Detect Master Group. Another of deSouches' responsibilities in completing Agent Assembly scenarios was determining the Master map. This is a necessary prerequisite for agents to start completing tasks that will earn them points. During the process of exploring the environment and bringing groups of agents together, situations may arise where deSouches learns that a group is capable of performing tasks. There are a sufficient number of agents who have worker roles, i.e. they can manipulate the blocks that make up the desired patterns, there are goal zones on the map and dispensers are known. In our case, we set the required number of agents in the worker role to three, we required at least one goal zone, as well as one role zone and dispensers of at least two types. If any such group map satisfies this, it becomes a Master map, the corresponding group becomes a Master group. From now on, every other group that can join this group will join it, and every group newly formed in this way becomes the Master group.

Detect Dimension of Master Map. Another deSouches' responsibility is estimating the size of the environment. Since it is cyclic, agents cannot detect its edge and it may appear infinite to them. Our approach how to decide the width and height of the grid is based on the fact that the immobile part on the map is the dispensers. For the Master map, deSouches uses dispensers to estimate the width and height of the environment when in a certain number of cases (in our case set to three) the dispensers are in the same horizontal position but at a certain vertical distance that is the same for all the three cases. Thus, deSouches then assumes that these are the same dispensers that the agent encountered when it crossed the edge. The height of the area is estimated in a corresponding manner.

3.3   Task Fulfilment by Agent Groups

The behavior of the system, or rather the deSouches policy, changes when a Master group is established. From this point on, it is already clear which group will be active and perform tasks. deSouches is now trying to find a coalition of agents to work on the tasks. The information about possible tasks deSouches receives from the system via situated agents, who receive this information from the competition system and then report it towards deSouches as a strategic option. It then searches each cycle, if any tasks are active, for a one - to four-agent coalition of free agents in that group that would be able to perform any of the tasks now (Fig. 4). By free agents we mean those agents in the group in the role of worker who are not currently ordered to participate in the assembly of a task. Related to this is the change in deSouches' assignment of goals to situated agents. If an agent in the Master group has nothing to do and asks deSouches for a goal assignment, then as long as it is still in the default role, it will have to go to the zone role, which must be at least one known role on the Master map, and accept some new role. Again, deSouches will decide what that role will be when it is needed. If the agent applying for the job is in the worker role, it will be ordered to roam and explore the environment. If the agent is in the digger role, it will be tasked with removing obstacles and attacking agents of other teams.

It is worth mentioning one more activity that deSouches performs during strategic decision-making. In each cycle, for all active tasks, it checks whether there is a strategic exception that will prevent the achievement of the task. And this could occur for two reasons. The first reason occurs when it is clear that the agents cannot accomplish the task in the time allotted because each task has a specified step up to which it is valid. The second reason is that the goal zone is no longer valid. This year, after a task is submitted, the goal zone can be

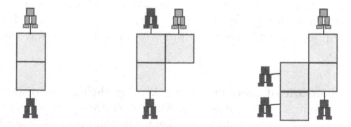

Fig. 4. An example of possible patterns made from two, three and four blocks. The green agent is the one tasked with committing the result. (Color figure online)

moved with some probability. Therefore, it is also checked each time whether the intended goal zone for the task submission still exists. If one of these exceptions occurs, deSouches will cancel the mission and release the allocated agents.

We now present the algorithm by which deSouches finds a suitable coalition of agents for the tasks. The inputs to this algorithm, in addition to a description of the desired pattern, are the free agents from the Master group, a list of dispensers that are listed on the Master map, and a list of goal zones. To avoid collisions of custom agents in goal zones, one goal zone is always considered for the currently solved tasks. In other words, the goal zones input to the algorithm are those to which no coalition is currently directed. Since goal zones tend to be a contiguous region that covers multiple positions in the grid, only one position is chosen among them. This is chosen according to the current state of the Master map so that the area around it is as free of obstacles as possible. With the inputs, we can search for a suitable coalition using the algorithm we present in the next section.

3.4 Building Coalitions to Accomplish Tasks

The essence of our solution is the creation of coalitions for given tasks. Since finding the optimal coalition structure, in general, is an NP-complete problem [10], and the number of agents in the system could be several tens, it was necessary to consider the time complexity of the assumed algorithm for forming such coalitions. The specificity of the problem that the coalitions are intended to solve gives us the opportunity to design a solution that has reasonable time requirements for an agent population on the order of tens of agents.

A coalition game is defined by a coalition structure that maximizes its value such that CS is a partitioning over A then $V(CS) = \sum v(C_i)$ [8], where $v(c_i)$ are values of individual coalitions in CS. The fundamental question is how to evaluate the coalitions. The number of points that agents in such a coalition can achieve is offered. The value of such coalition structure would be the sum of the points that each coalition can achieve. Other aspects that we could include in the value function would be the probability of achieving these points and the time in which these points are achieved. However, in working on the system for MAPC 2022, we have established only a simple principle such that the value depends on the number of steps its slowest member must take to complete its subtask. Thus, we will try to complete the task as quickly as possible, and the output of the coalition formation algorithm will be the coalition that promises to complete one of the given tasks the fastest.

We formalise the task of forming one coalition by having a set of agents in the form of their position on the map $A = \{a_1, a_2, ..., a_n\}$, a set of dispensers $D = \{(bt_1, \{dp_{1_1}, dp_{1_2})...\}, ...(bt_n, \{dp_{n_1}, ...\})\}$, where bt_i is the block type, which can be obtained from the dispensers at positions $dp_{i_1},, dp_{i_2}...$, a set of subtasks $T = \{t_1, t_2, ..., t_o\}$, where t_i is the block type for the subtask, and a set of goal zones' positions $G = \{g_1, g_2, ..., g_p\}$. Estimation of the shortest number of steps that agent a_1 needs to achieve a subtask from T is $c(a_1) = \arg\min_{dp_{pi}, g_j}(ds(a_1, dp_i) + ds(dp_i, g_j))$ where $ds(a, b)$ is Manhattan distance between positions a and b. If we specify block type and goal zone position, then arguments are also a set of appripriate dispensers for the type D and a goal zone position g we write $c(a_1, D, g) = \arg\min_{d_{pi} \in D}(ds(a_1, dp_i) + ds(dp_i, g))$. However, each agent must cater for different block from the task T. The choice of dispensers must be such that all the block types T are processed by the coalition. Therefore, we examine coalitions $A_i = \{a_{i1}...a_{io}\} \in A$ of size $|T|$ such that each agent has to bring one of the desired blocks. The cost of such a coalition which will submit the resulting pattern in goal zone g is then $v(A_i) = 1/max(c(a_{i1}, D_1, g)...c(a_{io}, D_o, g))$ where D_i to D_o are dispensers for requested block types t_1 to t_o and a_{i1} to a_{io} are agents that are obligated to bring these types of blocks.

Our coalition selection algorithm searches for the optimal coalition for each of the currently given tasks and selects the best coalition among them that is optimal for all given tasks. The algorithm for finding the optimal coalition for a single task T is shown below as Algorithm 2.

Algorithm 2: Coalition Algorithm for Agents Assemble

Phase 1;
foreach *agent* $a \in A$ **do**
 foreach *goal* $g \in G$ **do**
  foreach *subtask* $t \in T$ **do**
   d = bestDispenser(a,g,t);
   price = distance(a,d,g);
   taskCandidate.insert(t,a,d,g, price) ;   `/* insertSort */`

Phase 2;
CC = {} ;
repeat
 tc = taskCandidate.bestTaskCandidate();
 taskCandidate.remove(tc);
 foreach $C \in CC$ **do**
  if *tc is for agent not in C and the goal positions for tc and C are the same* **then**
   CC.insert(C ∪{tc});

 CC.insert({tc});
 `/* if any C from CC can complete T, return C`   `*/`
 foreach $C \in CC$ **do**
  if *C can complete T* **then**
   return C;

until *taskCandidate is empty*;

In the first part of the algorithm, for each given subtask and each goal area, each agent is given a dispenser over which it could execute the subtask from T. This dispenser does not have to be the closest to the agent, but it must be on the shortest agent-dispenser-goal zone path among all dispensers issuing a block of the desired type. Then we have the best possible candidate solutions for each agent, subtask, and goal zone. We then compose coalitions from these candidate solutions. Each time we select a candidate solution that has not yet been used and whose path length is the shortest among all other unused candidate solutions. With it, we first form a single-element coalition with this candidate solution, and second, we extend each already formed coalition with this candidate solution if the goal zones match. Each coalition will thus consist of candidate solutions that target the same goal zone. The algorithm terminates if any coalition is able to process all subtasks of the given task.

The number of iterations in phase 1 is obviously $|A| \times |G| \times |T| \times |D|$. It can be assumed that there are four types in T at most, i.e., that the desired pattern consists of at most four parts. This number is derived from the fact that more complex patterns have not been offered in the competition so far, and our system is not even able to compose patterns with more than four blocks. We set the maximum number of dispensers for each of the subtasks from experience to five, the same way we estimate the maximum number of goal positions. Thus, we estimated that finding the optimal coalition would require at most $100 \times |A|$ iterations, where $|A|$ is the number of agents (in the order of tens). Then several thousand iterations our system is able to perform in each cycle, since in the competition the time between each step was typically on the order of seconds. This was also confirmed after the implementation of this algorithm, which was not a computational burden on the operation of our system.

In total, there will be $|A| \times |G| \times |T|$ candidate assignments for individual agents to bring a block of the given type to the goal area (hereafter we will call this candidate solution) and based on them, we are trying to find a possible coalitions. We always add the next best candidate solution not yet added to the possible coalitions. If we had a set of k of candidate solutions, then the number of possible coalitions formed from these solutions would be 2^k. However, we only form coalitions where there are unique agents and the same goal position. Thus, if we expand the set of coalitions by adding a solution with agent a_i that points to the goal zone g_i, then firstly a single candidate coalition with this solution will be formed, and secondly, coalitions will be formed by adding this solution to such existing coalitions in which the agent a_i is not included, and the individual candidate solutions in the coalition point to the same goal zone g_i. In addition, we only extend coalitions that have less than $|T|$ members, because, by the nature of the problem solution, the coalition being sought will have exactly $|T|$ members. The number of coalitions for a four-block task that we can traverse is then given by the number of possible four-block coalitions from the agent population multiplied by a permutation of four, which covers all possible subtask assignments to these agents, because the cost of such a coalition also depends on which specific subtask from T is assigned to which agent.

This number is then equal to $4! * \binom{|A|}{4} = \frac{|A|!}{(|A|-4)!}$. While the number of possible coalitions to explore is still high and can be estimated as the fourth power of the number of agents, i.e., over half a million iterations for 25 agents, we have not approached such a number in practical use for competition. By incrementally building coalitions by adding the next cheapest candidate solution the first suitable coalition, where each subtask from T is processed, is also optimal. Therefore, the maximum number of coalitions we could find before we discovered the optimal coalitions was $\sum_{k=1}^{3} k! * \binom{|A|}{k}$ which for $|A| = 30$ is 24360 three-agent coalitions, 870 such two-agent coalitions, and 30 one-agent coalitions. Thus, our solution was found at the latest after the establishment of 25270 coalitions, which for today's serial computers is manageable in the time our system had in one step of the competition.

We give an example for two agents, a task demanding two blocks of different types and three goal positions. For both agents at a_1 and a_2, for both block types t_1 and t_2, and for all three possible goal positions, dispensers were found for which the path from the agent's current position through the dispenser location and the goal position is the shortest. Assume that for both types of tasks, there are, respectively, a group of agents knowing the location of dispensers D_1^1, D_2^1 and D_3^1 for the first type and D_1^2, D_2^2 and D_3^2 for the second type. After computing the optimal dispensers, we get a total of twelve candidate solutions as shown in Fig. 5. The number of steps required for every agent to move from its current position through the assumed dispenser to the goal zone is given below each illustration of these solutions. In the figure, solutions are numbered in a circle above the triangle.

After sorting the candidate solutions from cheapest to most expensive, we can start forming coalitions. In the first step, we add only one solution to form one coalition $\{\{8\}\}$. After adding the coalition marked as 11, we have the possible coalitions $\{\{11\}, \{8\}\}$. We could not extend the $\{8\}$ coalition with candidate solution 8 with candidate solution 11, since it is directed to the same goal zone, bud it is made by the same agent as is in 8. We cannot extend any of the existing coalitions with candidate solutions 3 and 1, so after adding them to the game we have possible coalitions $\{\{1\}, \{3\}, \{11\}, \{8\}\}$. We can combine the candidate solution 10 with the first one and we get $\{\{10\}, \{1\}, \{3\}, \{11\}, \{8\}, \{1, 10\}\}$ and coalitions with members $\{1, 10\}$ covers both types of blocks with different agents heading to the same goal position. And this is the take solution that is optimal according to our criterion and estimates the transport of both desired blocks in 35 steps.

At this point, we would like to have a short discussion about our solution. The evaluation of the coalitions is crucial for their correct determination and in our case, only an initial and rather naive approach was used. We do not compute the entire coalition structure but search for the optimal free agent coalition in a given cycle. However, this does not guarantee an optimal coalition structure of agents, because there may not be an optimal coalition as recommended by our algorithm, in the optimal coalition structure of agents at the specific time.

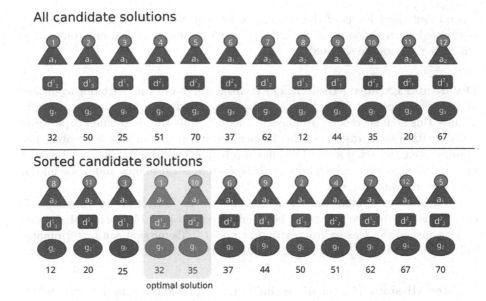

Fig. 5. Coalition Search Example

Although this statement is obvious, as an example we can consider some problems where the grand coalition value is say $v(A) = 8$ and the coalitions B, C, which are disjunctive decompositions of A, have values $v(B) = 5$ and $v(C) = 4$. Then the optimal coalition structure is formed by coalitions B, C and not by coalition A, which however our system would recommend. We also do not take into account the dynamics of the environment. By examining it, agents may find that the coalition is not optimal because the system has changed. For example, they may discover a new dispenser or even a separate deferred block, or agents may add other agents to the agent group if this (master) group is merged with another group. The above shortcomings are thus a topic for further improvement of the system for MAPC tasks. We anticipate that the coalition solution may be suitable for other multi-agent tasks if the Agent Assemble task is not repeated in the next edition. If it does, we will try to ensure that at each point in time, our system knows the optimal coalition structure of our agents to improve its performance. We will now return to the deSouches system and present our solutions for MAPC at other levels of the system.

3.5   Coordinator Agents and Missions in the System

Most of the goals specified by deSouches need some missions. We have mentioned three missions in the text above. First, a mission for exploring the environment and coordinating groups, then a mission for clearing the environment of obstacles, and we have devoted the main part of this section to creating missions for task completion. Introducing the different missions and their execution at the second and third levels of the deSouches system, we start with those that are performed by a single agent in order to explore and clear the environment in which the agents are situated.

Divide and Explore Mission. The coordinator is working with one agent and all it does is repeat the 'Explore' goal assignment, whether the previous effort to achieve this goal succeeded or failed. An agent fulfils this goal when it performs a walk within some distance. This is specified when the mission is created, and in our system, we set it around a value of ten. The direction is calculated using a pheromone algorithm, which improved the system performance and made finding the Master group faster.

Compared to random walks where we found the Master group for a 70 × 70 environment with twenty agents between steps 100 and 150, using pheromone we established the Master group around step 50. This mission can be terminated only by deSouches by using the agent for another mission.

Fighter Mission. This mission is similar to the previous one in that one and the same goal is given whether its previous follow-up was successful or unsuccessful. This mission is executed by all agents who adopted the 'digger' role at the time they adopted the role and, unlike the previous mission, it is executed throughout the entire runtime of the system. The goal given to the agents is 'Go And Shoot'. The agent walks randomly and if an obstacle or foreign agent appears within its firing range, it will fire at it. To avoid being blocked from firing at a foreign agent, who may already be knocked out for a few steps due to the fire and thus there is no point in attacking it further, the agent keeps a record of who it has ever fired at. Based on these records, he deduces whether to attack the enemy or pursue other targets.

Block Missions. Unlike previous missions, block missions for two or more blocks are performed in coalitions. We have described how deSouches forms a coalition in the Subsect. 3.4 above, and we now discuss the individual goals that agents must achieve during the mission and their possible coordination.

Whether the product is made up of one, two, three or four blocks, it is always the job of each agent solving this block mission to find a block of the desired type, transport it to a goal position, and connect its block to the other blocks. If the mission is for a task with more than one block, agents end their activity after linking their block to another block or blocks by disconnecting from their block, except for one agent who remains attached to its block until the entire pattern is composed and can be submitted. In Fig. 6 we have demonstrated the behavior of the coordinator for a two-block mission. One agent has to execute the sequence of goals 'Detach All', 'Get Block From Dispenser', 'Go To Position', 'Connect' and 'Submit'. The names of these objectives are, we hope, self-explanatory. The first agent first gets rid of everything attached to it, if there is such a thing, just in case. It then walks to the dispenser that was found while searching for the coalition, picks up the block, walks with it to the given location at the goal zone, connects its block to the other agent's block, and submits the block. The other agent does the same, but only until it connects his block to the other block and disconnects from it (part of the goal 'Connect' is to disconnect from his block).

You can see two things on the automata. First, the transition between the 'Go To Position' and 'Connect' goals is barrier synchronised. The 'Connect' goal can only be issued to both agents at once. If one agent has completed its 'Go to Position' objective and the other has not yet, the first agent must wait. You can also see the coordinator's behavior if either goal fails, or an event occurs where the agent is subjected to an attack (clear event) that causes it to lose any attached block. If it fails to travel to a goal zone, it performs a random walk and tries again to reach that goal. In the event of a clear event, the agent must backtrack to reach the dispenser for a new block. In the diagram, it is the connection above the depicted states.

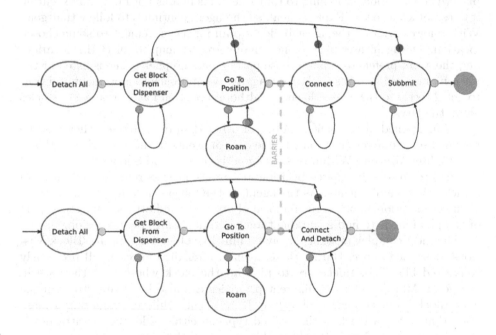

Fig. 6. Two Blocks Mission Control Automata

3.6   Situated Agents Level

The goals that are given to the agents in this realisation follow from the missions mentioned above, and there are also two atomic goals that are given directly by deSouchces. We begin our description of the situated agents behavior with one of them. This is the 'Force Detach' goal, which we mentioned in the introduction of Sect. 3.2, and which is given to all situated agents immediately after their creation. Its purpose is that, if our system needs to restart during a match, the agents start with no blocks attached and can proceed as if the match had just started. To accomplish this, plans for disconnecting blocks are created sequentially in all directions, and after the last plan is executed, the goal is considered accomplished, and the agent then asks deSouches for more work.

Since it is almost certain that a Master group is not established after four actions, then the agent is assigned to the 'Divide and Explore Mission' if it is not in the 'digger' role, or the 'Fighter Mission' if it is in that role. The second case can occur when the system is forced to restart during a match and the agent realises that it is a digger. In the case of the 'Divide and Explore Mission', the agent is repeatedly given the 'Explore' goal. This goal is not just about exploring the environment by walking around, but the agent can perform other activities during these walks. During the re-evaluation of plans, it can build a plan to change roles if it is standing in the goal zone and its role is still the default. It then asks deSouches to tell it which role to adopt and builds a higher priority plan with one action, switching to that role. This plan is not final and executing it does not achieve the 'Explore' goal, so the agent continues to follow that goal. With a lower priority, the agent builds a plan for its movement to some chosen location. The agent uses pheromones on our group's map to select this location, and the agent prefers to explore those parts where no pheromone is listed or the pheromone is old. It takes a relatively aggressive approach to movement and tries to get directly to the chosen location, although it often has to remove obstacles along the way.

As mentioned, if an agent is in one of other than default roles, they may be assigned some different missions. In the case of agents in the 'digger' role, this is the 'Fighter Mission'. Within this, the goal is to 'Go And Shoot' the essence of which is to go to a designated position and in the process remove obstacles and attack other teams' agents. As the agent in the 'digger' role has a larger range of the clear action, which is the removal of obstacles and attacks on agents, part of the planning is to find a suitable target within a range of this action.

The most complex missions involving multiple objectives are the 'Block Missions' described above. During these, agents, after disconnecting all previously connected blocks for safety, try to pick up the block whose type they are in charge of. Multiple plans of different priorities can also be created to fulfil the 'Get Block From Dispenser' objective. If an agent, while re-evaluating a plan, finds that it has a block of the desired type on either side, then it attaches it and the goal is achieved. However, this is only if there are no other agents of its team standing around the block. Then they respect the right hand rule with priorities north, east, south and west. An agent only attaches a block when there are no other agents of its team standing next to the block in the higher priority direction. The agent waits otherwise. If it can join the block, it creates a plan to join the block and by successfully executing the plan, the 'Get Block From Dispenser' goal is met. The agent proceeds similarly if it is standing next to a dispenser and intends to pick up a block from it, but then the plan includes both the request from a dispenser action and the subsequent attach action. A third possible situation is that the agent stands directly on the dispenser and then tries to take one step outside of it in some direction. If neither of the above applies, the agent searches for the nearest dispenser that dispenses a block of the desired type and sets off towards it. Here we use the 'Approach Type' subplan declaration. This plan is constructed by method A* as the optimal sequence of steps to reach the position where the object of the desired type, in this case, the dispenser, is located, and this plan is executed unless a higher priority plan is constructed. The most flexible dispenser should be the one that was considered when the coalition was built. In our implementation, however, we always had the agent search for the nearest suitable dispenser in case a new and more suitable dispenser was discovered.

The mission continues by entering the goal 'Go To Position'. This goal is similar to the 'Approach Type' goal, but the position is given here precisely because it was set when the team for this mission was assembled. Again, the agent plans the path using the A* method. Now we want to point out that the path found takes into account the block attached to the agent and also the desired rotation of the block at the goal position. However, this can be tricky in situations where there are obstacles and other agents at the goal position and the execution of the path may not be and often has not been, successful. Therefore, we have incorporated a 'Roam' goal into the mission, which is given to the agent when such a failure occurs. As part of its execution, the agent attempts to take a few steps aside and then reach the position again for the re-assigned goal 'Go To Position'. The remaining targets are for connecting the individual blocks and then submitting them by the selected agent.

Finally, we mention one more goal that deSouches specifies as atomic. If a master group is established and some agents have not managed to change their role from 'default' to 'worker' or 'digger', deSouches instructs such agents to reach the role zone and change the role. For this 'Change Role' goal, they again use the 'Approach Type' subgoal, this time with the desired type at the goal location corresponding to the role zone, and the agent, once it reaches this location, asks deSouches to tell it what role to adopt, and then adopts it.

4   Evaluation of Participation in the Tournament

In total, our system played twelve games against four teams, so each team played each other in three games. As could be observed, the settings of each match varied in terms of duration, i.e., number of steps, map size, and number of agents per team. Overall, we placed third out of five teams with a score of 19 points. We won six games out of twelve, drew one, and lost five. In one case we recorded zero points, the most points we recorded in our last appearance was 1640 points, which was the most points anyone recorded in this tournament. Although some task parameters were already estimable after the warm-up matches with Paula Böhm from the school organising the competition, namely the number of agents and the size of the area in each match, we did not set these parameters and let the agents act without such estimates, even though the team would have gained some advantage. We observed the following facts from the matches. As expected, we didn't have many chances in the first matches, which lasted only 400 steps. Since our solution required some initial familiarisation with the system, the agents had only a very short time to work on the tasks. This then meant that we only won once and lost three times against four opponents. As the number of steps increased, our handicap with the initial warm-up decreased. In the other eight matches, which were played at six hundred and eight hundred steps, our team did much better, losing only once and by only thirty points, to GOALdigger, who finished second in the end. We played more close results, even drawing with the same team, beating the GOAL-DTU team in one of our matches by only forty points and beating the later overall winners MMD by eighty points.

It could be observed that not only our team but also the MMD team recorded significantly higher scores in cases when the opponent was not doing well. Although we tried to coordinate our agents so that each group submitted scores at different goal zones, having multiple teams working at the same locations introduced collisions and neither team was as efficient as in situations where they had this space to themselves. It is the improvement of precommit manoeuvring that is the challenge for us to improve the performance of our solution.

5   Conclusion

Even though our system has finished worst in the overall competition so far compared to the systems we have used in previous competitions, we do not see our new system as a step in the wrong direction. While the original system was able to perform the tasks well, our system did not perform downright worse. In addition, we had to deal with new aspects that were added to the assignment this year. The norms that our system did not consider would have been ignored anyway by the system we used in previous years, but without the coordination of the individual agents in the mission, the rather reactive approach would have had problems and would not have been able to perform the tasks without major modifications. We are also aware of a number of shortcomings and opportunities for improvement in this year's deSouches system, ranging from improvements to the coalition planning algorithm to better end-of-task execution. We found it beneficial to use our system in situations where it was advantageous to be reactive to emerging stimuli as well as in line with the goals currently being pursued. For a more general use of our system, it would be necessary to specify the individual functionalities of the system more precisely, to create an environment and support for programming, including a suitable graphical environment, and a set of libraries on which the solution would be based. As we anticipate continuing our participation in this competition, we will continue to work on the development of the deSouches system.

Acknowledgement. This work was supported by the project IT4IXS: IT4Innovations Excellence in Science project (LQ1602).

A   Team Overview: Short Answers

A.1   Participants and Their Background

Who is part of your team? This year, members of the teams were František Zbořil, František Vídeňsky and Ladislav Dokoupil

What was your motivation to participate in the contest? We have participated in the previous two years and we intended to continue this year, even though our main man from previous years is no longer on the team. We wanted to try some new strategies for the current scenario and have some fun competing.

What is the history of your group? (course project, thesis, ...) The course on agent and multi-agent systems has been taught at our school for more than ten years, during which a number of diploma and bachelor theses have been written. This year our team consisted of a professor, one PhD student whose thesis topic are BDI systems, and one Master's student who focused on environment search in his Bachelor's thesis.

What is your field of research? Which work therein is related? In particular, BDI agents, interpretation of BDI languages and modeling of distributed systems.

A.2   Statistics

Did you start your agent team from scratch, or did you build on existing agents (from yourself or another previous participant)? The system used in the competition has been developed for the 14th edition in 2019. This system has been modified in accordance with the current competition rules.

How much time did you invest in the contest (for programming, organising your group, other)? Approximately six man-weeks

How was the time (roughly) distributed over the months before the contest? Half of that time was in the month before qualifying and the other half was between qualifying and competition.

How many lines of code did you produce for your final agent team? Our implemented system has approximately 12,000 lines, most of which have been created previously for earlier years and about one-third for this year.

A.3   Technology and Techniques

Did you use any of these agent technology/AOSE methods or tools? What were your experiences?

Agent programming languages and/or frameworks? We specified Java as the programming language in the competition entry form, and did not specify any other system. However, we use the JADE library in our solution but only for managing agent threads and our system is a custom work inspired by BDI systems but also multi-agent approaches like JaCaMo.

Methodologies (e.g. Prometheus)? No

Notation (e.g. Agent UML)? No

Coordination mechanisms (e.g. protocols, games, ...)? Yes, agent coordination consisted of forming coalitions for assigned tasks. In each cycle, a coalition was sought for free agents that were not currently working on one of the tasks. This was a crucial conceptual idea for our solution this year.

Other (methods/concepts/tools)? Nothing significant to note here.

What hardware did you use during the contest? We ran the system on regular PCs and laptops. During the competition we used Acer Predator Helios 300 laptop

A.4   Agent System Details

Would you say your system is decentralised? Why? It is not decentralised completely. deSouches assigns missions to other agents, which the agents in the group then execute. Based on the missions, goals are assigned to individual agents, which they execute autonomously until they meet them or if their efforts fail. Thus, the missions again have a central element that works with the result of the agents' efforts. It also synchronises the agents, e.g., assigns additional goals and informs the controlling agent about the completion of the mission.

Do your agents use the following features: Planning, Learning, Organisations, Norms? If so, please elaborate briefly. Planning takes place in each cycle for the assigned goals. The agent may re-evaluate its plan, or if it is unable to make any plan for the goals, it informs the mission coordinator. Among the classical algorithms, we use A* for path finding in the environment. To organise agents, as we have already mentioned, a central agent is used to explore opportunities and create coalitions of agents for them, if possible.

How do your agents cooperate Agents work together at the mission level by informing the mission coordinator of their success or failure in achieving their assigned goals and are assigned additional goals by the coordinator on that basis.

Can your agents change their general behaviour during run time? If so, what triggers the changes? Yes, as we have already stated, the central agent analyses the current situation and assigns missions to agents accordingly. Initially, the agents synchronise and explore the environment, later they focus on completing the tasks if the right teams can be formed for them.

Did you have to make changes to the team (e.g. fix critical bugs) during the contest? We made some changes after the warm-up matches. We did not make any more changes during the competition.

How did you go about debugging your system? What kinds of measures could improve your debugging experience? We debugged mainly by doing a lot of system runs and observing the behavior of the agents, including what tasks they followed and how successful they were. At this point, we can't think of any major suggestions for improving the debugging options.

During the contest, you were not allowed to watch the matches. How did you track what was going on? Was it helpful? Based on the agents, maps are created for the groups they are in. We can display these maps on our side. We also have an overview of which tasks which agents are performing and how they are performing them. It was only useful during the competition in that this satisfied our curiosity.

Did you invest time in making your agents more robust/fault-tolerant? How? We tuned the robustness based on our experience with our system and experimenting with different settings. This was done incrementally and there is still room for improvement.

A.5   Scenario and Strategy

How would you describe your intended agent behaviour? Did the actual behaviour deviate from that? The basic idea was to first create as large a group of agents as possible that share a map and are synchronised in terms of knowledge of their positions relative to the other agents in the group. Then, if a group was large enough and knew about dispensers and goal zones on its shared map, it was labelled as a mastergroup. Coalitions were then sought for agents in this group that were capable of completing the current task assignments. These groups were sought as optimal given the expected distance they must travel to pick up a block and transport it to a predetermined goal zone. Our agents have mostly behaved according to these principles.

Why did your team perform as it did? Why did the other teams perform better/worse than you did? It seemed that teams that didn't rely on just one specific task might have had an advantage. This is the approach we have taken in previous years and this year we tried to be more specific in the assignments of tasks to agents. Also, the need for initial synchronisation cost quite a bit of time/steps and that was our disadvantage. For the next competition we intend to combine both approaches.

Did you implement any strategy that tries to interfere with your opponents? When the agent had a role in which he could attack opponents, he did so. However, since it was clear that several such attacks were needed to gain an advantage by such an attack, this was not relevant to our system and there were only a few agents with this role in our team. Moreover, they were primarily intended to clear the environment of obstacles.

How do your agents coordinate assembling and delivering a structure for a task? For each possible structure up to four blocks, we have predefined positions of the agents that deliver the blocks. If all the agents reach them, the blocks are connected and the product is submitted by one of them.

Which aspect(s) of the scenario did you find particularly challenging? The scenario as a whole was a challenge. We can't single out one aspect. For us the biggest problem was probably getting to the right places in the goal zones. There was often a lot of traffic and agents were in each other's way. Therefore, the ability of the agents to solve this problem fundamentally affected the performance of our system.

What would you improve (wrt. your agents) if you wanted to participate in the same contest a week from now (or next year)? We have a number of ideas on how to improve the functioning of our system. For example, re-evaluating coalitions already formed or better maneuvering before submitting a task.

What can be improved regarding the scenario for next year? What would you remove? What would you add? The scenarios get more interesting every year. This year we have not been too concerned with norms because we felt that the penalties for violating them were low and behavioural changes in line with norms would be irrational. This may change by next year, as may the wider range of roles. Agents needed to be in one of the roles available to complete tasks, which could change for next year, making the competition more interesting but more difficult to solve.

A.6   And the Moral of it is ...

What did you learn from participating in the contest? As in previous years, the creation of a multi-agent system for non-trivial tasks is a complex and quite challenging activity.

What advice would you give to yourself before the contest/another team wanting to participate in the next? As this was our third participation, we had already learned our lesson. Not to underestimate the functioning of the whole system when the opponent is present and to make sure that the system is able to cope with possible connection failures, which we fortunately did not encounter this year.

Where did you benefit from your chosen programming language, methodology, tools, and algorithms?
Since we were building our system from scratch, the disadvantage was that we had to invest a lot of time in creating a basic system. On the other hand, we could adapt the multi-agent architecture to the competition.

Which problems did you encounter because of your chosen technologies? Again, we mention the need to create it completely. That is why there were and probably still are untuned parts in it, which in already finished and time-tested systems work flawlessly.

Which aspect of your team cost you the most time? Certainly debugging the system and verifying its functionality.

A.7   Looking into the Future

Did the warm-up match help improve your team of agents? How useful do you think it is? The warm up match was crucial to our team's performance in the competition. It helped us uncover some fundamental flaws in our system setup. Without it, our results would have been much worse.

What are your thoughts on changing how the contest is run, so that the participants' agents are executed on the same infrastructure by the organisers? What do you see as positive or negative about this approach? In previous years, it happened that teams lost connection with the organisers' server, which led to inconvenience and the need to cope with it. This year we have not encountered this and therefore have no objection to this method of running matches.

Do you think a match containing more than two teams should be mandatory? We wouldn't say it's mandatory, but it would certainly make the competition more interesting. We can even imagine some form of knockout phase if the number of teams is even larger next time.

What else can be improved regarding the MAPC for next year? The organisers have our full confidence that next year's event will again be at least as interesting, motivating, beneficial and entertaining as it has been so far.

References

1. Bellifemine, F.L., Caire, G., Greenwood, D.: Developing Multi-agent Systems with JADE. Wiley, Hoboken (2007)
2. Bordini, R.H., Hübner, J.F.: BDI agent programming in AgentSpeak using *Jason*. In: Toni, F., Torroni, P. (eds.) CLIMA 2005. LNCS (LNAI), vol. 3900, pp. 143–164. Springer, Heidelberg (2006). https://doi.org/10.1007/11750734_9
3. Brooks, R.: A robust layered control system for a mobile robot. IEEE J. Robot. Autom. **2**(1), 14–23 (1986)
4. Dastani, M.: 2APL: a practical agent programming language. Auton. Agent. Multi-Agent Syst. **16**(3), 214–248 (2008). https://doi.org/10.1007/s10458-008-9036-y
5. Hindriks, K.V., de Boer, F.S., van der Hoek, W., Meyer, J.-J.C.: Agent programming with declarative goals. In: Castelfranchi, C., Lespérance, Y. (eds.) ATAL 2000. LNCS (LNAI), vol. 1986, pp. 228–243. Springer, Heidelberg (2001). https://doi.org/10.1007/3-540-44631-1_16
6. Hübner, J.F., Boissier, O., Kitio, R., Ricci, A.: Instrumenting multi-agent organisations with organisational artifacts and agents. Auton. Agent. Multi-Agent Syst. **20**(3), 369–400 (2010)
7. Kaelbling, L.P.: A situated-automata approach to the design of embedded agents. ACM SIGART Bull. **2**(4), 85–88 (1991)
8. Rahwan, T., Michalak, T.P., Wooldridge, M., Jennings, N.R.: Coalition structure generation: a survey. Artif. Intell. **229**, 139–174 (2015)
9. Rao, A.S.: AgentSpeak(L): BDI agents speak out in a logical computable language. In: Van de Velde, W., Perram, J.W. (eds.) MAAMAW 1996. LNCS, vol. 1038, pp. 42–55. Springer, Heidelberg (1996). https://doi.org/10.1007/BFb0031845
10. Sandholm, T., Larson, K., Andersson, M., Shehory, O., Tohmé, F.: Coalition structure generation with worst case guarantees. Artif. Intell. **111**(1–2), 209–238 (1999)
11. Thangarajah, J., Padgham, L., Winikoff, M.: Detecting and avoiding interference between goals in intelligent agents. In: Proceedings of the 18th International Joint Conference on Artificial Intelligence, pp. 721–726. Morgan Kaufmann Publishers (2003)

12. Uhlir, V., Zboril, F., Vidensky, F.: Multi-agent programming contest 2019 FIT BUT team solution. In: Ahlbrecht, T., Dix, J., Fiekas, N., Krausburg, T. (eds.) MAPC 2019. LNCS (LNAI), vol. 12381, pp. 59–78. Springer, Cham (2020). https://doi.org/10.1007/978-3-030-59299-8_3
13. Uhlir, V., Zboril, F., Vidensky, F.: FIT BUT: rational agents in the multi-agent programming contest. In: Ahlbrecht, T., Dix, J., Fiekas, N., Krausburg, T. (eds.) MAPC 2021. LNCS (LNAI), vol. 12947, pp. 23–45. Springer, Cham (2021). https://doi.org/10.1007/978-3-030-88549-6_2
14. Wooldridge, M., Jennings, N.R., Kinny, D.: The Gaia methodology for agent-oriented analysis and design. Auton. Agent. Multi-Agent Syst. 3(3), 285–312 (2000)

The 16th Edition of the Multi-Agent Programming Contest - The GOAL-DTU Team

Jørgen Villadsen$^{(\boxtimes)}$ ⓘ and Jonas Weile

Algorithms, Logic and Graphs Section, Department of Applied Mathematics and Computer Science, Technical University of Denmark, Richard Petersens Plads, Building 324, 2800 Kongens Lyngby, Denmark
jovi@dtu.dk

Abstract. We provide an overview of the GOAL-DTU system for the Multi-Agent Programming Contest, including the overall strategy and how the system is designed to apply this strategy. Our agents are implemented using the GOAL programming language. We evaluate the performance of our agents in the contest and, finally, we discuss how to improve the system based on an analysis of its strengths and weaknesses.

1 Introduction

In 2020/2021 we participated as the GOAL-DTU team in the annual Multi-Agent Programming Contest (MAPC). We are using the GOAL agent programming language [1–4] and we are affiliated with the Technical University of Denmark (DTU). We participated in the contest in 2009 and 2010 as the Jason-DTU team [5,6], in 2011 and 2012 as the Python-DTU team [7,8], in 2013 and 2014 as the GOAL-DTU team [9], in 2015/2016 as the Python-DTU team [10], in 2017 and 2018 as the Jason-DTU team [11,12] and in 2019/2020/2021 as the GOAL-DTU team [13,14].

In 2022 we had the *Agents Assemble III* scenario which further expands upon the *Agents Assemble* scenario used in the 2019/2020/2021 contests. Several new features are introduced to add to the scenario from the previous iterations. One such addition is the possibility for agents to switch between different *roles* that each have a set of strengths and weaknesses; one role might be able to move faster but carry less load. Another addition is that *goalzones* are no longer static and can relocate during a simulation.

In this paper, we describe the strategy behind our implementation and evaluate our performance at the competition. The paper is organized as follows:

- Section 2 covers the overall strategy of our agents and our implementation.
- Section 3 evaluates our agents' performance in the contest.
- Section 4 reflects on the differences between the teams
- Section 5 makes some concluding remarks.

T. Ahlbrecht et al. (Eds.): MAPC 2022, LNAI 13997, pp. 151–164, 2023.
https://doi.org/10.1007/978-3-031-38712-8_6

2   The Strategy and Implementation of Our Agents

Our system for the agent contest is implemented in the multi-agent programming language GOAL [1–4] because GOAL has been our recent framework of choice for student projects as well as for several research collaborations.

In GOAL, each agent is an independent entity that can communicate with other agents through an extensive messaging system and perform actions to interact with the environment. These actions are scenario specific and defined for the particular environment that the agents operate in. The agent keeps both predefined and learned knowledge of the environment in a Prolog knowledge base, which constitutes the mental state of the agent. The agent then continually perceives its environment and updates its mental state based on the changes made to the environment. These changes could be the result of an action that the agent itself performed, or they could be the result of some other entity, including what we might call *nature* (i.e. changes that are not the result of some entity acting in the environment).

The agents operate by simple rule-based decision-making. Predefined rules determine the next action of the agent based on its current mental state and the state of the environment, thereby enabling the agents to react to changes in their environment.

2.1   Discovery

We employ different strategies based on the state of the simulation. Initially, in what we call the *discovery phase*, the agents are only tasked with exploring the map and locating dispensers, goalzones, rolezones, and each other. This is necessary because an agent only perceives objects and entities within its (very limited) field of vision, and all agents start out knowing nothing about the environment they are placed in. Agents then store the location of the resources they discover relative to their starting position, which means that all agents will have different coordinate systems. When two (or more) agents meet they will therefore try to establish a connection by learning the origins of the other agents, thereby enabling the agents to efficiently translate between their respective coordinate systems, allowing the agents to communicate about specific resources.

As agents do not perceive the identities of other agents that they encounter, the agents must instead verify their identities by comparing the perceivable objects in their shared field of vision. Thus, all agents continuously broadcast their immediate surroundings to all other agents during the initial discovery phase. Agents then check for broadcasts that match their own surroundings (including the location of the agents themselves), and if there are no other identical broadcasts, they can safely establish a connection to the other broadcasting agent. To optimize the process, agents will share their knowledge of the coordinate systems of all the other agents they have already connected to when establishing a new connection.

2.2 Task Plans

Once enough agents have connected to one another (we, somewhat arbitrarily, chose this to be half of the agents), a single agent is chosen to become the *task master*.

The task master is responsible for creating plans to solve available tasks in order to score points. The task master ranks the available tasks and tries to solve a specific task at a time. The first step in creating a plan is to request information from all other agents relevant for the task at hand. This includes their current attachments and knowledge of available resources necessary to complete the task. The other agents will then respond with their distance to each type of resource and an estimated delivery time.

The task master then collects all responses and checks whether it is feasible to solve the task by attempting to create a *task plan*. A task plan is a detailed description delegating each block of the pattern to a specific agent, specifying a point of assembly at which the pattern is to be assembled. If the task master is unsuccessful in creating a task plan for the task at hand, the task master will restart the process with an alternative task. On the other hand, if the task master successfully creates a task plan, the plan is sent to each agent that is to take part in executing the plan. Each of the agents receives only part of the plan, namely the steps that the agent is responsible for. An agent will only be assigned to deliver blocks of a single type, and from the task plan, the agent is able to infer exactly where it must position itself to deliver the blocks it is responsible for.

2.3 Solving Tasks

To solve a given task, an agent must first collect the necessary block types, and then move to the point of assembly. In order to efficiently solve tasks, the movement of the agents must be direct and fast. However, because the environment is extremely dynamic, the agents do not maintain an up-to-date representation of the map, and thus we cannot use simple path-finding algorithms without modifications.

Our approach is to mix a heuristics-based approach to global path-finding, with optimal local (i.e. within the field of vision) path-finding using A*. The heuristics based approach naively selects moves that bring the agent closer to its destination as long as possible. Once this simple approach is no longer possible, i.e. there might be something blocking the path, the agent chooses a *way point* among the locations within its field of vision. This way point is chosen to be the location within the agents' field of vision that is closest to the final destination. The agent then uses A* to find the optimal path to the way point within its field of vision, and once the agent reaches its way point, the process then starts over. This very simple approach to path-finding is only made feasible by the availability of the clear action. The possibility to clear any blocks that are in the way of the agent means that it will not get stuck in dead-ends; the agent can always clear its way out. However, there is of course an overhead cost attached to heavy utilization of the clear action, but we think that it is a relatively small price to pay in order to achieve such simple path-finding logic.

When the agent reaches the point of assembly for the task plan, it will position itself relative to the agent submitting the pattern, which will locate itself exactly at the predetermined point of assembly. This means, that assembling the pattern is fast and easy, but also extremely inflexible. The agents know exactly where to position themselves in advance, but if the predetermined point of assembly is blocked and cannot be cleared, the agents must find another place to assemble the pattern.

If, at any point during the execution of the task plan, an agent realizes that its individual plan is either unfeasible or cannot be performed within the agreed-upon time-frame, the agent will try to replan. As long as the agent is able to find a plan that can be performed within the time-frame, there is no need to inform the group of the change of plans. Otherwise, the agent will inform the group that the task is no longer solvable and invoke the taskmaster anew. Likewise, once the agreed-upon deadline for solving the task is reached, the default behavior for the agents is to simply drop the task. This ensures that agents will not be stuck waiting for a failed agent.

3   Evaluation of Matches

In this section, we evaluate all of our matches and highlight what goes wrong and what goes right. A match consisted of three simulations, and a simulation started automatically when the previous simulation finished.

3.1   GOAL-DTU VS GOALdigger

SIM1 (0 : 180)

Clearly, something goes wrong for our team of agents. Around step 200 there are three agents that seem to attempt to assemble the pattern for task 4, but it is clear that they do not agree on the exact coordinates for the point of assembly. Maybe something went wrong with inferring map dimensions, leading to a mismatch in coordinates. But this inference should have been disabled at the contest, due to exactly the concern that it might lead to such a mismatch. Because the simulations were run by another student on his local PC, there is however a chance, that it was accidentally left on.

Later in the simulation, there is a long period of time where the agents do not even try to assemble a pattern. This could be further proof that the inferred coordinates are way off, leaving the master agent unable to create any feasible plans.

Compared to our team, we see that GOALdigger performs significantly better. It appears that the strategy of the GOALdigger team is to focus on the simple tasks—all of the 180 points that GOALdigger scores in this simulation are scored by submitting single-block patterns. However, we also see what seems to be an (unsuccessful) attempt to submit a more complex task, see agent 17 from step 160 and onward.

SIM2 (0 : 370)

In general, agents seem to move rather well even in maps like this one that are mostly blocked; the agents creates a path forward by clearing blocks and finding small passages. However, to highlight an instance where this is not the case, consider agent 19 at step 320. Evidently, the "explore score" that prioritizes different moves according to a number of heuristics is not properly tuned. The agent simply rotates in place for many turns before finally finding another path.

Otherwise, this simulation is very similar to simulation 1. We notice the same exact problem; namely that agents do not even bother trying to assemble any patterns, probably due to a mismatch in coordinate systems.

The strategy of GOALdigger also seems to be exactly the same as in the previous simulation. A clear majority of the points are attained by submitting single-block patterns; the GOALdigger team submits an impressive 31 tasks, 29 of which are single-block patterns, and the remaining two patterns are made up of two blocks.

SIM3 (520 : 410)

Unlike the previous two simulations, we actually succeed in submitting tasks and scoring points. In fact, we end up winning the simulation. We note, that most of our points are due to two submissions of the same complex pattern. This showcases some of the beneficial aspects of our simple strategy—the agents are very efficient at building complex patterns. However, this is only the case under optimal conditions.

We notice several occasions during the simulation where it gets extremely crowded at specific goalzones—especially the GOALdigger agents have a tendency to clutter. Crowded goalzones are a known weakness of our simple strategy, and it makes it difficult for our agents to successfully submit patterns. As an example (where the clutter is actually quite limited, but still our agents fail), consider agent 24 around step 360. The agent does not succeed in performing any action for a large number of turns, and instead simply times out. This could be due to problems with the path-finding algorithm. While observing agent 24, we also notice that it seems like two different groups of our agents are trying to assemble the same pattern at the same place, and they actually end up being in the way of one-another.

As another low-hanging fruit for improving our system, we see that our agents try to submit patterns in OLD goalzones. These old goalzones should simply have been removed from the knowledge base once an agent notices that they are no longer present. As an example, observe agent 18 during step 650 and on-wards. Clearly, the agents are trying to submit task 12, but the goalzone disappeared after step 361.

Finally, we notice that the GOALdigger team succeeds in submitting several two-block patterns; a lot more than in the previous simulations.

3.2 GOAL-DTU VS LI(A)RA

SIM1 (120 : 310)

We manage to submit a number of tasks, but we see a clear indication that our strategy is failing. Consider for example agents 4, 5, and 20 around step 225. It seems that their goal is to cooperate to build and submit task 5, but some slight error in the agreed-upon coordinates is stopping them from accomplishing this goal. The same scenario plays out just 45 steps later (at step 270), where two of the same agents, namely agent 4 and 20, fail at assembling task 6 due to the very same error. Fixing this miscalculation of relative coordinates should be top priority, but it also showcases another important problem—our agents *ought* to be more flexible. It should be easy for the agents to recognize this error, and then dynamically agree on a new point of assembly.

We see that the LI(A)RA team submits a large number of tasks compared to us, and seems to do so quite efficiently. Interestingly, however, the LI(A)RA agents fail to submit any patterns for more than 150 steps (between step 133 and 289), but it is not obvious as to why.

SIM2 (160 : 80)

Again, our agents fare reasonably well in a map with a lot of obstacles. Consider for example agents 8 and 18 from step 230 and on-wards. Both agents must clear their way through obstacles to complete the task, and they succeed in doing so in a quite efficient manner. However, agent 18 does perform some unnecessary clearing operations (where the agent does not even use the cleared space), and thus there is still room for improvement.

We also observe the same errors when trying to assemble patterns as in the previous simulation. From step 260, it seems evident that agents 5 and 9 wish to complete task 5. But despite being present in the goalzone with the necessary blocks, and getting within a single rotation from being able to complete the pattern, they never succeed in actually doing so. Here, our agents should be able to recognize the mistake in the agreed-upon plan, and then realize that agent 5 simply needs to perform a rotation in order to successfully complete the pattern.

SIM3 (0 : 270)

Our agents fail completely this simulation. They do not score a single point, nor do they even try to assemble/submit any task. Again, we think this is because of an error in inferring map dimensions, which can completely paralyze the agents.

3.3   GOAL-DTU VS FIT But

SIM1 (230 : 0)

We fare decently well in this simulation and end up winning it. However, we still see some of the problems touched upon in the previous matches. Further, it is very noticeable in this simulation how agents cannot decide on any tasks themselves—instead, only the taskmaster can delegate task plans. For simple 1 block patterns this approach is extremely inefficient, and we see several cases where agents could have completed tasks by themselves. As an example, consider agent 11 around step 90. The agent seems to be waiting for two other agents in order to complete task 3. However, the other agents fail to show up, and therefore agent 11 must drop the task. The agent actually fulfills all the requirements for task 5 but simply wanders out the goalzone with its block instead of submitting the task. This shows that our agents need more autonomy.

It is also observed, that once an agent is in place and waiting for remaining agents to complete a pattern, they completely ignore the threat of clearing events. Consider agent 3 around step 160. The agent is oblivious to the clear event and does not get out of the way, despite having to move only a single (or maybe 2) cells to get of the radius of the event. Agents should always try to avoid clear events, especially when they are about to complete a task.

SIM2 (630 : 670)

We perform fairly well this simulation but with the same problems of failing to complete task patterns. Consider for example agents 6, 8, 14, and 15 around step 470. The agents have built most of the complex pattern, but agent 8 fails to deliver the last remaining block just two rotations (or moves) away from completing the pattern. However, it seems that the reason is due to the path-finding algorithm failing/timing out and not a disagreement in coordinates. This follows because agent 8 does not skip its turns (as an agent would do once it is in place) but instead fails to perform any action. Completing this pattern would have meant winning the simulation.

We also notice that, again, the goalzones tend to get very crowded and that our agents do not deal well with this.

SIM3: (0 : 1640)

Once again, a complete meltdown of our system. It is identical to the previous matches where we do not get a single point.

However, we would like to use the opportunity to praise FIT BUT and their active use of roles—in this simulation, it really shows how they benefit from using the diggers to remove obstacles from the playing field in order to gain easy access to goalzones.

3.4 GOAL-DTU VS MMD

SIM1 (480 : 910)

We do fairly well, but are not nearly efficient enough. We observe several cases where we begin assembling a pattern but are not able to finish it in time. Further, we notice the large contrast to MMD that always have many agents building patterns in the same goalzone—we do not utilize the large goalzones well enough. We could easily have more agents work in the same goalzones at the same time.

SIM2 (150 : 780)

A lot of cases of agents trying to submit tasks in nonexistent (old) goalzones. This is a severe waste of resources, and leads to a game where we score very few points.

SIM3 (0 : 1520)

Yet another complete meltdown; see the descriptions of the previous simulations where we score 0 points.

4 Discussion

In this section, we retrospectively discuss and review some assumptions of our strategy, and then we take a brief look at the different teams that took part in this year's contest.

4.1 Strategy

Our strategy is very much developed with the specific scenario in mind (the *Agents Assemble* scenario), both in regards to the actual problem to solve, but also in regards to the specific parameters of the scenario. In particular, our implementation is based upon an implicit assumption that the number of agents in a map is fairly limited—in the history of this scenario, the maximum number of agents per team has been no more than 50. This allows us to take a centralized approached to task planning which, if the number of agents were to increase by a few orders of magnitude, would quickly prove to be inefficient.

Our centralized approach is also built upon an implicit assumption of the actual layout of maps; in order to select the taskmaster, at least half of the agents must be connected. By experience, this rarely takes more than 60 rounds, but in a very large map this might not happen within the duration of a single simulation.

It would be interesting to introduce simulations that challenge these kinds of implicit assumptions in the contest which would force competitors to create more general systems. One possible approach could be to have each competing team design a simulation for the contest (in addition to those provided by the organizers), which we expect would lead to less similarity between simulations.

4.2   Teams

Team	FIT BUT	GOAL-DTU	GOALdigger	LI(A)RA	MMD
Members	3	3	4	5	2
Time	6 man-weeks	30 h	1200 h prog.	80 h prog. + 40 h	896 h
Lines	12000	2000	10000	1100	5407
Platform	Java(+JADE)	GOAL	GOAL	Jason	Python
Returning	Yes	Yes	No	No	No

The table shows that the time each team has spent in order to prepare for the competition varies a lot. The hours spent differs as much as by a factor 40. However, it is also important to note that our team spent the least time preparing for this year's competition, but is a returning team. Thus, almost our entire codebase is reused from last year, but with a small number of updates. Likewise, the number of lines of code varies quite a lot between teams. We notice that the teams that have used dedicated multi-agent programming languages do not necessarily need fewer lines of code; both the two teams with fewest lines of code, as well as the two teams with the most lines of code, use such dedicated languages. Even within the same dedicated language, GOAL, the number of lines of code differs by a factor 5 between the two teams that use it.

5   Conclusion

During the contest, we observed some problems concerning robustness due to false information. When the problem did not occur, we generally achieved competitive scores. If an agent somehow incorrectly updates its location, this can lead to agents agreeing on incorrect dimensions of the map, and as a result the agents will be rendered useless. While this suggests that the system is not robust enough, one could also argue that, once false information is introduced into the system, we cannot expect coherent behavior.

Another observation is that, especially in larger maps with lots of agents, we have too many idle agents. Once the map is explored and an agent has connected two blocks, the agent will simply roam the map waiting to be assigned a task. Instead, the idle agents could be put to better use by e.g. protecting goalzones.

In conclusion, we are satisfied with our placement for the contest and with the improvements we have made to the system compared to last year, but at the same time, we have discussed several ways that the system could be improved. For the future we suggest to execute the agents on the same infrastructure by the organisers.

Acknowledgements. We thank the anonymous reviewers for helpful comments.

A   Team Overview: Short Answers

A.1   Participants and Their Background

Who is part of your team?

This year, 3 people were involved: Jørgen Villadsen (PhD), Jonas Weile (MSc student) and during the contest days also Markus Fridlev Schlenzig (BSc student). For earlier iterations of the code that we have built upon, also Alexander Birch Jensen and Erik Kristian Gylling have been involved.

What was your motivation to participate in the contest?

To study multi-agent systems in a realistic, but simulated, environment and to enhance our knowledge of the GOAL agent programming language.

What is the history of your group? (course project, thesis, ...)

Our team name is GOAL-DTU. We participated in the contest in 2009 and 2010 as the Jason-DTU team, in 2011 and 2012 as the Python-DTU team, in 2013 and 2014 as the GOAL-DTU team, in 2015/2016 as the Python-DTU team, in 2017 and 2018 as the Jason-DTU team, and in 2019 and 2020/2021 as the GOAL-DTU team. We are affiliated with the Algorithms, Logic and Graphs section at DTU Compute, Department of Applied Mathematics and Computer Science, Technical University of Denmark (DTU). DTU Compute is located in the greater Copenhagen area. The main contact is associate professor Jørgen Villadsen, email: `jovi@dtu.dk`

What is your field of research? Which work therein is related?

We are responsible for the Artificial Intelligence and Algorithms study line of the MSc in Computer Science and Engineering programme.

A.2   Statistics

Did you start your agent team from scratch, or did you build on existing agents (from yourself or another previous participant)?

As our starting point, we used the code from the competition last year—which in turn built upon the competition in 2020.

How much time did you invest in the contest (for programming, organising your group, other)?

We have spent approximately 60 h to further develop the code from the previous iteration.

How was the time (roughly) distributed over the months before the contest?

Most of the time was spent in August leading up to the qualification. After qualifying, no further improvements were made.

How many lines of code did you produce for your final agent team?

We have about 2000 lines of code.

A.3   Technology and Techniques

Did you use any of these agent technology/AOSE methods or tools? What were your experiences?

Agent programming languages and/or frameworks?
We used GOAL which is a quite easy and intuitive agent programming language.
Methodologies (e.g. Prometheus)?
No.
Notation (e.g. Agent UML)?
No.
Coordination mechanisms (e.g. protocols, games, ...)?
No.
Other (methods/concepts/tools)?
We used the Eclipse IDE for programming (it has a GOAL add-on).

What hardware did you use during the contest? We used a laptop.

A.4   Agent System Details

Would you say your system is decentralised? Why?
The team communicates via messages and channels to share information and agree on plans. The approach is mostly decentralized, but planning tasks are currently delegated to a single master agent.
Do your agents use the following features: Planning, Learning, Organisations, Norms? If so, please elaborate briefly.
The agents use planning to choose the tasks to pursue. A single agent is chosen to do the planning, but this agent relies on input from all other agents, and the planning agent is chosen dynamically at run time. The planning agent will search through assignment combinations and choose the most promising.
How do your agents cooperate?
The agents reactively decide on their actions based on the current percepts, their beliefs and their goals. They use predetermined rules and actions.
Can your agents change their general behaviour during run time? If so, what triggers the changes?
An agent will change its behaviour when it is chosen to take part in solving a task.
Did you have to make changes to the team (e.g. fix critical bugs) during the contest?
We chose not to make changes during the contest.
How did you go about debugging your system? What kinds of measures could improve your debugging experience?
We used log files to record the agents belief base and percepts.
During the contest, you were not allowed to watch the matches. How did you track what was going on? Was it helpful?
We only did basic logging to the console.
Did you invest time in making your agents more robust/fault-tolerant? How?
As evident from the competition results, we did not spend enough time on this aspect.

A.5   Scenario and Strategy

How would you describe your intended agent behaviour? Did the actual behaviour deviate from that?

First, to explore and have our agents find other agents, goal-zones and dispensers. Once most agents have connected, they collectively decide on a master agent to do planning. Once this agent has been found, it will continuously inquire the other agents about their available resources and try to create task plans. The task plan is sent to all agents involved in the plan, and these will try to solve it as efficiently as possible.

Why did your team perform as it did? Why did the other teams perform better/worse than you did?

We defined the overall strategy. The task-plans are created autonomously. We would have liked more flexibility for the agents to evaluate their strategy and correct this strategy as needed.

Did you implement any strategy that tries to interfere with your opponents?

We worked on some clearing strategies to defend goal cells, and to scare off opponents. However, they seemingly did more harm than good at the competition.

How do your agents coordinate assembling and delivering a structure for a task?

The planning agent creates a structured plan describing which agent should deliver what blocks, based on the input it receives from other agents. All agents involved in delivering a task then continuously check the plan to see if it remains feasible, updating the plan if necessary.

Which aspect(s) of the scenario did you find particularly challenging?

The map was made even more dynamic than preceding years, which was definitely a challenge.

What would you improve (wrt. your agents) if you wanted to participate in the same contest a week from now (or next year)?

If the contest was a week from now, we would mainly focus on bug fixing and thorough testing. If we had a whole year, we would work on changing the way we solve tasks and do planning—we would further decentralize it, removing most of the responsibility of the planning agent, and make the assembling of blocks more dynamic. Also, we should make better use of agents not partaking in solving tasks, as well as improving defensive strategies

What can be improved regarding the scenario for next year? What would you remove? What would you add?

We suggest to execute the agents on the same infrastructure by the organisers and then it would be interesting to decrease the time available for the agents to decide on their actions.

A.6   And the Moral of it is ...

What did you learn from participating in the contest?
We learned a lot about using GOAL to write multi-agent programs. We were reminded of the care it takes to develop and test in multi-agent environments.

What advice would you give to yourself before the contest/another team wanting to participate in the next?
Start early, because unexpected problems will occur. Have a clear testing strategy. The coordination between agents is working quite well and the A* path finding helps agents to move directly. Agents could be more flexible in helping each other and prioritizing other agents' tasks over their own when it is better for the team.

Where did you benefit from your chosen programming language, methodology, tools, and algorithms?
GOAL has built-in functionality that allows agents to communicate with one another and it has a predefined agent-cycle that is suitable for the belief-desire-intention model. A* was used by the agents to determine movement actions for short distances.

Which problems did you encounter because of your chosen technologies?
Writing thorough tests for GOAL code can be challenging,

Which aspect of your team cost you the most time?
Some unexpected problems (unrelated to the contest) ended up costing us a team member, and another team member had less time to work on the project than anticipated. This led to a large loss of potential time.

A.7   Looking into the Future

Did the warm-up match help improve your team of agents? How useful do you think it is?
It was not really useful due to the lack of time for improvements.

What are your thoughts on changing how the contest is run, so that the participants' agents are executed on the same infrastructure by the organisers? What do you see as positive or negative about this approach?
Yes, it would be great if the agents are executed on the same infrastructure.

Do you think a match containing more than two teams should be mandatory?
Maybe—perhaps if the agents are executed on the same infrastructure.

What else can be improved regarding the MAPC for next year?
We would prefer more or less the same scenario.

References

1. Hindriks, K.V., Koeman, V.: The GOAL Agent Programming Language Home (2021). https://goalapl.atlassian.net/wiki
2. Hindriks, K.V., de Boer, F.S., van der Hoek, W., Meyer, J.-J.C.: Agent programming with declarative goals. In: Castelfranchi, C., Lespérance, Y. (eds.) ATAL 2000. LNCS (LNAI), vol. 1986, pp. 228–243. Springer, Heidelberg (2001). https://doi.org/10.1007/3-540-44631-1_16
3. Hindriks, K.V.: Programming rational agents in GOAL. In: El Fallah Seghrouchni, A., Dix, J., Dastani, M., Bordini, R.H. (eds.) Multi-Agent Programming, pp. 119–157. Springer, Boston (2009). https://doi.org/10.1007/978-0-387-89299-3_4
4. Hindriks, K.V., Dix, J.: GOAL: a multi-agent programming language applied to an exploration game. In: Shehory, O., Sturm, A. (eds.) Agent-Oriented Software Engineering, pp. 235–258. Springer, Heidelberg (2014). https://doi.org/10.1007/978-3-642-54432-3_12
5. Boss, N.S., Jensen, A.S., Villadsen, J.: Building multi-agent systems using Jason. Ann. Math. Artif. Intell. **59**, 373–388 (2010). https://doi.org/10.1007/s10472-010-9181-2
6. Vester, S., Boss, N.S., Jensen, A.S., Villadsen, J.: Improving multi-agent systems using Jason. Ann. Math. Artif. Intell. **61**, 297–307 (2011). https://doi.org/10.1007/s10472-011-9225-2
7. Ettienne, M.B., Vester, S., Villadsen, J.: Implementing a multi-agent system in Python with an auction-based agreement approach. In: Dennis, L., Boissier, O., Bordini, R.H. (eds.) ProMAS 2011. LNCS (LNAI), vol. 7217, pp. 185–196. Springer, Heidelberg (2012). https://doi.org/10.1007/978-3-642-31915-0_11
8. Villadsen, J., Jensen, A.S., Ettienne, M.B., Vester, S., Andersen, K.B., Frøsig, A.: Reimplementing a multi-agent system in Python. In: Dastani, M., Hübner, J.F., Logan, B. (eds.) ProMAS 2012. LNCS (LNAI), vol. 7837, pp. 205–216. Springer, Heidelberg (2013). https://doi.org/10.1007/978-3-642-38700-5_13
9. Villadsen, J., et al.: Engineering a multi-agent system in GOAL. In: Cossentino, M., El Fallah Seghrouchni, A., Winikoff, M. (eds.) EMAS 2013. LNCS (LNAI), vol. 8245, pp. 329–338. Springer, Heidelberg (2013). https://doi.org/10.1007/978-3-642-45343-4_18
10. Villadsen, J., From, A.H., Jacobi, S., Larsen, N.N.: Multi-agent programming contest 2016 - the Python-DTU team. Int. J. Agent-Oriented Softw. Eng. **6**(1), 86–100 (2018)
11. Villadsen, J., Fleckenstein, O., Hatteland, H., Larsen, J.B.: Engineering a multi-agent system in Jason and CArtAgO. Ann. Math. Artif. Intell. **84**, 57–74 (2018). https://doi.org/10.1007/s10472-018-9588-8
12. Villadsen, J., Bjørn, M.O., From, A.H., Henney, T.S., Larsen, J.B.: Multi-agent programming contest 2018—the Jason-DTU team. In: Ahlbrecht, T., Dix, J., Fiekas, N. (eds.) MAPC 2018. LNCS (LNAI), vol. 11957, pp. 41–71. Springer, Cham (2019). https://doi.org/10.1007/978-3-030-37959-9_3
13. Jensen, A.B., Villadsen, J.: GOAL-DTU: development of distributed intelligence for the multi-agent programming contest. In: Ahlbrecht, T., Dix, J., Fiekas, N., Krausburg, T. (eds.) MAPC 2019. LNCS (LNAI), vol. 12381, pp. 79–105. Springer, Cham (2020). https://doi.org/10.1007/978-3-030-59299-8_4
14. Jensen, A.B., Villadsen, J., Weile, J., Gylling, E.K.: The 15th edition of the multi-agent programming contest - the GOAL-DTU team. In: Ahlbrecht, T., Dix, J., Fiekas, N., Krausburg, T. (eds.) MAPC 2021. LNCS (LNAI), vol. 12947, pp. 46–81. Springer, Cham (2021). https://doi.org/10.1007/978-3-030-88549-6_3

LI(A)RA Team - A Declarative and Distributed Implementation for the MAPC 2022

Marcelo Custódio, Michele Rocha, Ricardo Battaglin, Giovani P. Farias,
and Alison R. Panisson[(✉)]

Department of Computing (DEC), Federal University of Santa Catarina (UFSC),
Araranguá, Brazil
alison.panisson@ufsc.br

Abstract. With the increasing computational power and the evolution of the distributed computing paradigm and artificial intelligence techniques and methodologies, computing is becoming increasingly distributed and intelligent. The multi-agent paradigm is one of the most powerful paradigms for implementing distributed artificial intelligence. There are multiple (multi-)agent-oriented programming languages, platforms and methodologies to implement these systems, and the Multi-Agent Programming Contest aims to provide challenging scenarios in which researchers can explore their preferred programming languages, platforms and methodologies to implement multi-agent systems, collecting benchmarks, etc. In this paper, we describe the multi-agent system implemented by the LI(A)RA team for the Multi-Agent Programming Contest 2022, including details about the system's implementation, the technologies and methodologies used, and also discuss the team's results.

Keywords: Artificial Intelligence · Multi-Agent Systems · Agent-Oriented Programming Languages · Multi-Agent Programming Contest

1 Introduction

The multi-agent systems paradigm emphasises the thinking of systems as multiple intelligent entities. This paradigm is becoming very popular, not only because of the rise of the use of artificial intelligence techniques but also because it naturally meets the current demand to design and implement distributed intelligent systems such as smart homes, smart cities, and personal assistants, for instance, also facilitating the integration between those systems. Nowadays, we are able to argue that multi-agent systems are one of the most powerful paradigms for implementing complex distributed systems powered by artificial intelligence techniques [11], for example, incorporating argumentation-based reasoning and communication [22,24], modelling and reasoning about uncertain information and theory of mind [27,31], and many other techniques.

T. Ahlbrecht et al. (Eds.): MAPC 2022, LNAI 13997, pp. 165–194, 2023.
https://doi.org/10.1007/978-3-031-38712-8_7

Multi-agent systems are built upon core concepts such as distribution, reactivity, and individual rationality. To support the development of multi-agent systems, a large number of tools have been developed, such as agent-oriented programming languages and methodologies [4]. Consequently, practical applications of multi-agent technologies have become a reality, many of them solving complex and distributed problems [10,23,32,33]. In addition, it also allows the execution of various tasks and makes it possible the integration with various technologies, for example, chatbot technologies [8,9].

The Multi-Agent Programming Contest (MAPC) was created with the aim of exploring the potential of multi-agent systems, providing challenging scenarios to explore agent-oriented programming languages, platforms and methodologies for developing multi-agent systems. Also, MAPC provides reference problems in which different researchers can compare their results, such as benchmarks. MAPC 2022 brought the Agents Assemble III scenario, including a normative system, the idea of agents roles, and complex tasks agents should exhibit attitudes of collaboration and coordination in order to score points. In this paper, we describe the solution proposed by the LI(A)RA team for the MAPC 2022 scenario. LI(A)RA is a project, created in 2022, for teaching agent technologies for undergraduate students at the Federal University of Santa Catarina. The project also aims to research the software engineering process behind participating in the contest. The proposed solution was implemented using Jason Platform [5], focusing on (i) a purely declarative implementation, which aligns with the purpose of the original language, and (ii) distributed mechanisms for coordination and collaboration.

This paper is organised as follows. First, in Sect. 2 we describe the Agents Assemble III scenario used during the Multi-Agent Programming Contest 2022, pointing out the differences between this year's scenario and the previous ones, also highlighting the main challenges in this new scenario according to our point of view. In Sect. 3, we describe the implementation of LI(A)RA's solution for the MAPC 2022 scenario, including the methodology applied during development and the agents' strategies implemented according to different aspects of the Agents Assemble III scenario, for example, movement strategies, synchronisation strategies, among others. In Sect. 4, we describe our results in the MAPC 2022 contest. Finally, in Sect. 5, we present our conclusions, pointing out some future directions our team intend to adopt.

2   The Agents Assemble III Scenario

In 2022, the Multi-Agent Programming Contest brought a revision from the scenario presented in the previous MAPC 2019[1] and 2020/2021[2], named the Agents Assemble III. The main difference regarding the previous year's scenario was: (i) considering roles for agents and establishing different capabilities for agents according to their roles. Also introducing role zones, which are places

---

[1] https://multiagentcontest.org/2019/.
[2] https://multiagentcontest.org/2020/.

Fig. 1. Example of the Agent Assemble World. (Color figure online)

in the environment agent could adopt and change roles; and (ii) a normative system in which agents would be punished according to they violate the norms established during the simulation.

In the Agents Assemble III scenario, agents are situated in a grid world environment with limited local vision, and they are required to organise and coordinate themselves to assemble and deliver complex structures made of blocks, which are called "tasks". In Fig. 1, we can observe an example of an instance of the Agents Assemble III World, in which we are able to observe the following aspects:

1. blue numbered small squares and green numbered small lozenges represent agents, in which agents with the same colour and format are from the same team. All matches are between two teams, which is why there are two teams[3] in the grid world in Fig. 1.
2. large blue and red translucent lozenges represent role and goal zones, respectively. Role zones (large blue translucent lozenges) are regions in which an agent is able to change its role, choosing among the different roles available during a particular match, which will enable it to execute particular actions during the simulation. Goal zones (large red translucent lozenges) are regions in which agents are able to deliver tasks. Agents are required to be at a goal zone in order to deliver tasks, also respecting the specificity of each task (form of the structure made of blocks, relative position of the agent delivering the tasks, etc.).

---

[3] Future versions of the contest may allow matches among more than 2 teams.

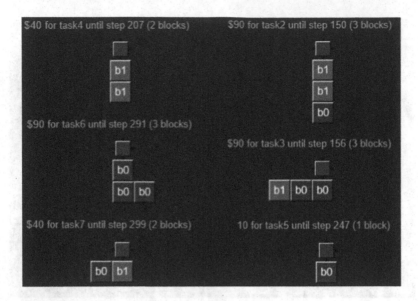

Fig. 2. Examples of Tasks.

3. black blocks are obstacles that agents cannot go through, they can deviate or clear[4] obstacles in order to move through the grid. For example, blue agent number 15 (at the bottom left in Fig. 1) is clearing an obstacle that was north of it (clear actions plot red outline lozenge in the environment).
4. blocks with different shades of yellow represent the dispensers. Dispensers can be used by agents to request blocks. When an agent requests a block from a dispenser, the dispenser generates a block over the dispenser, and the block becomes available to agents to attach it. Dispensers only generate blocks of their type, for example, a dispenser of the type "b1" only generates blocks of the type "b1". Figure 1 shows two different dispensers, one of the type "b1" and one of the type "b0".
5. finally, we also are able to observe, in Fig. 1, agent 19's range of vision, highlighted by the lighter region around it. Agents have a limited local vision, and an agent is able to observe only those things within its range of vision. For example, agent 19 is perceiving the adversary agent 19, the goal zone, and obstacles within its range of vision.

There are many challenges associated with the MAPC 2022 scenario, some of them already known from previous contests, and new challenges consequence of the addition of roles and normative specifications. Below we emphasise the most challenging aspects of the MAPC 2022 scenario according to our point of view.

- **The absence of absolute position:** one of the most challenging aspects of the MAPC 2022 (also 2019 and 2020/2021) scenario is the absence of abso-

---

[4] Clear actions are only available for some roles agents can adopt during the simulation.

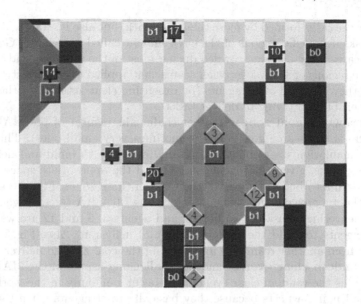

Fig. 3. Example of a Crowded Goal Zone.

lute position. It means, all agents start in a different position on the computational grid which implements the environment, and all of them understand they are at the coordinates $x = 0$ and $y = 0$ at the beginning of the match. Consequently, when agents reach important regions of the world (for example, goal zones and dispensers), the perspective of those things' position is different from each other. For example, the dispenser "b1" in Fig. 1 is at `position(3,-12)` ($x = 3$ and $y = -12$) for blue agent 19, and at `position(-7,-1)` for the blue agent 4 (considering that Fig. 1 shows the configuration of the match at the start point, in which agents understand they are at the coordinates $x = 0$ and $y = 0$).

- **The uncertainty of success when executing actions:** another challenging aspect of the MAPC 2022 scenario is that agents randomly fail to execute their actions. It means, an agent only knows if its actions had the expected result after executing the actions and perceiving its success during the next step of the environment simulation. For example, when an agent executes the action to move north, it is expected the agent to leave its current position, let's say `position(10,10)`, and ends at the north of it, i.e., at `position(10,9)`. However, at the current configuration of the scenario, the agent only knows if it actually moved after, when it perceives the next step of the simulation (it requires the agent to perceive if it had succeeded in executing that action), perceiving a change in its position.

- **The complex tasks:** another challenging aspect of the MAPC 2022 scenario are the complex tasks, ranging from task formed by 1 to 4 blocks in different configurations. Figure 2 shows some examples of tasks that appeared during a match. Not only do agents need to cooperate and coordinate to build and

deliver the tasks formed by more than one block, but also it requires delivering
the tasks in specific regions of the environment called goal zones. Goal zones
were scarce, they became crowded during most of the matches, and they also
became regions of interest by other teams that applied aggressive strategies in
which they attacked other agents (by executing clear actions at other agents
and their blocks) trying to deliver tasks.

- **The crowded goal zones:** another challenging aspect of the MAPC 2022
  scenario is the scarce goal zones (sometimes very small ones). This aspect
  of the simulation was problematic in finding space to build and deliver the
  complex tasks, given that agents should find the appropriate space between
  other agents to build and deliver the task on those zones. Figure 3 shows an
  example of a crowded goal zone, in which the LI(A)RA (green) agents 4 and
  2 are delivering a task of two blocks, and agents 3, 9 and 12 are waiting for
  other agents to build the complex task and deliver it. Also, Fig. 3 shows 4
  agents from another team also approaching the goal zone to deliver tasks.
- **The random clear events:** another challenging aspect of the MAPC 2022
  scenario is the random clear events that occur randomly in the world. They
  are challenging aspects because they basically reset agents when they occur
  over agents, taking the energy from the agents and (mostly of the time)
  destroying the blocks they were carrying.
- **Selecting one action by step:** an aspect of the MAPC 2022 scenario that
  changes how to implement the system is that agents are able to execute only
  one action by step of the simulation, then, if the simulation has 600 steps,
  agents will execute at most 600 actions during the simulation. While it makes
  the matches fair in the sense all agents from all teams will execute at most
  the same number of actions, it also changes how we implement agents, being
  necessary to think about a strategy in which agents will choose one action
  for each step, sending the action at the correct time, i.e., sending their 30th
  action between the 30th and 31st step of the simulation.

3 Implementation

3.1 Technology

To implement the LI(A)RA team's solution for the Multi-Agent Programming
Contest 2022, we have used the Jason platform [5]. Jason extends the AgentS-
peak(L), an abstract logic-based agent-oriented programming language introduced by Rao [30], which is one of the best-known languages inspired by the
BDI (*Beliefs-Desires-Intentions*) architecture [6], one of the most studied architectures for cognitive agents. Also, Jason is part of the JaCaMo Framework [3],
which allows us to implement complex multi-agent systems encompassing all
dimensions necessary, named agents, environment, and organisation.

In Jason, besides agents are implemented based on the BDI architecture [6],
they also are defined with a plan library that provides the know-how for agents,
inspired by the procedural reasoning system (PRS) [14], providing an architecture that combines practical reasoning and planning, in which agents are able

to handle challenging tasks in a dynamic environment. The agents' knowledge is defined through beliefs and, as usual, the knowledge available for agents may not necessarily be complete or accurate, considering the environment may be large and may change the agent has not perceived.

In Jason, beliefs and goals are represented by predicates and a set of n terms of first-order logic, as follows:

```
predicate(term_1,term_2, ..., term_n)
```

For example, the triggering event `role(worker)` is composed of the predicate 'role' and the term 'worker', meaning the agent has perceived it is playing a role named worker.

Furthermore, predicates can be annotated with meta-information related to that information, as introduced in [5] also used by others [16,17,21]. The syntax for annotated predicates is as follows:

```
predicate(term_1,term_2, ..., term_n)[ann_1,ann_2,...,ann_n]
```

where each `ann_i` represents the SPSVERBc5th annotation for that particular predicate, with the following syntax:

```
functor(term'_1,term'_2, ..., term'_n)
```

where an atom (called functor) is followed by a number of terms (called arguments). This extension of the language provides more expressiveness, as pointed out by [21] in the context of argumentation. A common meta-information originally used in Jason Platform [5] is the source of information, for example:

```
likes(john,icecream)[source(mary)]
```

described that `mary` has said that `john` likes ice cream, i.e., `mary` is the source of the information `likes(john,icecream)`.

In Jason, agents are able to represent the information they believe to be true, for example, `likes(john,icecream)`, and information they believe to be false, for example, `¬likes(john,icecream)`, and, using negation as failure, they are able to query information they have no knowledge about, for example, `not(likes(john,icecream))` and `not(¬likes(john,icecream))`, representing that the agent does not know if `likes(john,icecream)` is true or false.

Plans are composed of a triggering event, a context, and the body of the plan, which represent a recipe (set of ordered actions and sub-goals) to achieve that particular goal. The body of a plan may include updates to the belief base, actions and (sub)goals. Triggering events are used to react to the addition (or deletion) of beliefs or goals. The context establishes the precondition for the plan, defining what must be true in order for the plan to be executed. The following example shows the abstract syntax of Jason plans:

```
triggering_event : context <- body.
```

For example, agents would be able to react to the perception of a role zone, creating a goal to move to that particular role zone using the following plan:

```
+roleZone(X,Y)[source(percept)] :
        not(movintToRoleZone(_,_)) &
        my_expected_role(MyRole) &
        not(role(MyRole))
    <-
        +movingToRoleZone(X,Y);
        !moveTo(X,Y,rolezone).
```

in this particular plan, the context for executing this plan requires that the agent is not moving to any role zone, i.e., not(movintToRoleZone(_,_)), and it is playing a role during the simulation that is different from the expected role it should be playing (given the strategy adopted by our team), i.e., my_expected_role(MyRole) & not(role(MyRole)).

In the agent's plan library, there may be several plans to react to the same triggering event corresponding to a goal, an external event, etc. and they represent choices an agent can make to achieve their goals. While sophisticated plan selection functions can be implemented, originally, in the Jason Platform, plans are analysed using the order they have been declared in the plan library of an agent, similar to architecture with vertically layered priorities [18].

For example, the piece of code below contains 4 plans that implement 4 different ways an agent may achieve the goal !moveTo(X,Y), implementing a very simple movement strategy that could be used in MAPC 2022 scenario. When an agent creates a goal, for example, !moveTo(10,20), it will verify which plans could be used to achieve that particular goal, i.e., which plans apply at that current moment of its execution. Then, the agent will use the first plan which applies to try to achieve its goal. Considering a particular scenario in which the agent is at position(5,10), then there are two plans the agent could use to achieve the goal moveTo(10,20), named plan1 and plan3. However, considering the original implementation for the plan selection, the agent will prioritise always horizontal movement over vertical movement, i.e., going east first, executing the action move(e), until reaching position(10,10), then the first plan will not be applicable anymore, and the only applicable plan will be the plan3, when the agent will go south, executing the action move(s), until reaching the position position(10,20), achieving its goal.

This plan selection mechanism specifies a very important aspect of the technology, which must be considered in order to adequately implement strategies. For example, the example below shows a very simple movement strategy, and it could implement a different movement strategy by just reordering plans 3 and 4 first, prioritising vertical movement over horizontal ones.

```
+!moveTo(X,Y): position(XMy,YMy) & XMy < X <- move(e). //plan1
+!moveTo(X,Y): position(XMy,YMy) & XMy > X <- move(w). //plan2
+!moveTo(X,Y): position(XMy,YMy) & YMy < Y <- move(s). //plan3
+!moveTo(X,Y): position(XMy,YMy) & YMy > Y <- move(n). //plan4
```

Another important aspect of a multi-agent system is communication. In Jason platform, agents are able to communicate using already implemented internal actions with the following format:

.send(receiver,performative,content)

in which receiver is the agent (or set of agents) that will receive that particular message, performative indicates the performative used in that particular message, which will provide the intention behind that communication, providing meaning for that communication together with the content of that message. For example, an agent named ag_11 is able to tell other agents about a role zone it found during its execution using the following message:

.send([ag_1,ag_2,ag_3],tell,roleZone(10,20))

in which the agent sends a message to agents ag_1,ag_2 and ag_3, telling that it has found a role zone at coordinate (10,20), i.e., roleZone(10,20). All agents will receive that information and they will believe that roleZone(10,20)[source(ag_11)]. Although Jason platform provides a set of predefined performatives with well-defined semantics [35] based on the KQML [12], other performatives can be easily added, extending those already available, for example, to allow sophisticated dialogues based on argumentation [25,26,28,29].

Furthermore, an agent program can be implemented in different modules/files and integrated into a single agent, each module providing part of its knowledge and capabilities [15,20], i.e., part of its beliefs and plans, respectively. Although there are many sophisticated manners to approach modules of agent programs, as pointed out by [20], we use a very simple approach in which agent knowledge and plans can be implemented in different files and after that integrated into an agent program. For example, imagine we implemented strategies for moving, attacking, and exploring the MAPC scenario in different files named: move.asl, attack.asl and explore.asl. Then, in order to have an agent that integrates the strategies for moving[5] and exploring, we only need to include both files as part of the agent program as follows:

```
{ include("move.asl")    }
{ include("explore.asl") }
```

In case we would have an agent that integrates the strategies for exploring and attacking, we would include the correspondents files as part of the agent program as follow:

```
{ include("explore.asl") }
{ include("attack.asl")  }
```

---

[5] Note that we have multiples implementations for the movement strategies, in which an agent is able to create a goal to move to a specific location, !moveTo(10, 20), but also referring what it is expected to find there if necessary, for example, a role zone !moveTo(10, 20, rolezone).

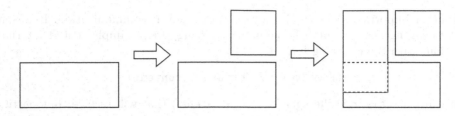

Fig. 4. The Incremental Approach.

3.2 Methodology

The multi-agent system was implemented using an *incremental approach*. Incremental approaches, also called *evolutionary approaches*, are widely acknowledged in the literature and they arise from the need for flexibility in the process of development. The incremental approach consists of incremental developments, where parts of the software are postponed in order to produce some useful set of functions earlier in the development project [7]. The basic idea in the incremental approach is to expand increments of an operational software product [2]. That means, each stage of development, is not intended to produce a complete system, but to produce multiple versions of the system, in which each new version adds new functionalities. Figure 4 shows a generic representation for the incremental approach, in which new "*modules*" are added to the system.

There are many specific models that may be accommodated under the incremental approach. One of the most interesting is the *Extreme Programming* (XP) [1], which normally is used in projects with uncertainty or changing requirements, and it is an example of *agile approaches* [13], which aim at supporting changes and rapid feedback during software development.

We found this approach very adequate for our team, given the technology used, as described in Sect. 3.1, and the methodology used to implement our solution, in which all members implemented parts of the system, aligning the project during a weekly meeting. Also, XP requires comprehensive documentation, which was a goal for our team.

It is important to note that an incremental approach allows us to think about the system in a more modular way, in which modules of behaviour/capabilities can be implemented and tested, individually and integrated. In particular, we have implemented the modules presented in Table 1, implementing different strategies used during the MAPC 2022, which we will discuss in the next section.

A challenge for an incremental and modular approach to development is the documentation and standardisation of code. While the documentation was basically made towards commentating on the code, all developers shared a table of predicates used during implementation, presented in Tables 4, 5, and 6. One of the benefits of using a declarative programming language is that the code provides most of the semantics necessary to understand it, but even though, the developers have shared those tables containing a short description of all predicates used in the agents' code.

Table 1. Modules Implemented.

Module Name	Description
"move.asl"	movement strategies
"memory_updates.asl"	memory update strategies
"strategy.asl"	decision-making strategies
"collect_blocks.asl"	strategies for collecting blocks
"adopt_role.asl"	strategies for adopting roles
"exploration.asl"	exploration strategies
"complete_task.asl"	strategies for completing tasks
"synchronism.asl"	strategies for synchronising agents
"task_delivery_organization.asl"	strategy for task organisation
"connect_and_deliver.asl"	strategies for connecting and delivering tasks
"after_event.asl"	strategies for dealing with effects caused by events
"change_round.asl"	strategies for changing the round

This approach of sharing the used predicates also is important when programming different modules, even from the perspective of a single developer, because predicates declared, added, or defined in a particular module may be necessary for other modules. For example, the module named "**strategy**" uses predicates declared all over the other modules, most of them basically keeping the information of what that particular agent is doing in that particular step of the simulation, corresponding to the general strategy for our agents we will describe in the next section.

3.3   Strategies

An important aspect of our implementation, which also defines most of how we implemented our strategies, is that all agents are instances of the same code. On the one hand, this aspect of the implementation makes it more difficult to think of a solution. On the other hand, it explores the implementation of agents that show characteristics of adaptability, autonomy, and flexibility. Also, it is aligned with the characteristics of the MAPC 2022 environment, in which agents are able to execute one action by step of the simulation, deciding which action to execute based on the information they perceived during the previous steps. That means agents will execute a new action towards reacting to the perception of a new step in the simulation, deciding what to do based on their own execution (considering all information it acquires) during the match.

Considering both aspects of the scenario and implementation, we adopt a strategy in which agents react to the perception of each step of the simulation than reasoning about what they should do based on the current state of the environment around each agent and its previous actions and perceptions, memorising what they are doing at that particular step, and then executing the selected action in the environment. When they perceive the next step of the simulation, they remember what they were doing in the previous step, reasoning about the next action to execute according to that information.

In our strategy, agents may reach a state in which they remember they are doing concurrent activities, for example, the activities of *exploring* and *helping*, indicating they remember to be *exploring* the environment and also *helping* other agents to complete a task in the previous steps of the simulation. To deal with concurrent goals, we implemented a plan library with priorities based on the memory of agents. That means, for example, agents should always prioritise finishing a task in which they are helping other agents than exploring. The piece of code below shows an example of how this strategy is implemented:

```
+!step(S): helping(A,T,B,X1,Y1,X2,Y2,P) <- ....   //priority 1
+!step(S): collectingBlocks(X,Y,P)       <- ....   //priority 2
              .
              .
+!step(S): exploring  <- ....                      //priority n
```

In the example above, we show part of the agents' plan library with n plans, in which the agent will prefer to select plan 1 than plan 2 (if plan 1's context applies). In this example, agents prioritise *helping* other agents than collecting blocks, and *exploring* has the lower priority in the example above.

In the MAPC 2022 scenario, there is information that is worth agents remembering and information that we believed not to be worth agents remembering, given the dynamics of the environment. For example, in our implementation, agents remember the position of important components, such as role zones, goal zones, and dispensers. Even though the goal zones disappeared eventually, they were less dynamic than obstacles and blocks. We choose to implement agents that will not remember the position of those things with a higher probability of disappearing or changing position. Further, it is the memory (its beliefs) that make agents, which are all instances of the same code, show different behaviour. This is because those memories will enable the context of other plans, with higher priority, in the agent plan library.

For example, all agents start with the goal of finding a role zone to change their roles according to our strategy, which will enable them to execute a set of predefined actions in the environment of the contest. When an agent knows the position of a role zone, it will move towards that zone, otherwise, it will explore the environment to find a role zone, and then move towards the zone to change its role. The piece of code below shows an example of this strategy:

```
//plan1
+!step(S): my_role(R) & not(role(R)) & roleZone(X,Y)[source(memory)]
       <- !moveTo(X,Y).

//plan2
+!step(S): my_role(R) & not(role(R))  <- !explore.
```

In the example above, first, the agent tries to execute the plan1, but if it does not know the position of a role zone then that plan does not apply, i.e., it does not have any valid unification for `roleZone(X,Y)[source(memory)]`. In the case `plan1` does not apply, the agent tries to execute the `plan2` (if that context applies), in which the agent creates a goal for exploring the environment, i.e., `!explore`. When that agent finds a roles zone, exploring the environment, it will memorise the information of the coordinates of the role zone it found, i.e., `roleZone(X,Y)[source(memory)]`, then the context of the `plan1` will apply, and then the agent will select that plan during the next step of the simulation, starting to move towards that role zone using that plan, i.e., creating the goal `!moveTo(X,Y)` in which X and Y are the coordinates to the role zone.

A strategy for implementing the proposed solution, adopted by our team, was implementing plans from lower priority to higher priority, in which higher priority plans have a dependence on beliefs (memories of what the agent is currently doing) achieved by the complete execution of lower priority plans. That means the context of plans with higher priority depends on the memories that only will be obtained during the execution of plans with lower priority. In the example above, the memory `roleZone(X,Y)[source(memory)]` will be obtained by executing the `plan2`, in particular, the plan to achieve the sub-goal `!explore`. Then, after knowing that information, the context of `plan1` will apply and that will be the selected plan in the next step of the simulation, given it has priority over the `plan2`.

Using this development strategy based on the priority of plans, we implemented specific strategies for different activities agents should execute during the matches, among them: **movement and exploration strategies** and a **strategy for dealing with norms**, a **synchronisation strategy based on encounters**, a **strategy for sharing information**, a **strategy for creating groups of agents**, and a **strategy for delivering tasks**. We discuss them below.

Movement and Exploration Strategies. During some test matches, we observed that obstacles, in general, were very disturbing for agents trying to move. Also, the proportion of obstacles increased according to the simulation changed from one round to another. Considering that obstacles should be disturbing for agents from other teams too, we focused on implementing a movement strategy that cleared as less obstacles as possible (different from most of the other teams, from this and previous years of the contest), keeping the obstacles on the grid world to disturb other agents trying to move on the environment.

The first aspect of the movement strategy implemented was the **exploration**, in which agents should explore the environment until being able to do something useful for the team, for example, carrying blocks and helping others to build complex tasks. At the beginning of a match, agents start to explore a particular direction, for example, north – `exploring(n)` – and, aiming to avoid clearing obstacles, they deviate obstacles going to side directions prioritising clockwise, i.e., in case an agent is exploring to the north and there is an obstacle at the north of agent, but there is no obstacle at east, then it would go east until be able to go north again. In case there is an obstacle at the north and east of the agent, then it goes west (only if didn't come from that direction in the previous step of the simulation). Otherwise, when the agent is blocked by obstacles at the north, east, and west, then the agent executes the clear action targeting the obstacles in the north, allowing it to move to the north. This exploration strategy avoids clearing so many obstacles while also avoids agents to move in circles (or even being trapped at some small portion of the grid world).

A complexity to movement strategies, in the scenario of MAPC 2022, is related to agents moving while carrying blocks. As a coherent simulation, the scenario establishes that obstacles block agents either for obstructing the agent trying to move directly or for obstructing blocks attached to agents trying to move. That means, when agents are moving with blocks attached to them, they have to worry about obstacles obstructing not only their path but also the blocks' path to which they are attached. For example, if the agent has a block attached to the east of it, and the agent is trying to move north, then the agent needs a clear path both north of it and north of the block. However, if the agent has a block attached south of it, and it is trying to move north, then the agent does not need to worry about obstacles blocking the block.

Considering the complexity of moving with blocks, our team thought about two strategies (i) first, we believe to be the more common, is to use the same strategy for exploration, but also clearing obstacles obstructing blocks attached to the agent in order to move; and (ii) second, which we end using, is to rotate the block attached to the agent to the opposite direction the agent is moving, i.e., if the agent is moving north, it rotates the block to the south. The second alternative was more attractive to our team because it aligns with our strategy of clearing fewer obstacles as possible. Also, this strategy of moving with blocks attached to the agent in the opposite direction it is moving also become a very elegant **movement strategy**. Figure 5 shows an example of an agent using this strategy, in which agent 2 approached the dispenser b1, collected a block and it is moving away without clearing many obstacles. It makes hard, for other agents, to approach the dispenser than when the agents clear all obstacles on the way, because the dispenser will still be surrounded by obstacles.

Strategies for Dealing with Norms. Analysing the phenoms related to norms, we observed that by limiting agents to carry at most 1 block, we avoid most of the penalties applied when breaking the norms. Also, this strategy aligns with the movement strategy that works only for agents carrying a unique block.

Synchronisation Strategy Based on Encounters. An important aspect for agents to work together in the scenario proposed in the MAPC 2022 was the need for synchronisation of agents, regarding their coordinates. This issue comes from the characteristic of the scenario in which there is no absolute position in the grid world from the perspective of agents. That means, agents start the simulation at different positions on the grid and each agent believes it started at position zero – position(0,0). That means, when agents move and find important elements on the grid, for example, dispensers of blocks, they will have

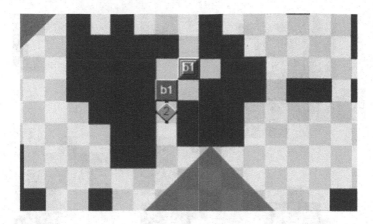

Fig. 5. Example of movement clearing few obstacles to collect a block.

a different perspective of the position of those elements. In order to coordinate tasks, cooperate and share information it was necessary to implement a strategy for synchronisation.

There would be centralised solutions for synchronisation, but in order to keep our implementation completely distributed, we implement a synchronisation strategy focusing on encounters. That means, when agents encounter each other in the grid world, they are able to communicate and synchronise their relative positions, creating filters for the position of those teammates they encountered during a match. We also used this idea of encounter to create groups of agents, which are dynamic and the process depends on these encounters.

For example, in Fig. 1, agents 3 and 4 are inside each other range of vision, which means they can perceive each other. This is what we call an encounter – when both agents are inside each other range of vision.

The synchronisation strategy occurs as follows: when an agent perceives another agent inside its range of vision, it executes a broadcast message, informing it can perceive the teammate at the coordinates (XMate,YMate) regarding its current position (XMy,YMy) during the step S of the simulation, also keeping a believe found_mate(XMate,YMate,XMy,YMy,S) with that information. At the next step of the simulation, S+1, the agent verifies if there is any match from the broadcasts it receives from other agents and those teammates found and stored by itself, comparing the relative position as follows:

```
found_mate(XO,YO,XOA,YOA,S)[source(TeamMate)] &
found_mate(XF,YF,XMA,YMA,S)[source(memory)] &
((XF+XO) == 0 & (YF+YO) == 0)
```

in which XO, YO, XF and YF are the position they found each other, thus if the difference between those values is equal to zero, that means the agent TeamMate is the same agent found by it at that step of the simulation. By understanding whom it has found, the agent is able to create a filter using the following equation:

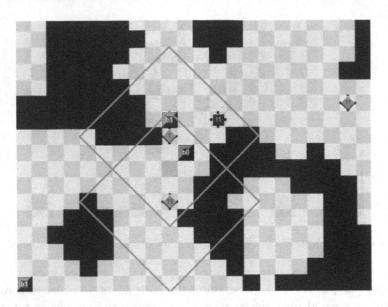

Fig. 6. Example of an encounter.

```
mate_filter(TeamMate,((XF+XMA)-XOA),((YF+YMA)-YOA))[source(memory)].
```

in which it calculates the relative position of the other agent regarding its position.

Note that there are two different pieces of information they are able to infer from this communication process: (i) when agents enter inside the range of vision of each other, they only perceive there is another agent from the same team inside their range of vision. Thus, they communicate the relative position they found the teammate, using that information to understand which agent they have found (both agents execute the same process and they are able to understand they found each other); and (ii) when agents understand they found each other, they are able to create the filter for the relative position of the teammate, using that filter always it is necessary, for example, translating the coordinates of information received from teammates to its relative position using the filter. Figure 6 shows an example of agents 1 and 19 encountering each other, in which the green lozenges are their range of vision.

Strategy for Sharing Information. After creating filters for other agents' coordinates, agents are able to share information regarding the position of important elements. We implement a strategy in which agents share information about the coordinates of dispensers, goal zones, and role zones. Other elements we identify to be very dynamic, and it would not be worthy to share that information, for example, obstacles that could easily be cleared by other agents (from the same team or from the other team).

The implemented strategy for sharing information is as follows: (i) when an agent finds an element it is worthy to share its coordinates, for example, a dispenser, it sends to all agents it knows a filter the position of that element, already applying the filter, translating the coordinates to the relative position of the receiver of that message, also sending the list of agents it is sharing the information; (ii) when an agent receives a message sharing the information of an element from the grid world, with a list of other receivers, it stores the information in its belief base, and it verifies which other agents (who are not in the list) it knows the filter (those it could also share the information and did not receive yet), then it sends the coordinates of that element applying the filter for each receiver, but now without a list of receivers; (iii) when an agent receives a message sharing the information of an element from the grid world, but without the list of other receivers, it only stores that information in its belief base.

That means agents propagate information on two levels. The first level is when an agent shares information about a relevant element itself found in the grid world, and the second level is when agents share information that was shared by agents who found those relevant elements in the grid world. This strategy was used considering the strategy for creating groups of agents we will discuss next, in which agents only share information with groups directly connected by members.

Strategy for Creating Groups of Agents. We create a strategy in which agents form groups dynamically, depending on the encounters that occurs during each match. The basic idea is that agents which encounter each other will belong to an implicit group, and they are able to collaborate. An agent is able to belong to more than one implicit group of agents, for example, imagine that agent ag1 encounters agents ag2, ag3, ag4 and ag5, then ag1 is able to collaborate with each of those agents individually and request collaboration from all of them. However, ag2 only will be in the same implicit group of agent ag3 if it encountered ag3 during the match.

We choose to implement this strategy for creating implicit groups of agents because of other decisions we made regarding other strategies, for example, focusing only on delivering small tasks (with less than 3 blocks). Thus fewer agents are required to deliver a task, and we realised that the encounters that occurred during the matches were enough to form groups large enough to deliver those tasks.

Strategy for Delivering Tasks. We implemented a relatively simple task delivery strategy. When an agent is able to contribute to completing a new task, it queries all agents belonging to its implicit group, asking the distance required to them to help deliver the task in a particular goal zone, according to the protocol[6] shown in Fig. 7. Then, when other agents are able to help (they are not helping another agent with another task), they answer the query informing the distance needed to reach the goal zone with the necessary block. Then, the

---

[6] The inspiration for this protocol comes from the Contract Net Protocol [34].

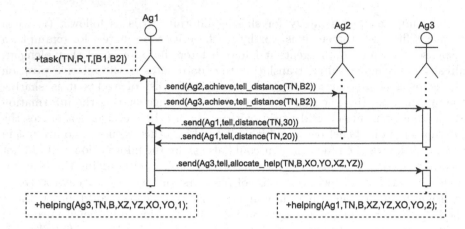

Fig. 7. Allocation Help Protocol.

agent which requested help chooses the close agent to help it, informing the winning agent, and they start moving towards the goal zone to deliver the task.

Figure 8 shows an example in which agent 7 will deliver the task2 (from the task border at left of the figure) which is worth $40. Note that tasks also have the requirement of a specific position for the agent that will deliver the task, in the case of task2, it requires the agent to be north of the block b0. Also, we are able to observe in Fig. 8, agent 16 helping to build that task, positioning the block b1 according to the task2 requirement. Also, Fig. 3 shows agent 4 delivering the task3 with help of agent 2.

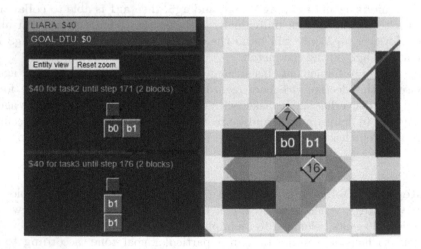

Fig. 8. Example of a task being delivered.

3.4   Tests

The test strategy was based on using different combinations for the multiple modules described in Sect. 3.2, executing the system, and observing the agents' behaviour and the score agents made during different simulations. During tests, we fixed some issues related to scenarios/situations we did not predict during the implementation. One of the issues fixed after executing some tests was related to strategies for avoiding and deviating from other agents, mainly in the crowded goal zones. Also, we realised that for some goal zones, agents which were not synchronised could try to deliver tasks at the same position, thus we implemented a strategy in which agents wait in a safe zone until their teammate approach to deliver the task they are helping.

4   Results

In the MAPC 2022, the LI(A)RA team ends in 4th place, tied with the GOAL-DTU team. During the contest, we won one round against the FIT BUT team, 2 rounds against the GOAL-DTU team (winning that match), and lose all rounds against GOALdigger and MMD. Our total score was 9 points (regarding the 3 rounds our implementation won). Table 2 shows the final scores for all teams.

Table 2. Final Scores.

Place	Team	Score
1	MMD	30
2	GOALdigger	22
3	FIT BUT	19
4	GOAL-DTU	9
4	LI(A)RA	9

Analysing the matches, our multi-agent system did not score many points against teams with more aggressive adversarial attitudes, which means, teams that implemented strategies for attacking agents from other teams. These attitudes were unexpected, given there is no history of this kind of attitude from other teams in the past, although the scenario is very favourable for this kind of attitude, in which agents can clear other agents taking their energy. Thus, competing with teams exhibiting these attitudes and having not expected such attitudes, our multi-agent system was vulnerable to other teams' attacks.

Attacking other agents during the match has shown to be a very interesting strategy, keeping agents responsible to attack others close to goal zones, in which they could not only take the energy of other agents but also destroy their blocks, which required the agents of other teams to search for blocks again. We intend to explore these attitudes in future participation in the MAPC.

Table 3 shows some estimated metrics about the teams' implementations collected by the organisers of MAPC 2022 and shared with all teams. In Table 3 is possible to note that: (i) our team had a larger number of developers, which we consider a challenge for this kind of development; (ii) our multi-agent system was developed in fewer hours than most of the other teams, we are the second team which expended fewer hours implementing the system, but GOAL-DTU has already participated in the previous year, then those metrics may be related only to increments made for this year scenario, while we started our implementation this year; (iii) our implementation is the shorter on; however, it is important to mention that it is difficult to count lines of code of different programming languages fairly; and (iv) we are the only team which use Jason platform.

Table 3. Estimated metrics.

Team	Members	Time	Lines of code	Platform	2020(-)
FIT BUT	3	240 h	12000	JAVA(+JADE)	Yes
GOAL-DTU	3	**30 h**	2000	GOAL	Yes
GOALdigger	4	1200 h	10000	GOAL	No
LI(A)RA	**5**	80 h + **40 h**	**1100**	**Jason**	No
MMD	2	896 h	5407	Python	No

5   Conclusion

In this paper, we described the LI(A)RA team's implementation for the MAPC 2022 scenario called Agents Assemble III. Besides summarising the main challenges related to the MAPC 2022 scenario from our perspective, we focused on: (i) describing the technology used to implement our multi-agent system; (ii) detailing the methodology used by our team to implement the multi-agent system, which was a modular and incremental approach; and (iii) describing the strategies we implemented for agents, according to different activities they could execute in the MAPC 2022 scenario.

There were very interesting behaviours that could be observed in the MAPC 2002 contest from other teams, for example, more competitive attitudes in the sense of attacking agents from other teams with the clear events, which surprised our team. We did not implement any strategy for agents to defend themselves from attacks, and we believe those attitudes were decisive in the final scores. Also, we realised our implementation may be shorter than all others, also we dedicate considerably less time to planning and implementing the multi-agent system than the teams with higher scores. Finally, we also did not finish the implementation of all modules we intended during the planning phase, which also may have compromised our scores.

We intend to participate next year, starting the planning phase early, dedicating more time to the implementation phase, also exploring approaches for creating modules of agent-oriented programs already developed over the Jason Platform, as the approach presented in [19].

Table 4. Predicates used in the implementation.

Predicate	Meaning
my_role(Role)	a belief describing the role that particular agent should adopt during the match. The variable Role will unify with the name of the role that agent will adopt during the match, for example, the role worker, i.e., my_role(worker)
maxBlocks(X)	it stores the information of the max number of blocks agents will carry during the matches, X will unify with such max number of blocks. Different agents may be able to carry different numbers of blocks according to the strategies developed
goingDirection(X)	it represents a memory of which direction an agent is going, for example, goingDirection(n) indicating the agent is going north
role(X)	it describes the role of a particular agent during a match
position(X,Y)	it describes the current agent position, it is also an agent memory that holds updated, considering there is no absolute position in the MAPC's scenarios
attached(X,Y)	it describes that there is something attacked to an agent at coordinates X and Y
lastActionResult(X)	it describes the result of the last action executed by that agent
lastAction(T)	it describes the last action executed by that agent
lastActionParams(L)	it describes the parameters of the last action executed by that agent
team(T)	it describes the team of the agent
collectingBlocks	it represents a memory that the agent is collecting blocks
carryingMaxBlocks	it represents a memory that the agent is carrying the max of blocks it is capable to carry
roleAbleBlocks	it represents that particular agent is able to carry blocks, i.e., it plays a role able to collect and carry blocks
carryingBlock	it represents a memory that the agent is carrying blocks
has_block(T)	it represents a memory that agent has (it is carrying) a block of the type T
movingToDispenser(X,Y,T)	it represents the memory that the agent is moving to a dispenser at coordinates X and Y, and this dispenser has blocks of the type T

Table 5. Predicates used in the implementation.

Predicate	Meaning
movingToRoleZone(X,Y)	it represents a memory that the agent is moving to a role zone. X and Y are the coordinates of a role zone the agent is currently moving to it, e.g., movingToRoleZone(-20,35)
movingToGoalZone(X,Y)	it represents a memory that the agent is moving to a goal zone; (X,Y) is the goal zone coordinate the agent is currently moving to it, e.g., movingToGoalZone(10,25)
obstacle_at(X,Y)	an inference that represents obstacles inside the agent's field of view
obstacle_cannot_clear_at(X, Y)	an inference that represents obstacles that cannot be cleared inside the agent's field of view
collectingBlocks(X,Y,T)	it represents a memory that the agent is collecting blocks from a particular dispenser at coordinates X and Y of the type T
roleZone(X,Y) [source(memory)]	it represents a memory related to the coordinates of a role zone that the agent found during its execution
roleZone(X,Y) [source(percept)]	it represents a perception of a role zone inside the agent's field of view
goalzone(X,Y) [source(memory)]	it represents a memory related to the coordinates of a goal zone that the agent found during its execution
thing(X,Y,dispenser,P) [source(memory)]	it represents a memory related to the coordinates of a dispenser that the agent found during its execution
thing(X,Y,T,P) [source(percept)]	it represents a perception related to things inside the agent's field of view. Things can be dispensers, entities, etc.
closest(goalzone, X, Y)	an inference that allows agents to find the coordinates of the closest goal zone
closest(rolezone, X, Y)	an inference that allows agents to find the coordinates of the closest role zone
closest(dispenser, T, X, Y)	an inference that allows agents to find the coordinates of the closest role zone

Table 6. Predicates used in the implementation.

Predicate	Meaning
task(T,Time,R,E) [source(percept)]	a perception for a task T, in which the agent has available the duration and reward related to that task
norm(N,I,F,R,Number) [source(percept)]	a perception for a norm
cost(Distance,BlockType,TName) [source(TeamMate)]	informs the distance a teammate needs to help to build a particular task, contributing with the block BlockType
allocate_help(T,B,XZ,YZ,XO,YO) [source(TeamMate)]	a belief the agent is trying to allocate a particular agent to help it
mate_filter(TeamMate,XFilter,YFilter)	a filter that allows agents to translate coordinates to the relative coordinates of other agents
requested_collaboration(T,XZ,YZ,XO,YO,B)	a belief for all requested collaboration regarding tasks
cannot_deliver(TName)	a belief that the agent cannot deliver a particular task, that means, the agents already reasoned about that task and concluded it cannot deliver it
helping(Ag,T,B,XZ,YZ,XO,YO,N)	a memory that the agent is helping another agent to complete a particular task
found_mate(XMate,YMate,XMy,YMy,S) [source(memory)]	a temporary belief used to synchronisation strategy, keeping the information of a teammate the agent found in the grid world
inform_position(T,XT,YT,Parameters) [list(List),source(TeamMate)]	used for informing the position of elements found by agents in the grid world
waiting_away(Ag,TName,XMy,YMy,S)	a belief that the agent is waiting away from the goal zone
submitting(_,_)	a memory informing the agent is submitting a particular task

16th Multi-agent Programming Contest: All Questions Answered

LI(A)RA Team
Federal University of Santa Catarina

A   Team Overview: Short Answers

A.1   Participants and Their Background

Who is part of your team?

We are 3 undergraduate students, named Marcelo, Michele and Ricardo, from the Computer Engineering program at the Federal University of Santa Catarina (UFSC), under supervision by Professor Alison R. Panisson and PhD Giovani P. Farias. Alison and Giovani have about 10 years of experience in multi-agent systems programming, and the students have bout 1 year of experience. Students are learning about multi-agent systems in undergraduate courses and at the LI(A)RA project, which focuses on teaching multi-agent systems technology.

What was your motivation to participate in the contest?

Giovani and Alison have participated in MAPC in the past, and they always thought about creating a project focusing on teaching multi-agent technologies to students (undergraduate and graduate students), in which they could apply the knowledge from this learning to MAPC problems. One of the more evident motivations is evaluating the multi-agent platforms, languages, and methodologies to develop complex multi-agent systems.

What is the history of your group? (course project, thesis, ...)

LI(A)RA project was created in February of 2022 by Professor Alison at UFSC, in collaboration with the LIA (Academic League of Artificial Intelligence) focused on teaching and exploring multi-agent systems technologies.

What is your field of research? Which work therein is related?

Alison and Giovani are both researchers in the field of multi-agent systems. Alison's main research interest is multi-agent (software agents and humans) communication using argumentation. Giovani's main research interest is multi-task planning.

A.2   Statistics

Did you start your agent team from scratch, or did you build on existing agents (from yourself or another previous participant)?

We started from scratch, about 2 months before the contest.

How much time did you invest in the contest (for programming, organising your group, other)?

Alison has spent about 80 h of programming (during his vacation time), and the group has spent about 40 h discussing strategies, previous papers from MAPC, and organising the infrastructure to develop and test the system.

How was the time (roughly) distributed over the months before the contest?
During about 5 months the group had meetings to talk about strategies and the previous papers from MAPC. Alison implemented the system 2 weeks before the qualification phase.

How many lines of code did you produce for your final agent team?
About 1100 lines of code

A.3 Technology and Techniques

Did you use any of these agent technology/AOSE methods or tools? What were your experiences?

Agent programming languages and/or frameworks?
We used purely Jason.

Methodologies (e.g. Prometheus)?
Usual software engineering methodologies, with incremental and modular components (in the case of Jason agents, an incremental and modular plan library).

Notation (e.g. Agent UML)?
Table of predicates with their meaning and decision-making flowcharts.

Coordination mechanisms (e.g. protocols, games, ...)?
A complete decentralised mechanism, using communication protocols, for synchronising and organisation (similar to Contract Net Protocol).

Other (methods/concepts/tools)?
Although Jason provides a series of structural programming structures, we opted to make the code more declarative as possible, respecting the original declarative programming paradigm of the language.

What hardware did you use during the contest?
To run our agents in the contest, we used an Avell A52 LIV notebook, with the following specifications:

- Processor: Intel Core i5-10300H (4.5 GHz max clock);
- Graphics Card: NVidia GeForce GTX 1650Ti (with 4GB GDDR6 dedicated RAM);
- Memory: 16 GB DDR4 [2 × 8 GB - Dual Channel] @3200 MHz;
- Hard Drive: SSD M.2 NVME 500 GiB;
- Wireless Card: Intel Dual Band Wireless-9462 + Bluetooth 5.1.

A.4 Agent System Details

Would you say your system is decentralised? Why?
Completely decentralised, no central mechanisms were utilised.

Do your agents use the following features: Planning, Learning, Organisations, Norms? If so, please elaborate briefly.
They use simple strategies organised by priority of plans in their plan library, in which plans are enabled by a mechanism of memory.

How do your agents cooperate?

They synchronise when find each other, requesting help to complete tasks when they are able to participate in those tasks, verifying the best match in the group of agents that can help.

Can your agents change their general behaviour during run time? If so, what triggers the changes?

Yes, they use a mechanism of memory to influence their behaviour. All our agents are instances of the same code.

Did you have to make changes to the team (e.g. fix critical bugs) during the contest?

We opted to keep our original code during the contest without any change.

How did you go about debugging your system? What kinds of measures could improve your debugging experience?

Debugging is normally hard. We basically executed the system, analysed the executions, and did inspections on agents and environment state to find and fix bugs.

During the contest, you were not allowed to watch the matches. How did you track what was going on? Was it helpful?

We did not track what was going on (unfortunately we only were able to organise the system execution during the contest)

Did you invest time in making your agents more robust/fault-tolerant? How?

Yes, identifying possible problems during tests.

A.5   Scenario and Strategy

How would you describe your intended agent behaviour? Did the actual behaviour deviate from that?

Agents dynamically adapted their behaviour according to the result of exploration of the environment and the whether or not they were able to meet other agents at the same time.

Why did your team perform as it did? Why did the other teams perform better/worse than you did?

We consider our implementation was about 35–40% complete, which is resulting from the fact the team started to implement the system very late. We consider we had a very good result considering the state of our implementation and the fact it was the first year the team participated in the contest. One behaviour we did not predict from other teams and it make a great difference was agents attacking others to avoid other teams delivering tasks (We believe it was the first time teams used this kind of *aggressive* strategies) and it worked very well for them (against us).

Did you implement any strategy that tries to interfere with your opponents?

We did not. Others who implemented got an advantage in matches, which seems an interesting direction to pursue during the next contests.

How do your agents coordinate assembling and delivering a structure for a task?

They used a coordination protocol, similar to the contract net protocol, in which one agent was responsible to coordinate the delivery.

Which aspect(s) of the scenario did you find particularly challenging?

Using no absolute position for agents was the most challenging aspect.

What would you improve (wrt. your agents) if you wanted to participate in the same contest a week from now (or next year)?

We would finish our implementation, which was about 35–40% complete.

What can be improved regarding the scenario for next year? What would you remove? What would you add?

We found the scenario very challenging. We would suggest 3D (three-dimensional) tasks, and also agents would have the capability to defend themselves from clear events (some agents would have this capability according to their roles).

A.6   And the Moral of it is ...

What did you learn from participating in the contest?

From the technological point of view, we learned that the platform provides enough to implement this kind of complex multi-agent system to solve complex problems (dynamic, non-deterministic, etc.).

From the software engineering point of view, we were able to use an incremental approach to develop "modules of behaviour", all put together when instantiating agents. All our agents had the same code (same implementation to all our agents), which also is a very interesting achievement.

We found it very difficult to coordinate the team during implementation, but it is because we had a very short time to implement our system (about 2 weeks only)

What advice would you give to yourself before the contest/another team wanting to participate in the next?

Start the implementation as soon as you can, but first study the scenario in detail to plan how to implement your multi-agent system. Also, studying the scenario will provide you with a short of strategies (choices) we will eventually make.

Where did you benefit from your chosen programming language, methodology, tools, and algorithms?

Mostly because of our experience with the language, but it also is very elegant (declarative language) and we would like to check if we could keep it as declarative as possible (we succeed in this).

Which problems did you encounter because of your chosen technologies?

Our system become slow with many agents on regular laptops, and we had to execute it from a better machine (but nothing very powerful like a server). I believe other teams had the same problem independent of the technology they used.

Otherwise, the technology fulfilled our needs.

Which aspect of your team cost you the most time?

Testing. Some situations we would like to test cost many simulations in which we had to wait for the specific situation to happen to verify if our implementation was efficient. We did not explore more sophisticated manners to test our implementation (re-configuring the server, for example).

A.7 Looking into the Future

Did the warm-up match help improve your team of agents? How useful do you think it is?

We did not change our code after the warm-up, but it was useful to verify the connection with the server, the performance of our machine executing the system, etc.

What are your thoughts on changing how the contest is run, so that the participants' agents are executed on the same infrastructure by the organisers? What do you see as positive or negative about this approach?

I believe it would be very positive, giving us better benchmarks in which the infrastructure is not a variable anymore.

Do you think a match containing more than two teams should be mandatory?

I believe it depends on the scenario. 2019–2022 scenarios would have more than a team and it would have been fun. For other scenarios, we are not sure if it would make sense.

What else can be improved regarding the MAPC for next year?

We are very excited about next year's contest and we have no more suggestions. Thank you for organising it and keep it up.

References

1. Beck, K.: Extreme Programming Explained: Embrace Change. Addison-Wesley Professional (2000)
2. Boehm, B.W.: A spiral model of software development and enhancement. Computer **21**(5), 61–72 (1988)
3. Boissier, O., Bordini, R.H., Hubner, J., Ricci, A.: Multi-agent Oriented Programming: Programming Multi-agent Systems Using JaCaMo. MIT Press, Cambridge (2020)
4. Bordini, R.H., Dastani, M., Dix, J., Seghrouchni, A.E.F. (eds.): Multi-Agent Programming, Languages, Tools and Applications. Springer, Heidelberg (2009). https://doi.org/10.1007/978-0-387-89299-3
5. Bordini, R.H., Hübner, J.F., Wooldridge, M.: Programming Multi-agent Systems in AgentSpeak Using Jason. Wiley, Hoboken (2007)

6. Bratman, M.: Intention, Plans, and Practical Reason. Harvard University Press, Cambridge (1987)
7. Cernuzzi, L., Cossentino, M., Zambonelli, F.: Process models for agent-based development. Eng. Appl. Artif. Intell. **18**(2), 205–222 (2005)
8. Engelmann, D., et al.: Dial4JaCa – a demonstration. In: Dignum, F., Corchado, J.M., De La Prieta, F. (eds.) PAAMS 2021. LNCS (LNAI), vol. 12946, pp. 346–350. Springer, Cham (2021). https://doi.org/10.1007/978-3-030-85739-4_29
9. Engelmann, D., et al.: Dial4JaCa – a communication interface between multi-agent systems and chatbots. In: Dignum, F., Corchado, J.M., De La Prieta, F. (eds.) PAAMS 2021. LNCS (LNAI), vol. 12946, pp. 77–88. Springer, Cham (2021). https://doi.org/10.1007/978-3-030-85739-4_7
10. Engelmann, D.C., Cezar, L.D., Panisson, A.R., Bordini, R.H.: A conversational agent to support hospital bed allocation. In: Britto, A., Valdivia Delgado, K. (eds.) BRACIS 2021. LNCS (LNAI), vol. 13073, pp. 3–17. Springer, Cham (2021). https://doi.org/10.1007/978-3-030-91702-9_1
11. Engelmann, D.C., Ferrando, A., Panisson, A.R., Ancona, D., Bordini, R.H., Mascardi, V.: Rv4jaca - runtime verification for multi-agent systems. In: Cardoso, R.C., Ferrando, A., Papacchini, F., Askarpour, M., Dennis, L.A. (eds.) Proceedings of the Second Workshop on Agents and Robots for reliable Engineered Autonomy, AREA@IJCAI-ECAI 2022, Vienna, Austria, 24th July 2022. EPTCS, vol. 362, pp. 23–36 (2022)
12. Finin, T., Fritzson, R., McKay, D., McEntire, R.: KQML as an agent communication language. In: Proceedings of the Third International Conference on Information and Knowledge Management, pp. 456–463 (1994)
13. Fowler, M., Highsmith, J., et al.: The agile manifesto. Softw. Dev. **9**(8), 28–35 (2001)
14. George, M., Lansky, A.: Reactive reasoning and planning: An experiment with a mobile robot. In: The Proceedings of the Sixth National Conference on Artificial Intelligence, pp. 677–682 (1987)
15. Madden, N., Logan, B.: Modularity and compositionality in Jason. In: Braubach, L., Briot, J.-P., Thangarajah, J. (eds.) ProMAS 2009. LNCS (LNAI), vol. 5919, pp. 237–253. Springer, Heidelberg (2010). https://doi.org/10.1007/978-3-642-14843-9_15
16. Melo, V.S., Panisson, A.R., Bordini, R.H.: Meta-information and argumentation in multi-agent systems. iSys-Braz. J. Inf. Syst. **10**(3), 74–97 (2017)
17. Melo, V., Panisson, A., Bordini, R.: MIRS: A modular approach for using meta-information in agent-oriented programming languages. In: Nineteenth International Workshop on Trust in Agent Societies (2017)
18. Müller, J.P., Pischel, M., Thiel, M.: Modeling reactive behaviour in vertically layered agent architectures. In: Wooldridge, M.J., Jennings, N.R. (eds.) ATAL 1994. LNCS, vol. 890, pp. 261–276. Springer, Heidelberg (1995). https://doi.org/10.1007/3-540-58855-8_17
19. Ortiz-Hernández, G., Guerra-Hernández, A., Hübner, J.F., Luna-Ramírez, W.A.: Modularization in belief-desire-intention agent programming and artifact-based environments. PeerJ Comput. Sci. **8**, e1162 (2022)
20. Ortiz-Hernández, G., Hübner, J.F., Bordini, R.H., Guerra-Hernández, A., Hoyos-Rivera, G.J., Cruz-Ramírez, N.: A namespace approach for modularity in BDI programming languages. In: Baldoni, M., Müller, J.P., Nunes, I., Zalila-Wenkstern, R. (eds.) EMAS 2016. LNCS (LNAI), vol. 10093, pp. 117–135. Springer, Cham (2016). https://doi.org/10.1007/978-3-319-50983-9_7

21. Panisson, A.R.: M-arguments. In: 2020 IEEE/WIC/ACM International Joint Conference on Web Intelligence and Intelligent Agent Technology (WI-IAT), pp. 161–168 (2020)
22. Panisson, A.R., Bordini, R.H.: Knowledge representation for argumentation in agent-oriented programming languages. In: 2016 5th Brazilian Conference on Intelligent Systems (BRACIS), pp. 13–18. IEEE (2016)
23. Panisson, A.R., et al.: Arguing about task reallocation using ontological information in multi-agent systems. In: 12th International Workshop on Argumentation in Multiagent Systems, vol. 108 (2015)
24. Panisson, A.R., McBurney, P., Bordini, R.H.: A computational model of argumentation schemes for multi-agent systems. Argument Comput. **12**(3), 1–39 (2021)
25. Panisson, A.R., Meneguzzi, F., Vieira, R., Bordin, R.H.: Towards practical argumentation in multi-agent systems. In: 2015 Brazilian Conference on Intelligent Systems (BRACIS), pp. 98–103. IEEE (2015)
26. Panisson, A.R., Meneguzzi, F., Vieira, R., Bordini, R.H.: Towards practical argumentation-based dialogues in multi-agent systems. In: 2015 IEEE/WIC/ACM International Conference on Web Intelligence and Intelligent Agent Technology (WI-IAT), vol. 2, pp. 151–158. IEEE (2015)
27. Panisson, A.R., Sarkadi, S., McBurney, P., Parsons, S., Bordini, R.H.: On the formal semantics of theory of mind in agent communication. In: Lujak, M. (ed.) AT 2018. LNCS (LNAI), vol. 11327, pp. 18–32. Springer, Cham (2019). https://doi.org/10.1007/978-3-030-17294-7_2
28. Panisson, A.R.: A framework for reasoning and dialogue in multi-agent systems using argumentation schemes. Ph.D. thesis, Pontifícia Universidade Católica do Rio Grande do Sul (2019)
29. Panisson, A.R., Meneguzzi, F.R., Fagundes, M.S., Vieira, R., Bordini, R.H.: Formal semantics of speech acts for argumentative dialogues. In: 2014 Proceedings of the 13th International Conference on Autonomous Agents and Multiagent Systems, França (2014)
30. Rao, A.S.: AgentSpeak(L): BDI agents speak out in a logical computable language. In: Van de Velde, W., Perram, J.W. (eds.) MAAMAW 1996. LNCS, vol. 1038, pp. 42–55. Springer, Heidelberg (1996). https://doi.org/10.1007/BFb0031845
31. Sarkadi, Ş, Panisson, A.R., Bordini, R.H., McBurney, P., Parsons, S.: Towards an approach for modelling uncertain theory of mind in multi-agent systems. In: Lujak, M. (ed.) AT 2018. LNCS (LNAI), vol. 11327, pp. 3–17. Springer, Cham (2019). https://doi.org/10.1007/978-3-030-17294-7_1
32. Schmidt, D., Panisson, A.R., Freitas, A., Bordini, R.H., Meneguzzi, F., Vieira, R.: An ontology-based mobile application for task managing in collaborative groups. In: Markov, Z., Russell, I. (eds.) Proceedings of the Twenty-Ninth International Florida Artificial Intelligence Research Society Conference, FLAIRS 2016, Key Largo, Florida, USA, 16–18 May 2016, pp. 522–526. AAAI Press (2016)
33. da Silveira Colissi, M., Vieira, R., Mascardi, V., Bordini, R.H.: A chatbot that uses a multi-agent organization to support collaborative learning. In: Stephanidis, C., Antona, M., Ntoa, S. (eds.) HCII 2021. CCIS, vol. 1421, pp. 31–38. Springer, Cham (2021). https://doi.org/10.1007/978-3-030-78645-8_4
34. Smith, R.G.: The contract net protocol: high-level communication and control in a distributed problem solver. IEEE Trans. Comput. **29**(12), 1104–1113 (1980)
35. Vieira, R., Moreira, Á.F., Wooldridge, M., Bordini, R.H.: On the formal semantics of speech-act based communication in an agent-oriented programming language. J. Artif. Intell. Res. **29**, 221–267 (2007)

Author Index

T. Ahlbrecht et al. (Eds.): MAPC 2022, LNAI 13997, p. 195, 2023.
https://doi.org/10.1007/978-3-031-38712-8

Printed in the United States
by Baker & Taylor Publisher Services

Printed in the United States
by Baker & Taylor Publisher Services